Tourism Discourse

Tourism Discourse
Language and Global Mobility

Crispin Thurlow
University of Washington, USA

Adam Jaworski
Cardiff University, UK

First published 2010 by
PALGRAVE MACMILLAN

Palgrave Macmillan in the UK is an imprint of Macmillan Publishers Limited, registered in England, company number 785998, of Houndmills, Basingstoke, Hampshire RG21 6XS.

Palgrave Macmillan in the US is a division of St Martin's Press LLC, 175 Fifth Avenue, New York, NY 10010.

Palgrave Macmillan is the global academic imprint of the above companies and has companies and representatives throughout the world.

Palgrave® and Macmillan® are registered trademarks in the United States, the United Kingdom, Europe and other countries.

ISBN 978–1–403–98796–9 hardback

This book is printed on paper suitable for recycling and made from fully managed and sustained forest sources. Logging, pulping and manufacturing processes are expected to conform to the environmental regulations of the country of origin.

A catalogue record for this book is available from the British Library.

A catalog record for this book is available from the Library of Congress.

10   9   8   7   6   5   4   3   2   1
19   18   17   16   15   14   13   12   11   10

Printed and bound in Great Britain by
CPI Antony Rowe, Chippenham and Eastbourne

Contents

List of Figures and Tables

Figures

Tables

Acknowledgements*

This book is based on a research project, started in the Autumn of 2001, under the heading *Language, Communication and Tourism as a Global Cultural Industry* enabled through funding from the Leverhulme Trust (grant no. F/00 407/D) to the Centre for Language and Communication Research, Cardiff University, for a larger programme of research on *Language and Global Communication*. We continue to be enormously grateful to the Leverhulme Trust for providing us with this opportunity to pursue research. We would also like to thank our Leverhulme programme colleagues at the Centre for Language and Communication Research and especially the programme directors Theo van Leeuwen (now at the University of Technology, Sydney) and Nik Coupland for their support throughout the time we've been working on this project. Our special thanks go to our project colleagues Virpi Ylänne and Sarah Lawson. As Associate Researcher on the project between 2002 and 2005, Sarah was very helpful in collecting, coding and preparing some of our project data. Virpi, our colleague in the Centre for Language and Communication Research has co-authored Chapters 3 and 5 of this book.

The completion of the book was made possible through the collegial support of Jerry Baldasty in the University of Washington's Department of Communication and through two indispensible visits to the Whiteley Center, an extraordinary writing retreat on San Juan Island in the Puget Sound, as well as a study trip to The Hill, Abergavenny, South Wales, generously funded by the Centre for Language and Communication

---

* We are grateful to be able to reproduce a number of visual materials for the purposes of our analysis and critique. We wish to thank, in particular, the following for their permissions: Jonathan Meader and Crown Publishing (cover of *The Wordless Travel Book*, Figure 6.3), Martha Aleo (photo of Zulu beadwork, Figure 2.29), the New Zealand Tourism Board (website banner, Figure 6.2), JAT Airways (route map, Figure 1.4), the *Sunday Times* (newspaper extracts, Figures 4.3, 4.4, 4.5, and 4.6), the *Guardian* (newspaper extracts, Figures 4.1 and 4.2), King Features Syndicate (Hagar the Horrible cartoon, Figure 5.2). Every effort was made to trace copyright holders, but if any have been inadvertently overlooked the publishers would be pleased to make the necessary arrangements at the first opportunity.

Research at Cardiff University. Thank you so much. We are incredibly grateful to the Kathy Cowell and her colleagues at the Whiteley Center for their generous, friendly assistance.

Along the way, we have had help from various research assistants with collecting, coding, preparing and transcribing the diverse and extensive materials which serve as the empirical basis of our work, and others who have helped with the final preparations of the manuscript. Thank you, Ayo Banji, Ody Constantinou, Aboubakar Sako, Klas Prytz, Ulla Räisänen, Nicole Hofmans, Georgina Thomson and Chris Harihar.

One of the other privileges of working in such a transdisciplinary topic over the last several years has been exchanging ideas with old colleagues and getting to know and, sometimes getting to work with, a wide range of new ones. We are grateful for the ideas they shared with us and for their encouragement – whether direct or indirect it has always been indispensible. Thank you, Nik Coupland, David Dunn, Małgorzta Fabiszak, Gavin Jack, Mimi Kahn, David Machin, Nigel Morgan, Aneta Pavlenko, Alison Phipps, Ingrid Piller, Annette Pritchard, Theo van Leeuwen, John Urry and Alison Wray.

Between us, we are grateful also to the numerous tourists, travel representatives and industry workers who have not only facilitated our fieldtrips but who have also answered our endless questions. A special thank you goes to Phoday Touray in Gambia. Perhaps more than anyone, however, we are grateful to our known and unknown hosts, recognizing that, as a traditional isiZulu saying puts it, *umuntu ngamuntu ngabantu* – a person is a person because of other people.

Speaking of which, and last but not least, our love and gratitude go to our families without whom none of this would have been possible or worthwhile. For Crispin, this is Jürg, Joe and Jay. For Adam, this is Ania and Maja. Thank you for tolerating the extravagant working hours, the long absences and for claiming to still like us as much as before we started work on this book (and the other two!).

Introduction
Mediating Global Mobility: Language, Tourism, Globalization

> Contemporary tourism involves travel, however temporary and fleeting, by Western peoples on a massive scale to the margins of empire and to the peripheries of modernity; it is one of the greatest population movements of all time.
>
> (Bruner, 2005: 10)

> Signalling new freedom for some, globalizing processes appear as uninvited and cruel fate for many others. Freedom to move, a scarce and unequally distributed commodity, quickly becomes the main stratifying factors of our times.... A particular cause for worry is the progressive breakdown in communication between the increasingly global and extraterritorial elites and the ever more 'localized' rest.
>
> (Bauman, 1998: 2–3)

This book is about the role and nature of language and communication in tourism as a global cultural industry. Over the last 20 or 30 years, the academic study of tourism as a site of cultural exchange and production has been gathering a tremendous momentum, with some of the most important contributions being made by scholars from sociology, anthropology, geography and cultural studies. There has also been a growing critical/cultural perspective arising from within the traditionally business-orientated field of hospitality and leisure management. In writing *Tourism Discourse*, our primary goal has been to start setting out a new field within language and communication studies, which we refer to as 'the sociolinguistics of tourism'.[1] In other words, we are hoping to be able to make a contribution to our own field by considering what tourism, as a powerful domain of contemporary social

1

life, has to say about the textual representation, mediatization and organization of social life more generally and of language in particular. If, as Ed Bruner (quoted above) suggests, tourism really is 'one of the greatest population movements of all time', it is high time sociolinguists and discourse analysts pay it some attention. In contributing to our own field, however, we would also like to think that we can offer a complementary perspective to the field of critical tourism studies that is uniquely linguistic and communicative. In doing so, we hope to situate the linguistically oriented analysis of discourse squarely within an already transdisciplinary body of work so centrally concerned with tourism as a site of cultural production and exchange. In either case, our ultimate concern is with the particular ways that language and communication (or, as we explain shortly, discourse) constitute and frame identities, relationships and communities in the context of tourism.

As critical discourse analysts, we are additionally committed to understanding how communicative processes manifest and reproduce matrices of power and ideologies of difference in the broader context of 'advanced' or 'global' capitalism. In undertaking the research which forms the basis of *Tourism Discourse*, we have also come to see for ourselves how, as a central hallmark of so-called 'globalization', mobility for pleasure or leisure serves as a powerful channel and agent for the manoeuvres of global capital. It is in this way that we too mean to describe, explain and interpret tourism as one of the major forces shaping social, political and cultural processes in the world today. And, if Zygmunt Bauman (quoted above) is correct, there is a role to be played – however modest – by people who understand something of the way human communication works.

There are thus three institutions which serve as the theoretical and social cornerstones of our discussion in this book: 'language', 'tourism' and the global economy – for now, just 'globalization'. In this introductory chapter, we offer a brief account of what we understand and mean by each of these; a more substantial theorizing of all three unfolds in stages through the book. While the inclusion of items into a list unavoidably signifies some kind of order and 'relation of equivalence' (Fairclough, 2003), we do not mean to imply an over-simplistic relationship between language, tourism and globalization, nor do we mean to prioritize one or other of them. Ultimately, however, it is our general contention in writing *Tourism Discourse* that tourism and globalization are inherently discursive in nature; that tourism is deeply complicitous in the ideologies of globalization, and vice versa; and that language is powerfully shaped by/in the discourses of both tourism and globalization. We mean to demonstrate each of these ideas by considering six case studies of common textual practices – or globalizing genres – in tourism. For now, however, we start by briefly addressing what is, for us, the most intimidating of our three cornerstone concepts.

Globalization and global capitalism

> You cannot, in my view, even be a practising social scientist of any sophistication if you do not grasp or master the debate about globalization. It is probably the most significant debate now going on in the social sciences and in politics too.
>
> (Giddens, 1999: 2)

> ... the highly polysemic notion of 'globalization' [serves] to dress up the effects of American imperialism in the trappings of cultural ecumenicism or economic fatalism and to make a transnational relation of economic power appear like a natural necessity.... 'globalization' is not a new phase of capitalism, but a 'rhetoric' invoked by governments in order to justify their voluntary surrender to the financial markets.
>
> (Bourdieu and Wacquant, 2001: 4)

Supposedly, we are living in what Anthony Giddens (1999) terms a 'runaway world', a world characterized by unpredictability, risk and uncertainty. Central to academic and lay attempts to rationalize, explain and influence this runaway world is the notion of globalization. Nevertheless, in what Held and McGrew (2000) describe as the stance of the 'global sceptics', there are other commentators such as Pierre Boudieu and Loïc Wacquant (quoted above; see also Callinicos et al., 1994; Hoogvelt, 1997) who strongly refute the idea that there is anything especially new in globalization other than the re-orderings and concomitant impacts of advanced or post-industrial capitalism – which is to say, global capitalism. In this sense, therefore, a more critical/cultural position is taken with regards globalization, which itself is viewed as a rhetorical or discursive move to frame, explain and legitimate the global political economy – especially insofar as it privileges those countries who stand to gain most. Certainly, as Giddens again points out, there are demonstrable, material realities to global interconnectedness – most notably, transnational trading of goods, services and information, and the so-called 'media revolution' brought about by new, high-speed communication technologies. However, there is little doubt that the cultural dimensions of globalization are heavily implicated in, and bound up with, the forces of global capitalism. In fact, much theorizing about the processes alluded to by 'globalization' maintains that it is the cultural dimension of globalization which warrants even greater attention than the economic and commercial ones (Waters, 1995).

In making sense of globalization for ourselves, and from our particular perspective as researchers of language and communication, we have necessarily leaned towards an interest in the cultural dimensions of globalization. Nonetheless, we do recognize that a too partisan approach to one or other dimension of globalization can only fail in its attempt to understand such a complex, contested phenomenon. Like others, therefore, we prefer to think of globalization as a dense and fluid network of transnational 'flows' (Appadurai, 1990, 1996) and 'concentrations' (Smith, 2000) of people, technologies, financial resources, information, media images, ideologies and symbolic resources. While these flows and concentrations may span the globe, they do not necessarily cover it – nor do they span it in equal measure. This recognition runs counter to the core mythology of globalization, which often persuades us that its reach is not only extensive but also comprehensive; instead, globalization is a story about contemporary social and economic life which conceals substantial material and symbolic differences/inequalities. Another popular idea about global forces is that their impact is not only ubiquitous but also impartial; and yet these forces are evidently not neutral but always subject to economic privileges, political power and historical oppressions. Echoing the sentiments of Bauman above, well-known critic of globalization Naomi Klein (2002) rightly observes that global capitalism opens windows for some (a few) but just as quickly raises fences for (many) others.

Certainly, at the level of human interaction, we ourselves are less certain of the kind of social-cultural interconnectedness invoked by popular notions such as the 'global village', which appears to remain more at the level of ideological myth than universal, material reality. At least this is what we have seen in the work we are presenting here. It is for this reason precisely that critical discourse analysts are typically engaged with examining the discursive (or rhetorical) nature of globalization – the sense in which it is less a material reality and more a framework for talking about, and justifying, material realities and inequalities of global capitalism. Specifically, like Norman Fairclough (2003: 4; also Bourdieu and Wacquant, 2001), we are inclined to think of 'globalization' as a neoliberal discourse used to account for, and often to justify, the kinds of re-orderings brought about by advanced or post-industrial capitalism. In this sense, and as we will show in the chapters which follow, globalization is sometimes more 'aspirational' than it is 'actual', with people commonly 'talking' globalization into existence for strategic ends – and, usually by those who stand to benefit materially and politically from the re-orderings of capital. Certainly, there is a non-discursive reality to global capital just as there is a colonial history; nonetheless, the meanings and ideologies of global capitalism are only known by the way people talk or write about it. And this talk/writing – this discourse – is powerful not only in representing the global political economy but also in realizing it. Globalization, for us, is therefore a discourse, an ideological formation or cultural narrative that reveals and conceals the more tangible workings of global capitalism, all of which runs central to the global cultural industry that is tourism.

Tourism and global mobility

> Touristic culture is more than the physical travel, it is the preparation of people to see other places as objects of tourism, and the preparation of those people and places to be seen. . . . the touristic gaze and imaginary shape and mediate our knowledge of and desires about the rest of the planet.
>
> (Franklin and Crang, 2001: 10)

Through its increasing – or increasingly complex – interconnectedness, globalization is essentially all about ever increasing mobility, not just of goods, images and information, but also, most obviously, of people (Robins, 2000 [1997]) – or what Appadurai (ibid.) calls the *ethnoscape* of globalization. Indeed, as Zygmunt Bauman (quoted earlier) argues, it is mobility that is *the* greatest hallmark of globalization – either in terms of the privileged travel-by-choice of elites (who he calls 'globals' or just 'tourists') or the enforced movements of economic migrants and refugees (or 'vagabonds'). These two mobile constituencies represent those who are privileged to experience global capitalism as an opportunity (or an opening of windows, Klein's terms) and those for whom it is an obstacle (a raising of fences). Nor is our notion of 'travel-by-choice' simply restricted to those who travel for leisure – that is, the conventional notion of tourist; it also includes business people, academics, NGO workers and those who may or may not travel for pleasure, but for whom travel is relatively pleasurable. Contemporary modes of travel are, after all, being designed more and more with the comforts and needs of these 'globals' in mind – arguably more so that anyone else (Thurlow and Jaworski, 2006). Besides, as Julia Harrison points out, business travellers too distinguish themselves from immigrants, refugees and others (who she calls 'transnationals') because business travellers (like academic travellers) are always secure in the knowledge that they will return home (Harrison, 2003: 37; see also Rojek, 1997).

As a crude measure of tourism's power, the United Nation's World Tourism Organization (WTO) reports that an estimated 924 million international tourist arrivals (leisure and business) were recorded in 2008 (WTO, January 2009).[2] Even with the 'global economic downturn' and the H1N1 flu pandemic at the time of writing this book, these tourism figures were not expected to fall significantly in 2009 (WTO, September 2009). Tourism is a surprisingly tenacious, if fickle, industry. Either way, 924 million is certainly a large figure – a vast movement of people, as Bruner (2005) rightly notes. And even if this 924 million were to represent actual tourists, as opposed to *arrivals*, it would account for less than 14 per cent of the estimated global population of 6.7 billion people. As it is, annual 'tourist arrivals' represents many of the *same* people travelling many times. These are, after all, business tourists, academic tourists, NGO tourists as well as leisure tourists – all those travellers privileged to return home at the end of their travels. Perhaps what is all the more striking about the scale of tourism, therefore, is that such a narrowly defined movement of people is capable of generating a staggering annual expenditure of well over US$856 billion worldwide in 2007. To be sure, however, these international tourists are, for the most part, European with, for example, US$928 and US$861 per capita expenditures in the United Kingdom and Germany for 2004, compared with US$299 in Japan, US$244 in the United States and US$15 in China (also WTO figures). In fact, according to the International Trade Forum, tourism has firmly established itself as the world's single largest form of international trade.

In spite of these remarkable numbers, scholars of critical tourism studies are, surprisingly, often forced to justify their scholarship to people clearly unable to see beyond their own personal experience of tourism as a frivolous, recreational activity. And yet, as such a huge global industry, there is surely no one whose life remains unaffected by tourism, be it those people privileged enough to tour or people who are 'toured'. In the way that Giddens (quoted above) talks about globalization, it seems almost irresponsible to assume that tourism should not somehow warrant serious scholarly attention. Indeed, it is precisely because of its scale and because it is not only an economic activity that anthropologists, sociologists, geographers and others have been committed to their detailed analyses of the social and cultural practices by which tourism is organized and experienced (to name just a few: Hutnyk, 1996; Selwyn, 1996; Morgan and Pritchard, 1998; MacCannell, 1999 [1976]; Abbink, 2000; Franklin and Crang, 2001; Urry, 2002; Kahn, 2003). And to be clear, like our own work here, none of this critical scholarship is done to support commercial stakeholders in 'doing' tourism better, although an underlying hope might be that they would do it more responsibly, respectfully and equitably (see Chapter 5).[3] Instead, critical tourism research usually seeks to demonstrate tourism's powerful role in reorganizing cultural practices, establishing ideologies of difference and perpetuating unequal relations of power (Favero, 2007). As such, many social theorists and cultural critics recognize that tourism does not merely reflect socioeconomic relations within and between countries, but is instrumental in organizing these relations (for example, Lash and Urry, 1994; Bauman, 1998; Kirshenblatt-Gimblett, 1998). And, in the case of tourism, the implications really are global. They are also discursive. Adrian Franklin and Mike Crang note (quote above) how tourism serves as a very influential and privileged lens through which many people come to make sense of not only a particular destination or people but of the world at large.

Without meaning to underplay the undeniable dialectic of economic and cultural life, it is ultimately an interest in cultural 'mimesis' (Waters, 1995) that underpins *Tourism Discourse*, and, specifically, the *memetic* transmission and uptake of the very distinctive semiotic resources and communicative practices deployed in the context of tourism as an elite mode of global mobility. Extending some of the ideas of Mike Featherstone (1991), Scott Lash and John Urry (1994: 193) argue that post-industrial or advanced capitalist societies have become fundamentally and heavily semiotic as shifts from manufacture-based to service-based economics is necessarily premised on an increased reliance on symbolic practices – language, communication, imagery and design (cf. Baudrillard, 1994; Hardt and Negri, 2000). This intensification and expansion of symbolic power is characterized by the increasing 'textual mediation' (Fairclough, 1999) or 'semioticization' (Graddol, 2002) of every area of contemporary economic and social life. As a major service industry, tourism too has undergone (and helped perpetuate) this major shift by which service-oriented economies in general render goods more discursively mediated, or increasingly semioticized. In fact, in the post-Fordist work order of late capitalist societies, tourism exemplifies a semiotically embedded service because, like advertising and marketing, a key part of what is actually produced and consumed in tourism is the semiotic context of the service (see also du Gay and Pryke, 2002; Negus, 2002; Urry, 2002). Not only does tourism involve face-to-face (or more mediated) forms of visitor-host interaction, like in many other types of service encounters, but the ultimate goods purchased by tourists during their travels are also images, lifestyles, memories and their narrative enactments (de Botton, 2002) – the fantasy and performance of 'going native', of adventure, of meeting new peoples, of exotic cultures and of unexplored places. Material goods such as souvenirs and artefacts, not unlike snippets of language formulae brought back from foreign trips, are themselves packaged and promoted as useful props in the enactment of these performances, and they serve as an extension of the tourist gaze (Urry, 2002) slowly turning into a tourist haze as the narratives continue 'back home'. It is precisely this way – in the talk and texts of tourism – that tourism discourse is organized and made meaningful. And, not least because of its scale, tourism discourse is a discourse with material, global consequences.

Language and discourse

> Symbolic capital, a transformed and thereby disguised form of physical 'economic' capital, produces its proper effect inasmuch, and only inasmuch, as it conceals the fact that it originates in 'material' forms of capital which are also, in the last analysis, the source of its effects.
>
> (Bourdieu, 1977: 6, 183)

> ... in every society the production of discourse is at once controlled, selected, organised and redistributed by a certain number of procedures whose role is to ward off its powers and its dangers, ... to evade its ponderous, formidable materiality.
>
> (Foucault, 1980: 52)

Wherever one chooses to locate the impetus for the increasing economic and political 'interconnectivity' (Thompson, 2000) identified by the label globalization, one of the key domains or experiences of 21st century living is unquestionably the concomitant exchange and spread of symbolic and cultural capital; nor is this globalizing flow neatly contained by the political ideologies of states ('ideoscapes') and mediatized cultural products of television, cinema and music ('mediascapes') proposed by Arjun Appadurai (1990). In writing and theorizing about globalization, much is often made of *communications* (with the 's') while very little is made of *communication* (without the 's'). For us, this marks the difference between mass media institutions and communication technologies, and the practices of everyday language-use and social interaction. In thinking about global flows, therefore, we are equally concerned with the more informal, 'on-the-ground' circulation of symbols, sign systems and other meaning-making practices that form what Crispin Thurlow and Giorgia Aiello (2007) call the 'global semioscape'. After all, it is at the level of the interpersonal, everyday exchange of meaning where the global and the local interface are negotiated and resolved, be it through processes of cultural absorption, appropriation, recognition, acceptance or resistance. This is precisely why we are interested in tourism, not only as a global cultural industry but also as a key site for intercultural exchange and for the banal enactments of globalization. It is precisely in this domain of social life that the potential for a properly linguistic or discourse analytic perspective on globalization lies (cf. N. Coupland, 2003a, 2010; Blommaert, 2003, 2009).

Host–tourist interactions and identities embody the very essence of globalizing processes.[4] It is in communication with each other, in every particular instant of contact, that hosts and tourists also negotiate the nature of the tourist experience, the meaning of culture and place, as well as their relationship to each other and their own identities. Any such interpersonal, face-to-face encounter is also heavily pre-figured at any number of stages of the tourist enterprise (for example, from reading holiday brochures, travel guides and newspaper travelogues, watching TV holiday shows, flicking through inflight magazines, visiting curio shops, selecting postcards from a rack) and in many different forms (for example, a hotel-based package or an activity holiday to 'grassroots' or adventure tours, to a luxury safari or exclusive cruise). In her account of the colonial, touristic histories (and production) of Tahiti, for example, Miriam Kahn (2003) shows how destinations are constantly imagined and re-imagined through stories, advertising, literature, fine art, cinema and so on.

Part of the impetus for our attention to the linguistic and discursive comes from within critical tourism studies itself. Writers like Adrian Franklin and Mike Crang (2001) and, more recently, Phaedra Pezzullo (2007) advocate the need for a more 'multi-sensory', 'embodied' understanding of tourism, and a concomitant reappraisal of its undue emphasis on the visual – typified by the sway of John Urry's (2002) hugely important, but often oversimplified and misunderstood, notion of the 'tourist gaze'. To some extent, any lack of scholarly attention to language is explained by nature of the tourist experience itself; in Cronin's

(2000: 82) words, 'sightseeing is the world with the sound turned off'. As Dunn (2005, 2006) further explains, tourists usually end up gazing simply because they cannot understand the languages spoken by the objects of their gaze. And yet, our own research would suggest that language is everywhere in tourism; language and languages sit at the very heart of the tourist experience, its representation and its realization, its enculturation and its enactment. Either way, analyses of language and social interaction in tourism studies have been noticeable by their absence.

Along with the increasing significance of ethnography as a mode for conducting social research, the study of discourse has had a powerful impact in changing not just language and communication scholarship but just about every major social science (for example, geography, sociology, psychology) and many fields in the humanities too (for example, literature, history, art) and even applied fields like business, education and medicine. Discourse analysis is both a theoretical framework for explaining how language 'works' in everyday use, and a collection of methods for investigating the social workings of language and the ways language constructs everyday social life. In these terms, language is not merely a vehicle for representing or *reflecting* social realities; rather, it is through language and other symbolic meaning-making activities that social realities come to be understood (to make meaning) and to be organized the way they are. In this sense, therefore, language (and languages) functions in concert with other more commonly recognized institutions such as the economy, government and education to establish, to maintain and to change the social order (cf. Cameron, 2009 [1990]). In short, and to follow Michel Foucault quoted above, language really does matter.

Nor is the analysis of discourse is simply about the study of language for its own sake.[5] Most discourse analysts are concerned with examining how micro-level phenomena such as specific textual practices or fleeting moments of conversation connect with, and help explain, macro-level social structures and processes. Given the increasingly textually mediated or semioticized nature of contemporary life, and the predominance of 'semiotic goods' such as branding and marketing, the analysis of discourse arguably promotes itself more now than ever before. In his very well-known treatise on *Language and Symbolic Power*, Pierre Bourdieu (1991 – see quote above) makes a compelling case for the complicity of discourse, economics and relations of power. Our intention in communication, he argues, is as much about the pursuit of symbolic profit (or, more famously, cultural capital) as it is about information exchange and mutual understanding. While there is always a materiality to language, in this case it is an economic materiality and advantage that is sought or achieved. Discourse is thus ideological not only in that it (a) construes and constitutes identities and relationships, and (b) represents and reproduces systems of belief and power, but also because it (c) establishes and maintains structures of inequality and privilege (see, for example, Billig, 1991, 1995; Fairclough, 1992; Hodge and Kress, 1993; Hall, 1996a; Blommaert and Verschueren, 1998; van Dijk, 1998). In *Tourism Discourse*, we want to show how it is possible to see all three of these discursive processes being strategically achieved in the representation, mediatization and organization of a range of tourist genres.

From the particular – but not exclusive – perspective of critical discourse studies, therefore, we share Theo van Leeuwen's (2002 [1993]: 167) understanding that, however 'ideologically innocent' they may appear, texts or small conversational moments can still be tremendously powerful in representing and reconstituting large areas of social life. From a methodological point of view, they are also very helpful in revealing the *effects* of power (Blommaert, 2005). It is this which makes critical discourse studies, although not without its limitations, such a valuable approach for investigating and thinking through the nature of tourism and/or globalization. In their everyday lives, few people get to read the same newspaper, the same inflight magazine, the same guidebook or to watch the same TV holiday show over and over again. Even fewer people regularly pore through a hundred inflight magazines, dozens of newspapers and tourist guidebooks, or pore over hours and hours of the same TV shows. (Nor is it everyone who is fortunate enough to spend time wandering the markets of Gambia.) It is really only scholars and media analysts who make a point of doing these kinds of things. The advantage of studies such as the ones we have undertaken here, therefore, is that they offer otherwise unique opportunities to see how a single issue – or a handful of specific issues – are reported, written about, talked about and displayed in many different texts, from many different locations and over an extended period. This in turn puts researchers like us in a better position to identify *some* of the more widespread, tenacious structural patterns, topical consistencies and cultural narratives. For critical scholars, it also helps greatly in revealing *something* of the discursive formations, 'regimes of truth' (Foucault, 1980: 131) and ideological assumptions by which textual practices – and the larger social practices of which they are a part – come to be institutionally organized and popularly understood.

How *Tourism Discourse* is organized

We have organized *Tourism Discourse* into six chapters, each of which deliberately addresses a different textual practice or generic format and, therefore, a different context of tourism. In focusing each chapter around a different text, we also highlight a series of different sociolinguistic or discourse analytic concepts and look to tie these with the most relevant social and theoretical issues arising in each case. Working across a range of different ways in which tourism is 'textualized' – that is, represented and organized discursively produced – we hope to be able to start mapping the globalizing processes and discursive strategies that underpin the symbolic economy and language ideologies of tourism more generally.

In Part I, we examine several examples of what we call 'discourses on the move' – instances of specifically touristic textual practices: inflight magazines (Chapter 1), trade signs and business cards in Gambia (Chapter 2) and holiday postcards (Chapter 3). In selecting these particular discursive forms of social (inter)action, we are able to compare the different textual practices and also to examine the more general 'texturing' of tourist identities and relations. In the case of inflight magazines, for example, the general rhetorical appeal is to a noticeably more elite, cosmopolitan lifestyle; holiday postcards meanwhile have typically always served a very much more bread-and-butter, egalitarian function in the tourist experience. This is not to say, of course, that the apparent ordinariness of postcards does not conceal an otherwise elitist identity display in relation to 'the folks back home'. The (re)presentation of these tourist identities is very much one of orientation rather than absolute categorization. As some kind of notional midpoint between these ostensibly elite and egalitarian practices, in Chapter 2 we turn our attention to the linguistic landscape created by the use of small business trade signs and business cards in Gambia. In each of these three cases, we are primarily interested in the way language is deployed multimodally as a semiotic resource for the performance of both tourist identities and global identities. As we shall show, the line between the two is far from clear.

In Part II, we then make an important material and conceptual shift from examining the touristic *use* of language (that is, discourse) to looking at the *representation* of language (that is, metalanguage). While we continue to examine three new tourist genres, our focus here is on textual practices where language is more or less explicitly thematized (cf. Johnson and Ensslin, 2007). As such, our primary theoretical concern is with the overlapping topics of metalanguage (see Jaworski et al., 2004) and language ideology (see Schieffelin et al., 1998; Blommaert, 1999) both of which direct attention to the ways in which 'language about language' (or discourse about discourse) is deployed as a resource for the scripting and policing of *other* people (cf. Thurlow, 2010). In Chapter 4, we see this at work in newspaper travelogues, while in Chapters 5 and 6 we examine the language ideologies of television holiday shows and guidebook glossaries, respectively.

All the communicative genres or text types examined in this book work together to establish the symbolic/cultural capital by which certain touristic 'regimes of truth' are established. Together, these different texts reveal the ways in which the tourism experience – and the world at large – is variously prefigured and scripted for tourists. Indeed, it is through their use or reading of these different texts that people not only learn what to see and do while on vacation, but also how to become tourists – and what it means to be a so-called 'global citizen'. Of course, this does not mean that tourists necessarily all 'take up' these texts in the same way, or make the same meaning out of them. It is with this in mind that, while moving through each of the chapters in Parts I and II, we also shift our attention from highly 'representational' genres like inflight magazines and newspaper travelogues towards the more 'interactional' genres such as postcards and guidebooks. At each point, therefore, the potential for tourists to engage with – to contest and rework – the texts increases. So, where inflight magazines and newspaper travelogues (or television shows) are largely institutional and directive, postcards (at least the backs of postcards) and guidebooks leave greater room for individual choice; their use is also situated more closely at the point of contact between visitors and hosts.

On being tourists ourselves

It has been an explicit agreement from the onset of our collaboration that we did not set out to sneer at tourists as some scholars and many travellers seem more than willing to do. Instead, in our efforts to understand the discursive meanings and organization of tourism, we have tried to regard tourists both sympathetically and critically – not always an easy balance to maintain. We have ourselves been tourists and continue to undertake, and participate in, many of the same practices – structural and textual – which we discuss here. Long before we came together under the auspices of the Leverhulme research programme (see our acknowledgements), both of us had been privileged to travel by choice for many years. Indeed, and as we have suggested above, academics are 'professional travellers' and unquestionably members of the global elite (cf. Bauman, 1998); international conferences and research meetings render us travellers-for-pleasure, even if it is for work. Besides, more often than not, the boundaries of work travel and tourism are nowadays very blurred (Lassen, 2006). Yes, we all cross borders; but for us, these crossings are largely autonomous, usually temporary and almost always secure – often comfortable and sometimes even luxurious. We too get to come home each time. What is more, like so many middle-class Europeans, we also regularly travel for leisure and have always enjoyed holidays abroad with family and friends, and holidays abroad to see family and friends.

None of this, of course, precludes us from being critical of these experiences and of the tourist experience in general. On the contrary, and as we have noted elsewhere (Thurlow and Jaworski, 2006), an honest consideration for the auto-ethnographic or self-reflexive has, we believe, given us added insight into the texts which interest us academically. It has also given us a way of being able to say at least something about the *reception* of the texts – an analytic step which critical discourse analyses too often omit. In other words, we have felt more confident in making certain claims about the impact and uptake of these genres because we ourselves are complicitous in them as active readers and participant observers. Likewise, we have 'sensed' the discourses which run through and constitute these various textual practice not simply because we are intellectually concerned by them or are empirically directed to them, but also because we recognize how we too have felt positioned by them and have actively – and sometimes even consciously – participated in sustaining them.

In putting *Tourism Discourse* together, we also realize that we have taken a fairly European or British perspective in terms of our data and, for the most part, we write about tourism from the particular experience of English-speaking tourists. Our justification for this is both prosaic and philosophical. To be frank, much of the data that underpins our discussion has been chosen partly because it was familiar, accessible and affordable. (Our most recent work on super-elite, luxury travel has proved to be a lot more challenging in this respect.) No account of tourism can or should discuss tourism as a monolithic practice. Arguably, there are as many tourisms as there are tourists, and it is only for analytic or commercial convenience that either come to be organized into 'types' or 'modes' of travel. As such, this book does not claim to speak of all tourisms or all tourists. Nonetheless, our goal has been to offer a unique perspective on the role of language and discourse in representing and organizing tourism as a global cultural industry; to this end, we have selected what we hope is a variety of reasonably typical texts and contexts by which to investigate and illustrate this perspective.

Part I

Discourses on the Move: The Genres and Symbolic Capital of Tourism

1
Elite Mobility and Global Lifestyles: Inflight Magazines

> Globalization can be thought of as a process (or set of processes) which embodies a transformation of the spatial organization of *social relations* and transactions – assessed in terms of their extensity, intensity, velocity and impact – generating transcontinental or interregional flows and networks of activity, *interaction*, and the exercise of power. In this context, flows refer to the movements of physical artefacts, people, *symbols*, tokens and information across space and time, while networks refer to regularized or patterned interactions between independent agents, nodes of activity, or sites of power.
>
> (Held et al., 2000: 55; our emphasis)

Discourses on the move

As David Held and his colleagues indicate in the quote above, globalization is inextricably bound up in – and constituted by – social relations, human interactions and symbolic exchanges. From our perspective, therefore, it is as much a communicative phenomenon as it is, say, an economic or political one. And what marks these communication processes as 'global' or, rather, as *globalizing* is their extent, intensity, speed and impact. For many people, this is probably most apparent in media communications and the rapid spread of global television formats like *Big Brother, Survivor, Deal or No Deal, Who Wants to be a Millionaire?* – not to mention TV soap operas and 24-hour newscasting (see Oren and Shahaf, 2009). In this book, however, we want to look at tourism not just as a site of *mediatized* cultural production and exchange but also to think about some more banal but no less globalizing genres, discourses and styles as key symbolic resources for the realization of different subject positions and relations of inequality in the context of globalization. In these first three chapters of *Tourism Discourse* we mean to demonstrate how the ideologies of tourism and globalization are inextricably linked to or through various genres, discourses and styles of contemporary, commercial travel representation. Each chapter examines a different example of these 'discourses on the move' which address a range of different tourisms, locations or sites, patterns of participation and degrees of mediation of the tourist experience.[1] It is, we believe, precisely these discursive actions, alongside the very act of 'going somewhere', which turn people into tourists. These textual formats and the social, communicative practices of which they are a part, also play a key role in generating the symbolic capital of both tourism and of global capitalism.

Discourses are 'on the move' in at least two ways: first, because the content and formats of tourism texts are constantly changing; second, because it is tourist texts (and textual practices) that circulate as much as it is the tourists themselves (cf. Lury, 1997). In this regard, we can think of discourse as a specific stretch of spoken or written text, an image or some other aspect of semiosis, or, in a more general Foucauldian sense, as a socially constructed system of representations and knowledge about different aspects of reality. In either case, tourism – and mobility more generally – is as much about the discursive representation and organization of movement as it is about the corporeal getting from A to B (Urry, 2007). Furthermore, as John Urry (2007: 48) states, '[b]odies navigate backwards and forwards between directly sensing the external world as they move bodily in and through it, and discursively mediated sensescapes that signify social taste and distinction, ideology and meaning.' Thus, alongside their technological infrastructures (for example, modes of transport), tourism and mobility are equally organized as a 'global culture industry' (Lash and Lury, 2007) offering semiotic signifiers of place, local people, nation, region or lifestyle through the production of mediating texts and interactions: guidebooks, magazines, radio and TV shows, blogs, advertisements, travelogues, postcards, logos, ritualized displays of welcome, wedding ceremonies, historical pageants, carefully choreographed service encounters, branded trinkets, music, fashions, food and drink labels, perfume and cosmetics packaging, and other mementoes – all of whose commercial value lies in their cultural *significance* as metonyms of the toured location, heritage or people. These signifiers work more or less effectively as styling devices for hosts and tourists alike to position themselves as viable participants – producers or consumers – in the business of travel.

In trying to pin down the central domains of globalization, and as a useful means of navigating the economic and cultural poles of the globalization debate, Appadurai (1990) famously describes the global *movements* (or flows) of information, people, technology, money and ideas (or ideologies) as a series of 'scapes': the mediascape, the ethnoscape, the technoscape, the finanscape and the ideoscape, respectively. In these terms, some of the textual practices we focus on in *Tourism Discourse* (the inflight magazine, the travelogue, television holiday programmes) obviously manifest the mediascape. However, they can also be viewed as a kind of textual nexus of mediascapes, finanscapes and ethnoscapes in their appeal to, and representation of, the interplay between the movement of global elites, the global accumulation of capital, and the heavily mediatized nature of globalizing worldviews. What interests us most about the specific texts we have chosen to look at is not only their ubiquity but also their ordinariness. These are precisely the kinds of textual practices that help to establish what Thurlow and Aiello (2007) call the 'global semioscape' – the more informal, less obviously mediatized circulation of words, images, design aesthetics. It is here, we will eventually suggest, that many of the routinized enactments of global capitalism are often to be seen – what we chose to call 'banal globalization' (see Conclusion).

Genre

In spite of its common and relatively unproblematic, lay usage, 'genre' has been theorized in different ways in a wide range of disciplines, for example, folklore studies, literature, linguistics and rhetoric (Chandler, 1997; Swales, 1990). For our purposes, we adopt the view that genres are distinctive types of communicative events or textual practices which are characterized in terms of (a) their central purpose, (b) their prototypical content and form and (c) their being conventionally recognized and labelled as such by the discourse community of which they are a part (Swales, 1990). Furthermore, although configured around obligatory, typical or optional elements (Lewin et al., 2001), the boundaries of genres are always flexible and invariably fuzzy. Indeed, most texts are hybrid or 'mixed-genre' (Fairclough, 1995: 89). For all their fluidity and hybridity, however, we are interested in seeing (or showing) how different types of tourism writing – like inflight magazines (Chapter 1), trade signs and business cards (Chapter 2), and postcards (Chapter 3) – become conventionalized and systematized, how their form and meaning are affected by their status as 'discourses on the move' in the global semioscape, and how they establish particular ways of knowing the world.

Every genre positions those who use it and participate in it, as interviewer or interviewee, as listener or storyteller, as reader or writer, as someone to be instructed or as someone who instructs. It is in this way that genres 'do' ideological work. Each and every textual practice provides or promotes a 'reading position', a subjectivity constructed by the writer for the 'ideal reader' (Kress, 1988: 107); and each of these positionings implies different – but not limitless – possibilities for response and for action. As Casey (1993, quoted in Chandler, 1997) proposes, genres work to construct ideologies and values by encouraging certain interpretations or readings, which, conversely, become routinized due to the reduction of the diversity of possible textual formats to just a few, rigid formats (cf. Fairclough, 1995: 86). It is in this way that the symbolic capital (Bourdieu, 1991) and semiotic landscape (Jaworski and Thurlow, 2010b) of tourism is maintained and reproduced across a number of textual practices. Thus, we argue, 'discourses on the move' inevitably construe their implied readers in a specific ideological position vis-à-vis both tourism and the world at large. As Appadurai notes of 'mediascapes', they 'tend to be image-centred and narrative-based accounts of *strips of reality* ... which help to constitute narratives of the "other" and proto-narratives of possible lives, fantasies which could become prolegomena to the desire for acquisition and movement' (Appadurai, 1990: 299, our emphasis). The same is equally true of the semioticizing practices of less mediatized texts or genres.

To this end, we have deliberately selected three genres which represent different scales of economic and sociocultural participation. They range from highly institutional and more obviously elite inflight magazines, to more private, egalitarian postcards sent back home by tourists. En route, we also consider trade signs and business cards in a poor African country which reveal the creative and strategic appropriation of elite (Western) genres and discourses only to index the gap between the affluent and the deprived areas of the world caught up in a network of global flows of tourists and capital. What we find across this selection is that genre may act as a textual 'common dominator' for comparing different semiotic resources deployed by various individuals and organizations in the process of constructing the social reality of tourism. Semiotic resources – languages or modes of representation – are hierarchically ordered and always more accessible to some than others (Bourdieu, 1991; Blommaert, 2005). Genres also cohere into single communicative acts (akin to speech acts) by combining different modalities – linguistic, non-linguistic, as well as contextual features (van Leeuwen, 2005). By referring explicitly to the analysis of multimodal texts such as magazines, van Leeuwen (2002 [1993]) nicely demonstrates the interplay between discourse 'genres' and discourse 'fields'. Hence, where relevant in our textual data, we pay attention to the discursive choices across different modalities, attending to our texts' linguistic, visual, material as well as contextual features of each text. In consequence, in our analysis of a range of 'discourses on the move', we aim to demonstrate how different textual genres re-contextualize the field of 'globalization'. This relationship between genre and field is perhaps most easily demonstrated in our first case study: the inflight magazine.

The inflight magazine

Without the airline industry it is unlikely that there would be any 'global' tourism to write about, and our sense of what globalization is would be very different indeed (cf. Urry, 2007). The rise of mass tourism since the end of the 1940s and the growth of commercial air travel have always been inextricably and powerfully linked. Whereas journeys by aeroplane had, until this time, been the preserve of a very small, wealthy elite, the development of larger and larger jet planes and the deceptively easy access to vast amounts of fossil fuel made it possible for more and more people to travel – and to travel even greater distances. Although all travel for leisure is to some extent elite (see Introduction), aeroplane travel these days is considerably more egalitarian than it used to be – not least thanks to the dramatic rise of the so-called 'low cost airlines' during the 1990s and in spite of the more recent emergence of ultra-luxurious, super-elite airline strategies (see Thurlow and Jaworski, 2006). The *International Air Transport Association* (IATA) in fact estimated that, in 2007, annual passenger numbers worldwide were over 2 billion with 2.75 billion predicted by 2011.[2] Nor is it the aeroplane itself that makes tourism what it is, but rather the complex of institutional, social and cultural practices to have emerged as a result. In fact, the workings of international airlines also resonate far beyond the confines of the aeroplane cabin and the airline industry itself, having an enormous impact on the organization of contemporary life in much the same way that the train and automobile did before (for example, Schivelbusch, 1986; Flink, 1988). It is for this reason precisely, suggest Scott Lash and John Urry (1994: 253), that the jet plane passenger can be viewed as the quintessential emblem of (post-)modernity (see also Munt, 1994; Morgan and Pritchard, 1998; MacCannell, 1999 [1976]). To be sure, the airline industry continually influences the social, cultural and economic structuring of the world in new and different ways; for example, in their appeal to age-old divisions of distinction, taste and luxury, airlines nowadays busily reworking and re-inscribing social divisions and inequalities anew (Thurlow and Jaworski, 2006).

As such a major stakeholder in tourism, the airline industry not only influences the global economic order but, as part and parcel of this, is obviously also very powerful in shaping the global semioscape and the identities of travellers. Like most multinational or international corporations, marketing for airlines hinges on careful strategies of differentiation, positioning, promotion and what is known as 'brand equity'. Part of this brand equity obviously relies on the usual assurances of safety and cost; however, an increasingly important part of the way airlines are able to achieve the kind of competitive brand they require is also to promote themselves as 'global' and to promise their passengers the cachet of being global citizens and travellers. While this has been a marketing strategy for some time the urge for airlines to extend their *global* reach is nowadays a matter of economic survival and national pride (Thurlow and Aiello, 2007). It is in this way, therefore, that globalization comes to be not only a matter of economic reordering, but also a lifestyle and marketing brand to be bought into and sold back to passengers. As such, it is both a material and symbolic resource: to render yourself and your product 'global' is to render it *de rigeur*. And it is the image of the globe-trotting cosmopolitan which feeds the core aspirational ideals of tourism's promotional literature, in much the same way that television holiday shows (see Chapter 5) strategically intersperse items about high-end, luxury destinations like Mustique, Monanco or Mauritius with the more readily accessible and familiar destinations of, say, package holidays in Spain and Greece. For this reason precisely, airline marketers seek to project a global image not only for themselves of course, but, in order to service their commercial interests, for their customers as well. In other words, it is by appealing to, and contributing to customers' desire to be global players themselves that airlines work to establish themselves as global players. It's a win-win situation.

Along with its media marketing and other branding strategies, one of the most ubiquitous and readily available textual practices by which the airline industry makes its contribution to both globalization discourse and tourism discourse is the inflight magazine. It is here that airlines perpetuate a particular version of the world and promote a particular *style* for travelling through it. The readership of inflight magazines is unquestionably the international traveller, and they are inextricably linked to international tourism as ubiquitous 'travel-lifestyle' publications (Spafax, 2000). Since becoming the stock-in-trade of the airline industry in the 1960s, inflight magazines have evolved to become increasingly glossy, editorially diverse consumer magazines. In fact, where the reading material airlines provided their passengers initially amounted to little more than destination and/or duty-free shopping booklets, since the 1960s inflight magazines have come increasingly to resemble newsstand consumer magazines. So, while the goal of inflight magazines is first and foremost to promote the airline's corporate image and, by the same token, to advertise the destinations it covers, they also form part of the broader package of inflight 'infotainment' offered to passengers. In this regard, they function on a par with video and audio presentations used to hold the attention of their otherwise captive audiences. And it is not as if no one ever reads inflight magazines. According to figures touted by the International Marketing Bureau, at least 60 per cent of frequent travellers are understood to read the magazines most of the time, while a further 36 per cent read them some of the time.[3] For us, these figures are reassuring from a methodological perspective since they help secure our analysis here in terms of assumptions about uptake and readership. Of course, for most lifestyle magazines, the reader demographic and the target demographic are not necessarily the same thing. In the case of the inflight magazine, however, over 80 per cent of target readers are men under the age of 55, almost all of whom are working either in the financial and business sector, manufacturing industry or governmental and professional occupations (Rhodes, 1999 – figures for Europe). This, it seems, is clearly the prototypical 'international business elite' (Robins, 2000 [1997]: 195), and, not surprisingly, it is their version of the world and their place in it which inflight magazines invariably depict.

As with each of the chapters in *Tourism Discourse*, we have chosen to leave any detailed account of our data and analytic procedures to the Appendix (see p. 238). The discussion of inflight magazines which follows is based on a sample of those produced by over seventy different international airlines. We recognize that some time has past since these particular inflight magazines were collected but it is our distinct impression that very little has changed in the generic textual and institutional practices of the inflight magazine – in spite of the severe economic pressures airlines have faced in the wake of the 9/11 terrorist attacks, the SARS and Swine Flu epidemics, and the 'global economic downturn'. While Dubai-based *Emirates* did make a high-profile decision in 2008 to cancel its magazine, and while other airlines have admittedly chosen to 'slim down' their magazines as a weight- and fuel-saving strategy, few airlines have chosen to follow suit. Indeed, an airline like British Airways has edged its High Life magazine even nearer to the high-end lifestyle magazine with issues being guest-edited by the likes of British television celebrity Michael Palin, well known for his series of BBC travel shows.[4]

What is immediately striking about inflight magazines is the uniformity of their composition, although one that is also characterized by an underlying intertextuality which positions the magazines consistently as a blend of travel brochure, lifestyle magazine, corporate catalogue and information leaflet. Inflight magazines are clearly examples of what Theo van Leeuwen (2002 [1993]: 190) would describe as 'spatially integrated texts' whose communicative functions, stages and strategies are highly standardized despite any apparent hybridity or intertextuality of inflight magazines, and efforts to 'localize' them to look different one from another for the purposes of commercial and national branding. Somewhat paradoxically, then, the magazines appear to be heterogeneous in drawing from different publishing genres, but at the same time being extremely consistent in how they do that. As Thurlow and Aiello (2007) note in their study of airline tailfin design, the limited semiotic repertoire of inflight magazines is curious because there are no formal or explicitly institutionally governed standards of practice, no rules which dictate the design and content of inflight magazines. Their uniformity and consistency across so many different airlines must, therefore, also be a normative matter of choice, political economy and/or ideology.

Inflight magazines typically offer a standard mix of feature articles concerned with travel and lifestyle choices, together with practical information about destinations, inflight entertainment (for example, games and guides) and airline news. It is this adherence to the same overall editorial format across so many airlines – apparently regardless of whether or not many of them are being produced by dedicated publishing companies – that makes the magazines recognizable as 'inflight magazines', establishing the genre and, in turn, becoming an essential service for branding an airline modern and competitive. Passengers can expect this standard, internationally recognized text, which may or may not be rendered local by topics or language; what is seldom tampered with however is the format. In this sense, therefore, the medium really does prove itself to be the message. Although we will complicate this formula later (see also Chapter 2), inflight magazines appear to exemplify the deployment of a global genre 'filled' with local discourse (see Machin and van Leeuwen, 2003). It is not so much what is in the magazines which is important, therefore, as the fact that the airlines have a magazine clearly identified by its ascription to a range of generic 'inflight magazine' features. In other words, it appears that the inflight magazine is a textual practice which marks an international airline as an 'international airline' – evidenced most obviously by their ubiquity.

Stylization and global lifestyles

From the perspective of critical discourse studies, the textual practices of inflight magazines are also ideologically revealing in their structuring of different subject positions for the institutions behind them (most notably, the airlines) and their intended readers. As has been mentioned, genres combine into coherent, yet multifunctional communicative acts. In this regard, critical discourse analysts tend to borrow from Halliday (1978) the tripartite distinction of communicative functions that all texts simultaneously fulfil: 'ideational' (representational), 'interpersonal' (managing identities and social relations) and 'textual' (creating coherence and cohesion in discourse; for example, Fairclough, 2003). It is the interpersonal function of inflight magazines that we are especially concerned with, or more specifically, their work in the construction of social identities for their parent airlines and their passengers. Before that, however, we want to introduce one key conceptual framework for thinking about the discursive construction of identities here in Chapter 1 but also elsewhere in the book.

In sociolinguistics, the term 'style' typically refers to linguistic variation with respect to speech and social characteristics – or simply, 'the range of variation within the speech of an individual speaker' (Bell, 2009 [1997]: 265). Traditionally, therefore, *style shifts* have usually been thought to occur in accordance with varying degrees of situational formality or informality (Joos, 1961), or the degree of attention paid to speech by the speaker (Labov, 1972). In these approaches, style has been treated as a correlate of rather simple and stable types of situations, and of speakers' demographic characteristics. However, in more dynamic approaches, style is not so much a stable attribute of a particular type of speaker or situation, but a reflexively managed resource for performing acts of identity (Le Page and Tabouret-Keller, 1985). It is in this tradition that Nik Coupland (1985, 2001, 2007, 2009), for example, has argued for style, especially *dialect* style, to be treated as an indispensable feature of interactionally strategic positioning of self and other in forging and enacting particular social personas, a form of self-identification and self-differentiation with particular groups or group-orientations.

A related though narrower concept is that of *stylization*, that is a knowing display of language style(s) deemed in a particular situation to be non-normative, unpredictable, or 'as if' (N. Coupland, 2001; Rampton, 1995). Stylization is typically theorized by tracing its origins to the work of Mikhail Bakhtin (1981, 1986) on multivoicing and as a manifestation of performative language use (Austin, 1961; Bauman and Briggs, 1990, 2009; Butler, 1990). According to Bakhtin, language is never monologic but always dialogic, which presupposes a rich mixing and multiplicity of 'voices', or 'heteroglossia', in all texts. Thus identities are not autonomous and separate but involved and intercorporeal – produced as a series of stylizations by appropriating, reworking and subverting different ways of speaking. (As we shall show shortly, inflight magazines are particularly good at exploiting this aspect of style.)

There is a fair degree of ambiguity in the use of such concepts as *styling* and *stylization*, the former being treated by Nik Coupland (2001) as more reflexive, metaphorical and stereotyped than the latter. Deborah Cameron (2000a) meanwhile notes how style may be used as a linguistic resource for performing an identity and refers to Allan Bell's (2009 [1997]) 'initiative shift' and Rampton's (1995, 2009a) 'crossing' to convey the sense of a person's adopting a way of speaking which is not their own – in other words, putting on a voice (that is, Coupland's *stylization*). In this way, styling, not unlike stylization, may involve a person styling him- or herself or styling another person to the same end. In her work on the commodification of communication in contemporary service workplaces, Cameron (2000a) finds workers modifying their speech not because they are able to make choices about their linguistic performance (*self* styling in the traditional sense), but because others give them a script and a way of delivering this script. To this end, the term *stylization* 'involves speakers giving a performance, the "script" for which has been written by someone else' (Cameron, 2000a: 327). In this context, stylization is a form of 'verbal hygiene' (Cameron, 1995) and the imposition of a style complete with its commodification as a work-related skill.

Retaining both Coupland's and Cameron's conceptualizations of *stylization* as a somehow scripted or imposed performativity, we also invoke the broader framework of Norman Fairclough's notion of *style* as the discursive enactment of identities (2003: 159):

> Styles are the discoursal aspect of ways of being, identities. Who you are is partly a matter of how you speak, how you write, as well as

a matter of embodiment – how you look, how you hold yourself, how you move, and so forth.

For us, the appeal of this broader semiotic relies on a less linguistic and more embodied performance (see Bourdieu, 1991, on *bodily hexis*). Indeed, we examine the kinds of stylization in/of inflight magazines in terms of 'discourse as multimodal social practice' rather than necessarily 'discourse as language-in-use'. With this in mind, the backdrop for our discussion of inflight magazines relates also to what Anthony Giddens (1991: 81) calls 'the primacy of lifestyle' in modern (often Western) societies. According to Giddens, the intensification of individual and societal doubt has resulted in what he characterizes as 'tribulations of the self' whereby people are forced to establish a sense of themselves in the face of – or in relation to – ever increasing commodification and the 'plurality of choice'. For our purposes, therefore, lifestyles entail a range of similarly routinized discursive and semiotic practices, which, as Giddens suggests, give 'material form' to narratives of identity.

So, to summarize, we take stylization to be the strategic (re)presentation and promotion of particular ways of being (or styles) involving language, image, social practice and material culture. If these different identificational meanings endure through repetition and routinization, they may, over time, become habituated and 'structurated' (Giddens, 1991) into a more extensive narrative of self and a *lifestyle* which in turn forms (or reshapes) one's *habitus* (Bourdieu, 1984). In these terms, inflight magazines, not unlike airlines' frequent-flyer programmes (see Thurlow and Jaworski, 2006) offer an opportunity for us to examine a social practice whereby individuals may be styling themselves as elite, but are also consciously and strategically *stylized* (or *styled*) by others – in this case, by the airlines and their marketers who promote a carefully managed elite lifestyle predicated on the mythology of super-elite, freedom of mobility, global citizenship, cosmopolitanism and conspicuous consumption. This, it seems, is what it means to be a global player – an identity and/or lifestyle that we see being produced through a number of different semiotic resources in inflight magazines: linguistic, visual and material.

Styling the global player: Putting themselves on the map

Of all the semiotic stylizing resources airline's use for communicating their image as global players, the route map is arguably the most vivid and most prevalent of these. It is also the single most defining *generic* feature of inflight magazines. While most magazines have at least two or three maps, others have as many as four, five or six. Some include *local* (for example, UK, France, USA, Japan) and/or *regional* (for example, Europe, South America, Middle East, Africa) maps; almost always, however, there is a *world* map. It seems it is as important – if not more important – that airlines present themselves globally as they do locally. Notwithstanding this, the presence of these maps is of less interest than their design which, on closer inspection, properly reveals the semiotic function of the route map.[5] It also reveals an interesting tension in the stylization of global elite.

As the route map from British Airways' *High Life* magazine illustrates (Figure 1.1), international airlines clearly want to be seen to be 'in the world' and to have 'global' networks of connections. Where imperial Britain famously used to paint world maps pink to demonstrate the extent of its colonial dominance, Britain's 'flag carrier' airline nowadays looks instead to criss-cross it in red (perhaps for clarity, airline connections are almost always marked by red lines on route maps). What is interesting is that these route markings are quite superfluous and really only approximate; as such, their rhetorical appeal seems to be to create an impression of the airlines entangling, even appropriating, the world in their own webs of commercial influence.

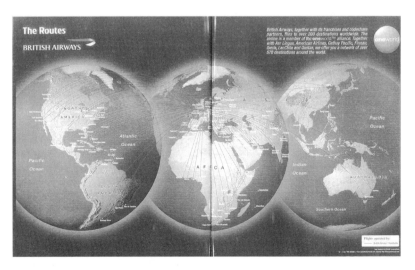

Figure 1.1   British Airways route map

Figure 1.2   ČSA route map

Of course, not all airlines have networks as widespread as British Airways. Even then, however, world maps are still displayed as a resource for positioning the airlines as global players.

As with the ČSA route map in Figure 1.2, smaller airlines create an appearance of a global *context* through the projection of their otherwise limited network onto a world map. Not surprisingly, ČSA, and many airlines operating on a similarly modest scale, seem to gain symbolic capital not so much from the density of their global network of connections, but through the illustration of connections to some of the major global cities, of which New York is the prime example. (We return to the issue of 'global cities' shortly.) To amplify their global reach yet further, however, airlines may also include any *anticipated* routes, as in the example of JAT (Figure 1.3), and the routes of all codeshare partners, as in the case of KLM/Northwest (Figure 1.4) where the world is almost lost beneath a mesh of international and domestic flight paths.

Of course, being perceived as 'global' is an important aspect of airlines' image-building, but being *central* in the globalized world is arguably even better. Maps are peculiar forms of representation, in that they usually represent the spherical, three-dimensional world drawn into a two-dimensional rectangle or ellipsis. As Jeremy Black (1997) explains, projections always involve distortions and are always political (see also Wood, 1992). For a long time, designs such the 16th century Mercator Projection or the 20th century Robinson Projection have struggled to

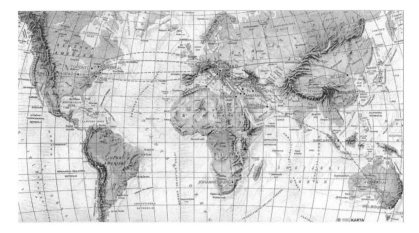

Figure 1.3 JAT route map

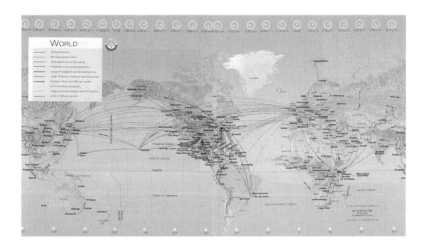

Figure 1.4 KLM/Northwest route map

bring as accurate and/or convincing a representation of the world as possible. What is interesting about both these familiar projections is that they usually represent the word in the same left–right, top–bottom orientation, the Americas appearing on the left, Europe in the top-centre position, New Zealand shown bottom-right and so on. Maps like this have become some of the most hegemonic ways of representing the world – they are, according to Black, the archetypal European projections. Edward Said (1979) too has famously commented on the ideological – in this case, Orientalizing – implications of these European visions for the countries which, de facto, become the 'Far East'.

Tellingly, in the style of McArthur's *Universal Corrective Map of the World* inflight magazine maps usually subvert this typical spatial arrangement of the world (except for most European airlines which are served well by the traditional maps), invariably centring their hub, capital or nation state.[6] Following Arnheim (1982), Gunther Kress and Theo van Leeuwen (1996: 206) note the privileging role of the centre in visual images, observing that information presented in the centre of images establishes it as 'the nucleus of the information on which all the other elements are in some sense subservient'. This effect is thus iconic and perceptual as well as symbolic in that attention is drawn naturally to the centre and that also centredness conventionally signifies importance (Aiello and Thurlow, 2006).

So, for example, the maps shown in Figures 1.5 and 1.6 demonstrate very clearly how, in order to position themselves at the heart of any global network, so-called 'flag-carriers' like Cathay Pacific and Quantas invariably centre their capital city as the hub of a vivid network of routes spanning out across the globe, not unlike the 14th century *Mappa Mundi* positioned Jerusalem as the centre of the universe.[5]

The impulse for airlines to project this global image and the compunction to adhere to the generic format of the inflight magazine are evidently strong. In the case of TunisAir (Figure 1.7), for example, we see how the desire to project a centred, global image may even require the depiction of large land masses, which have little to do with the

Figure 1.5   Cathay Pacific route map

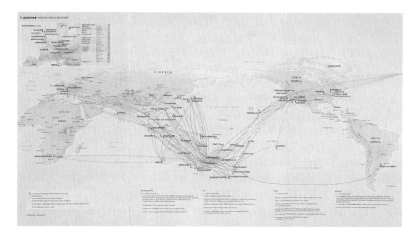

Figure 1.6   Qantas route map

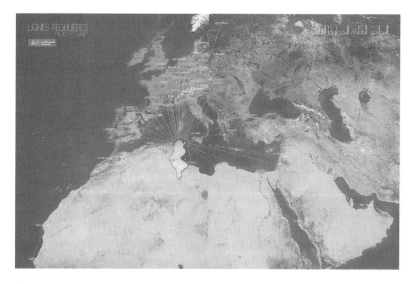

Figure 1.7   TunisAir route map

airline's network. The object of this visual rhetorical strategy is, once again, to appear to be spanning vast distances – especially insofar as this reach subsumes significant 'global' destinations. In the case of the TunisAir map, this also seems to bring with it a sense of the rather well defined division of the world into the rich and well-connected 'north' (depicted primarily in green), in contrast to the almost totally unconnected 'south' rendered in yellow, signifying the unpopulated, blank and anonymous 'desert'. A premium is therefore placed on the airline's connectedness to elite, and in this case predominantly European, destinations. As we discuss in more detail shortly, some destinations are invariably valued more highly by inflight magazines than others.

In their study of the transnational branding and marketing, Thurlow and Aiello (2007; also Aiello and Thurlow, 2006) consider how visual discourse can lend itself especially well to intercultural, cross-lingual communication. Perhaps more so than language, they argue, visual resources enable the coexistence of difference and similarity, specificity and genericity, and the local and the global. In part, this is because the iconicity and perceptual availability of visual signs makes certain aspects of images *potentially* recognizable and meaningful across cultures (as was the case with centring above). We suggest that route maps in inflight magazines function in much this way, being both perceptually salient and culturally meaningful. Accordingly, the same image can be given extremely similar meanings by people who do not otherwise share the same language. And this is obviously of great potential value for any airline serving an international, multilingual clientele.

There is nonetheless something of a paradox which underpins the design of route maps which also relates to the tension airlines must manage between being bearers of national pride (hence the 'flag-carrier') while also seeking to establish their global reach. In projecting an image of effortless reach, airline marketing must simultaneously depend on, and privilege, the nation state. Indeed, inflight magazines and the airlines they promote are situated at the epicentre of tensions between national (state-oriented) and international or commercial (worldwide) interests, which means that, on the one hand, they must position their hubs or capital cities and, by implication, their countries of origin at the privileged central place in the world; on the other hand, they must span as many international and intercontinental destinations as possible. This tension is managed graphically in a surprisingly consistent way in that route maps are apparently never political maps (that is, not representing individual countries by colour-coding). Although countries are strongly implied, not least by the names of city and airport destinations indicated on the maps, they do not depict national boundaries and show a 'world without borders' – itself a frequently used metaphor for globalization, and a resource for aeroplane passengers to imagine and position themselves as roaming the world freely, whether examining these route maps or following the plane flight's path on their 'personal' monitors for inflight entertainment. As we move through the rest of the book, this national–global tension emerges regularly, saying something important about the nature of tourists' identities and communities of practice under globalization.

Talking tourist: Exploiting the global language

The communicative strategies by which airlines establish their own and, indirectly, their passengers' global credentials are just as likely to be linguistic as they are visual. Before even opening an inflight magazine, readers are positioned through the strikingly narrow, predominantly English-language repertoire used to name magazines. While many magazines straightforwardly bear the name of the airline itself (for example, Garuda Indonesia's *Garuda* and Continental airline's *Continental*), nearly half of the magazines we looked at rely on something more creative and, usually, explicitly English such as Royal Jordanian Airlines' *Royal Wings*, KLM's *Holland Herald*, LOT Polish Airlines' *Kaleidoscope*. Other airlines draw on a repertoire of what might be seen as strategically cross-lingual names such as US Airways' *Attaché*, Air Canada's *enRoute*, EVA Air's *Verve*, EgyptAir's *Horus*, JAT's *Review* or SAS's *Scanorama* and Air Portugal's *Atlantis*. Both Air New Zealand and Ukraine International Airlines also rely on *Panorama*. Only a relatively small number of the magazines use an explicitly non-English (usually Arabic) name, often based on various greeting formulae – the quintessential tourist speech act (Jaworski, 2009). Examples of these include Kuwait Airways' *Alburaq* (Arabic 'lightening', Islamic equivalent of Pegasus), Ethiopian Airlines' *Selamta* (Amharic 'be at peace'), Royal Brunei's *Muhibah* (Malay 'friendship'), Sri Lankan's *Serendib* (an old Arabic name for Sri Lanka), Kenya Airways' *Msafiri* (Swahili 'traveller'), Thai Airways' *Sawadee* (Thai 'hello') and South African Airways' *Sawubona* (Zulua 'hello'). Certainly, to many Western, Anglophone passengers these are nominal sentiments that are likely to go largely unnoticed.

In using English names, some inflight magazines like Delta Airlines' *Sky* opt for names that allude to aspects of flight; other examples are Austrian Airline's *Skylines*, Finnair's *Blue Wings*, ANA's *Wingspan*, JAL's *Winds* and Turkish Airline's *Skylife*. Other magazines, however, choose names with a more deliberately cosmopolitan, jet-setter connotation such as Tarom's *Insight*, Estonian Air's *In Time*, Malaysia Airlines' *Going Places*, Sabena's *Passport* and Cathay Pacific's *Discovery*. In fact, this cosmopolitan *World Traveller* (Northwest Airlines) theme is generally popular, such as with BMI's *Voyager*, British Airway's *High Life*, Avianca's *Mundo* and United Airlines' *Hemispheres*. Both these types of fairly generic naming practice seem to play on the notions of effortless mobility, globality and the unhindered crossing of national boundaries. The predominant use of English, especially for magazines originating in largely non-English language environments, also seems to be an attempt by airlines to position themselves as 'global' by buying into the image of English as a world language.

Well over a third of the magazines we looked at were monolingual and, with one exception (Colombian airline *Avianca*'s Spanish-speaking inflight magazine), all of these were monolingual English. Of course, many of the airlines in our sample were from countries where English is the primary language or one of the official or national languages (that is, USA, UK, Australia, New Zealand, Ireland, West Indies, Zimbabwe, South Africa, Malta, Kenya, Ethiopia, Samoa, Canada, Brunei and Singapore). Nevertheless, and more remarkably, English is also the sole language used in the inflight magazines of the airlines of Romania, Sri Lanka, Scandinavia, Malaysia, the Netherlands, Iceland, Thailand, Belgium and Latvia – although, in the last three cases, small amounts of official national languages are used for inflight information or the welcome address. In the case of US airlines, both *Continental* and Delta Airlines' *Sky* magazine also use Spanish in addition to English for some passenger information (for example, safety instructions and visa forms).

Another third of inflight magazines opt instead for a more balanced, bilingual content, although the actual representation and use of the languages varies. In all these magazines English is the other language used, even appearing to take precedence over the national language in terms of the overall amount of copy (for example, the magazines of LOT Polish Airlines, Romania's TAROM, Korean Airlines and Ukraine International Airlines). One noteworthy semiotic/design choice taken up by the magazines of airlines like EL AL (Israel), Royal Jordanian, Gulf Air, Qatar Airways, Kuwait Air and Iran Air is to have their magazines readable from both 'front-to-back' for English and from 'back-to-front' to be consistent with Hebrew or Arabic orthography. In these cases, the coverage and content also tends to be evenly balanced between the two languages; however, in other such magazines (for example, Japan Airlines' *Winds*) the bilingualism is by no means as evenly balanced. While only four magazines might be classed as multilingual – Royal Air Maroc, MEA (Lebanon), Tunis Air and, with token amounts of Spanish, Portuguese and French used, American Airlines' *American Way* – a fifth of them appeared to rely on a less evenly balanced bilingualism and often the predominant language used is in fact English. The only magazines seen to rely more on their national language – in addition to Avianca's *Mundo* mentioned already – are Air France, EVA (Taiwan), JAL (Japan), Lithuanian Airlines and Aeroflot (Russia).

All of these different language choices made by inflight magazines point clearly to the predominant use of English alongside, or in preference to, other national languages as part of airlines' efforts to buy into the status of English as a world language and boost the airlines' status as 'global'. The reliance on English as a means *and* symbol of global communication is, of course, not unique to inflight magazines. Among others, Pennycook (1994) refers to the 'worldliness' of English, and Watts (1988, 2001) has commented about the cachet of English in ostensibly non-English-speaking countries; nor is this simply a matter of what House (2003) describes as 'language-for-communication' in contrast with non-English speakers' use of their first language as a 'language-for-identity'. English as a global semiotic resource, however unequally distributed or accessible, clearly serves both an instrumental, representational function as well as an identificational one.

Inflight magazines thus perpetuate the traditionally non-English speaking world's trend to appropriate English in order to position oneself – or one's passengers – as a global player (see Chapter 2 for another example of this). Relying increasingly on the international clientele and the rising English proficiency of their native populations, national carriers seem to not only cater for their potentially multilingual foreign passengers but also their 'internationalized' (through their competence in English) domestic customers. In this sense, anthropomorphizing descriptions of English as a colonizing or 'invading' language (for example, Phillipson and Skutnabb-Kangas 1999) not only misrepresent the sociolinguistics of language but also the historical and geographic realities of political-economy. Perhaps as an attempt to eschew the complicitous, globalist ideologies underpinning their ethnolinguistic concerns, critics of English too often fail to recognize or acknowledge the primary driving force behind the 'demise' or 'invasion' of their own varieties: advanced capitalism – a sentiment expressed by several other scholars commenting on the detrimental consequences of limited access to 'international' English by many (cf. Pennycook, 2006; Rassool, 2007; see also House, 2003, on the English as a lingua franca). Rather, the kind of English used in inflight magazines is typical of what Brown (1990) characterizes as 'cosmopolitan English' premised on a materialistic set of values in which international travel, not being bored, positively being entertained, having leisure and, above all, spending money casually and without consideration of the sum involved in the pursuit of these ends, are the norm (Brown 1990: 13, quoted in Anderson 2003: 92).

It almost goes without saying that a large proportion of all inflight magazine content is devoted to advertising, and, in this sense, they are not unlike any other type of commercial magazine. Also, unsurprisingly, the predominance of 'global' or multinational companies and brands among advertisers relies on the primary target audience of inflight magazines (middle-aged, male business people and professionals, see above) and their implied global interests and lifestyles (cf. Small et al., 2008). For our purposes, however, what is of greater interest is the choice of languages in advertisements; in particular, the undisputed emergence of English as the dominant language. Even in the inflight magazines with a non-English, monolingual, bilingual or multilingual language choice for the general editorial content (a quarter of those we looked at), predominantly English or English-only advertising accounts for over half of all advertising in inflight magazines.

As Jenny Cheshire and Lise-Marie Moser (1994), Ingrid Piller (2001a) and Helen Kelly-Holmes (2005) have argued in the case of advertising in predominantly non-English speaking publications, English is time and again used by international advertisers to buy into its powerful symbolic status (see Meinhof, 2004 on the linguistic indexing and stylization of foreignness in British TV commercials). In a somewhat less obvious case of local and national advertisers (for example, restaurants, hotels and so on, which are not part of multinational chains) promoting their services in inflight magazines, the use of English (whether the sole or second language) can be seen partly as earning the same symbolic capital as multinationals advertising in English, as well as a 'safe' way of reaching as wide an international audience as possible. As Piller (2001a: 153) expresses it, when it comes to addressing educated, business elites, English simply has the 'strongest linguistic currency'. This by no means implies that it is theirs exclusively, as we see from our marketplace data in Chapter 2.

That English is the language of international tourism and travel is unremarkable these days; what is more interesting, however, is to see how it is co-opted and re-semioticized in this particular context as part of such a consistent promotion of a global lifestyle. To quote Piller again: 'The use of English . . . iconically transcends [national and linguistic] confines and passes into a mythical global, unbounded realm where nothing but the sky is the limit. . . . The implied reader of bilingual advertisements is not a national citizen but a transnational consumer' (Piller 2001a: 173, 180). Just how truly transnational these consumer-citizens are remains to be seen. Indeed, our sense is that, at every turn, transcendence of the nation state remains more aspirational (or mythical)) than actual.

The power of global repertoires: Selling an elite lifestyle

As we saw with the route maps, it is not just the use and choice of printed language at play (or stake) here; the semiotic field of global capitalism is wide and includes different modalities, and in our case, most notably a combination of text and still images. Once again, this is apparent in the covers chosen for inflight magazines where different strategies are also used to appeal to tourists as 'transnational consumers' as Piller characterizes them (see Table 1–2 in the Appendix for the list of categories and distribution of cover images).

Accounting for over a fifth of all the cover images we looked at, inflight magazines rely heavily on the use of celebrities, especially international ones, and even more specifically those associated with the Hollywood film industry. For example, from our sample alone, film stars such as Jennifer Lopez (American Airlines), Keanu Reeves (EL AL), Jon Hurt (Aer Lingus), Angelina Jolie (Virgin Atlantic) and Sophie Marceau (British Airways) were featured, as well as two small inserts including Julia Roberts (Cathay Pacific) and Jackie Chan (Delta). The internationally renowned reggae artist Bob Marley appeared on the cover of BWIA (West Indies). Of course, celebrity endorsement is a well-established and well-tested marketing strategy.

The celebrity industry connects in very powerful ways with the tourism industry. To start, and as Graeme Turner (2004: 34) reminds us, '[c]elebrities are designed to make money.' The history of Hollywood-style stardom is one in which celebrities have become both commodities in themselves and vehicles for the promotion of commodity-driven lifestyles. Importantly, however, it is through their much publicized displays of material success that celebrities also 'vividly demonstrate the idea that satisfaction [is] not to be found in work but in one's activities away from work – in consumption and leisure' (De Cordova, 1990: 108). Often internationally recognizable brands, celebrities are especially influential because they glamourize the yearnings of ordinary consumers at the same time as appearing to be 'people like us' (Turner, 2004). And it is this quality which lends itself so well to the aspirational rhetoric of so much tourism promotion – and especially that of the airline industry. As we have noted elsewhere in relation to the promotional discourse of frequent flyer programmes: 'The goal [of aspirational marketing] is to keep people covetous of their ideal by carefully balancing opportunities for its realization (e.g. by acquiring or possessing a concrete manifestation of the ideal) and sustaining the impossibility of its attainment' (Thurlow and Jaworski, 2006: 115).

Just as other types of magazines and tabloid newspapers use celebrity photos on their covers to increase their sales, inflight magazines use celebrities as part of their commercial package to create an image for themselves and their passengers of glamour, desirability and global reach. For the inflight magazines, celebrities thereby function as yet another semiotic – and, specifically, metonymic – resource for global identification, along with the world maps, English-language names and content and multinational brand adverts. Tourists are also invited to imagine themselves moving through the world as the featured 'global celebrities' apparently do – a world without borders, a world of second homes and luxury vacations. Just as with airline frequent-flyer programmes, this constant 'texturing' of status is perfectly consistent with the logic of capitalism – a kind of planned symbolic obsolescence by which passengers (readers) can be held in a state always wanting to aspire to the next level of status as it is displayed by the celebrity tourist or needing to work harder to protect their existing status as tourists. We will show later (Chapter 5) how exactly the same role-model function is served by the use of celebrity tourists in television holiday shows.

The use of international celebrities, which, arguably, positions some inflight magazines and their airlines as global, is, to some extent, balanced by the foregrounding of local and national celebrities in some magazines. Rather than being contradictory, however, we interpret these tendencies as complementary, allowing airlines once again to straddle the tension between what Thurlow and Aiello (2007) characterize as national pride and global capital. Whether appropriating images of iconic, global celebrities or giving the same visual prominence to their national celebrities, positions national airlines 'in the world'. Although not always in the same league as the international stars mentioned above, it is possible also that national celebrities are used by inflight magazines because they are a less expensive option and showcase national achievements and 'high' culture. Some examples of the kinds of national celebrities we have seen include the Italian actor Giovanna Mezzogiorno (Alitalia), Finnish violinist Reka Szilvay (Finnair), Spanish Flamenco dancer Sara Baras (Iberia), Australian Olympic swimmer Grant Heckett (Qantas) and New Zealand adventure writer Stephen Lacey (Air New Zealand). The Sultan of Brunei was also the cover story for Royal Brunei's *Muhibah* magazine.

Although the focus of feature articles varies, sometimes focusing on a product (for example, wine), a geographic feature (for example, a river) or the history of a place, inflight magazines never fail to have at least one feature article on a travel destination – either international/foreign or national/domestic (these are typically covert advertisements of the airlines' own connections to the featured destinations listed at the end of the article; for a complete listing of feature articles devoted to *foreign* travel destinations, see Appendix). However, even though the representation of worldwide destinations is an important, generic component of these magazines, some destinations are evidently privileged over others. Indeed, along with the iconicity of English and celebrity icons, inflight magazines appeal also to the iconicity of place and, in particular, a metonymic repertoire of 'global cities'. Perhaps unsurprisingly, the most frequently featured cities are London, Madrid, New York and Paris, along with France, Australia, UK and USA as featured countries. In fact, in the seventy plus magazines we looked at, just three countries and their major cities (UK, London; France, Paris; USA, New York) accounted for a quarter of all the destinations featured. To these we might also add other destinations from the same countries: Manchester, Strasbourg, California, Chicago and Las Vegas. This pattern of geographic privilege is not accidental. Saskia Sassen (1991) in fact devotes a whole monograph to a discussion of New York, London and Tokyo as 'global' cities. For Sassen, what defines the cities as global is that they are the world's centres of international financial markets and the sites of the greatest concentration of capital and investment service transactions. Although in the case of our sample, Tokyo is surpassed by Paris, there is no apparent contradiction. Although it is also a G8 capital, Paris holds a tremendous amount of *cultural* capital due to the concentration of iconic architectural sites, works of art, places of entertainment, historical monuments and the myriad of discourses (including photographic and cinematic) constructing Paris as the city of love, glamour and beauty, and one of the top tourist destinations in the world. The United Nations' *World Tourism Organization* (see Introduction) regularly places France and Paris, in particular, as the world's top tourist destination.

Elite 'global cities' are, of course, often simply cities rich in economic capital (evidenced by the overall prevalence of G8 states) and those holding a considerable iconic status (or *cultural* capital) due to their importance as sites of global entertainment industry (cf. Sassen and Roost, 1999; and other contributions to Judd and Fainstein, 1999). For example, in addition to the 'select' destinations already mentioned, we find Australia, New Zealand, Spain (including Madrid, Barcelona), China (including Beijing, Hong Kong, Shanghai), Italy (including Rome, Milan, Venice), and then perhaps Japan (including Tokyo), Germany (including Berlin, Düsseldorf, Munich) and Hungary (including Budapest). Like celebrities, countries too have increasingly been branded and commodified (see Morgan et al., 2002). Countries – and their (capital) cities – accrue tremendous symbolic and cultural capital as a direct result of their economic capital. Research shows, for example, that consumers are more likely to purchase something if it comes from an industrial or Western country due to the stereotypical perception of quality or originality (Kotler and Gertner, 2002). This type of nation-state privileging is merely emphasized by the single feature on 'Africa' across our entire sample. In this regard, the role of English is again a central aspect of branding destinations as 'global' alongside the universal familiarity of their landmarks, cultural artefacts and financial importance.

The inflight magazine is clearly an ideal site in which countries or cities can advertise and thereby produce themselves – and they do so aggressively in what business scholars Philip Kotler and David Gertner (2002) call 'place marketing'. Airlines in turn are able to leverage the symbolic capital of these places through indirect association or through their direct link with them as flight destinations. This symbolic value is also on offer to the tourist, that is, the reader. If nothing else, inflight magazines are consistent in their cashing in on the cachet of 'global' destinations whether defined through their financial markets, iconic sites or the linguistic currency of English.

On being cosmopolitan: The imagined world of tourists

Although largely the preserve of Zygmunt Bauman's (1998) travelling 'globals', the airline industry is an otherwise largely modernist construct which ordinarily seeks to establish and promote a national identity and nation-based commercial interests. As has been evidenced by the proliferation of new national airlines in Eastern Europe since the collapse of the Soviet Union and Yugoslavia (see Wragg, 1998), it seems that no nation state regards itself as fulfilled unless it has its own *national* airline. Despite the enormous costs involved and widely publicized post 9–11 losses in revenue, national governments in Africa, Eastern Europe and, more recently, Western European countries like Switzerland and Belgium, are still heavily committed to setting up and/or retaining a 'flag carrier' airline – even if that 'national' airline is the financial property of another nation.

At the same time, of course, these flag carriers inevitably cross national borders and criss-cross an international landscape. Indeed, confronted by increasingly slim profit margins coupled with the deregulation of international airspaces (for example, over Europe and across the Atlantic), large international airlines have been busy forming themselves into shareholding and code-sharing alliances, and national airlines find themselves needing to market themselves as global carriers in order to extend their global(ist) reach. In fact, the major airline alliances (that is, *Oneworld*, *Star* and *SkyTeam*) mirror precisely the patterns of strategic, multinational co-operation and conglomoration that typify the global finanscape. For contemporary marketers and advertisers (see, for example, de Mooij, 1998: 23) the branding strategies of airlines are therefore necessarily predicated on establishing so-called 'global platforms' and 'local adaptations'. However, as most processes of economic and cultural globalization operate dialectically, even the transnational mergers of airlines do not necessarily mean the demise of their distinctly national identities and branding. For example, since the KLM and Air France merger in 2004, both airlines have maintained their role as national flag carriers and, significantly for us, continued to publish separate inflight magazines. And the same is true of the German Lufthansa-owned Swiss International Airlines.

One of the most characteristic features of mass tourism is the 'home-from-home' promise made by industry representatives. Certainly, we have found this to be a common theme in holiday travel shows (Chapter 5) where viewers are continually reassured that, however exotic and adventurous their destination, it comes with many of the familiar comforts of home. Arguably, nowhere is this more apparent than in business travel where great emphasis is placed on commercial tourists being able to move with as little disruption and challenge as possible from hotel room to hotel room, from airport lounge to airport lounge and so on. Perhaps, therefore, the uniformity of inflight magazines is part and parcel of this streamlining of the tourist landscape for the benefit of those people that Bauman (1998) refers to as 'globals' and 'tourists' as opposed to 'vagabonds'.

With that said, writers like Bauman often appear to make the mistake of over-simplifying this class of 'tourists', characterizing these 'first-world' inhabitants in terms of their cosmopolitanism and 'extra-territoriality' and holding business people, cultural managers and academics as representatives. In fact, air travel more than any other form of mass transport seems to typify *growing* inequalities based on the vast disproportions in the spread of global capital (Harvey, 2006; Thurlow and Jaworski, 2006). This is how John Urry puts it:

> For first-class passengers, air travel is integrally interconnected with limousines, taxis, air-conditioned offices, fast check-in and fast routing through immigration, business-class hotels and restaurants, forming a seamless scape along which nomadic executives making the global order can with less effort travel. For countless others, their journeys are longer, more uncertain, more risky, and indicative of their global inferiority in a world where access to network capital is of major significance within the emerging global stratification system.
> (Urry, 2007: 152; see also Cresswell, 2006: Ch. 9)

According to Bauman (1998: 89), for travelling elites 'state borders are levelled down'. However, while these people unquestionably enjoy the privileges of choice and ease of movement, they are, we believe, no less under the symbolic and literal sway of borders. Moreover, to categorize all travellers by choice as tourists conceals important differences. In much the same vein as Bauman, for example, Hannerz (1996: 102–103) talks about 'cosmopolitans' and reserves the label for the 'transnational' identity of those people who become involved in, and transformed by, a 'plurality of contrasting cultures' (see also Lash and Urry, 1994; also see our discussion of Ulrich Beck's *banal cosmopolitanism* in the Conclusion). For Hannerz, cosmopolitans are always willing to engage with a cultural Other, where, by contrast, what he calls 'metropolitan locals' or 'provincials' remain rooted in their territorial culture and always assimilate 'items of some distant provenance into a fundamentally local culture'. For most tourists or travellers, however, it is neither possible nor desirable to transcend territoriality.

Nonetheless, the 'global citizen' or the 'true' cosmopolitan is not, as Hannerz (1996) suggests, a real person – although surely such people exist. In keeping with Ulrich Beck's (2002) notion of 'abstract' or 'normative' cosmopolitanism, we are more inclined to view cosmopolitanism is very much one of many liberal discourses which run through the mythology of both tourism and globalization. It is in these terms that it is possible to think of people also *talking* globalization into existence – or, in the case of inflight magazines, printing it into existence. None of which is to deny the the centrality of aeorplanes, airports and airport cities in the material order of global capitalism (Urry, 2007: 155). The promise made by inflight magazines to both the jet-setter and the globe-trotter is an opportunity to buy into a way of life and a lifestyle which is, to use Piller's (2001a) terms, international, fashionable and sophisticated. Inflight magazines are thereby complicitous in establishing and perpetuating the *ideoscape* of globalization (Appadurai, 1990), although in terms of both (inter)national ideologies and ideologies of consumption. Whatever the destination of their passengers, global capitalism and the pursuit of global capital is the driving force behind inflight magazines and the promotion of most international travel and tourism. Globalization is, in effect, a sales pitch, and the 'global citizen' is both role-model and myth, which, in the service of global capital, are designed to persuade us to spend and consume.

It is in this way that inflight magazines also usefully reveal the complex interplay between the forces of post-industrial capital and the impact of 'global' culture – brought together by the shrewd opportunism of marketers who seize on globality as a strategic positioning for their companies. At the same time, national interests are showcased and globalized; such as in the centring of Sydney and Hong Kong in the route maps, and the promotion of Finnish violinist and local (non-chain) restaurants. Not only are they the mouthpiece of the airline but inflight magazines also appear to act as an important voice-piece for central discourses of globalization. To use van Leeuwen's (2002 [1993]: 178) distinction, the structure *of* the text is 'global' the structure used *in* the text is 'globalization'. Inflight magazines are therefore globalizing genres not only in their format and editorial content, but also in their function. They are, we suggest, instruments for representing the world in global terms but, more importantly, as *already* globalized.

In describing the globalist agenda which underpins inflight magazines, it is the cumulative effect of a number of different features which we have found notable; specifically, the consistency of their format and their continual appeal to a global identity or lifestyle. These magazines are thus both *textually* 'global' – in terms of their design and format – and *thematically* 'global'. More correctly, however, they are *globalizing* genres in the sense that they have a constitutive role in the processes of global capitalism and the discourses of globalization. In turning to the more strictly linguistic, this is perhaps most evident in the strategic deployment of English in naming the different magazines and in their extensive advertising content.

If contemporary life is shaped by so-called 'globalization', it is also marked by a 'crisis of identity' (Hall, 1996b) and the concomitant 'tribulations of self' of which Giddens (1991) speaks. And it is in the context of this type of uncertainty and (self-) doubt that lifestyle comes into prominence and that spaces open up for commodification and styliza-tion. The particular success of frequent-flyer programmes, although true in part of all loyalty schemes, is not only their recontextualization of global discourses, but also their ability to capitalize on social anxieties about identity in general and about status in particular (Thurlow and Jaworski, 2006).

In this sense, at first sight, inflight magazines are curiously demo-cratic. While most other semiotic signifiers of distinction between the areas of the plane designated as first-class, business and economy are different, from seat design, menus, food, crockery and cutlery, entertain-ment packages, free newspapers (no longer available in economy), flight attendants' politeness routines and so on, inflight magazines together with safety instructions are to be found in the seat pockets of all the passengers across the whole aircraft. One major difference being that while for most economy passengers the world presented in these pub-lications may be a temporary distraction and a gateway into the word of fantasy and aspiration, for their fellow passengers at the front of the plane, they are templates of their lifestyles and patterns of consumption likely to be continued once they get off the plane. As Small et al. (2008), following Morgan and Pritchard (2005a), argue inflight magazines are one of the tools used by airlines to socially sort their passengers on the basis of wealth and class.

As we noted earlier, Anthony Giddens (1991) has famously written about the 'dilemmas' or 'tribulations' of contemporary identities; how, in the face of seemingly opposing economic-cultural forces such as frag-mentation and unification, authority and uncertainty, we are all obliged to work harder than ever to establish a coherent sense of self. One conse-quence of these post-industrial pressures is the disconnect between our 'local lives' and what Giddens calls our 'phenomenal worlds', brought about by the fact that our immediate, everyday experiences are increas-ingly 'penetrated by distanciated influences' (ibid.: 187). There are two things that we might add to Giddens' observations. The first is this: phe-nomenal worlds are often also *imagined* worlds (cf. Anderson, 1983). If people experience their lives as global, this is the result of not only 'intrusions' from afar – be they material or mediated – but also because people *invite* the distant and *want* to envision themselves in, and con-nected to, faraway places. The romantic mythology of the global village certainly has a privileged tangibility for the richer citizens of the world, but it is also a story that many others like to tell as we shall show in Chapter 2. The second comment we have regarding Giddens' 'phenome-nal worlds' is that we are less sure they are as 'truly global' as he suggests.

In the case of tourists, for example, there is pleasure precisely in the fact that the imagined world of travel is also always grounded locally, either by contrast or by similarity. The enjoyment and privilege of tourism is that one remains somehow rooted in or connected to one's home base, one's national identity, just as the thrill of international jet-setting is that there are national borders to be crossed and countries to be tallied in passports. The imagined world narrated by inflight magazines is simultaneously local and global, national and international, parochial and cosmopolitan.

2
Borrowed Genres and the Language Market: Trade Signs and Business Cards

> While clearly most people across the world are not global tourists *qua* visitors, this does not mean that the places that they live in and the associated images of nature, nation, colonialism, sacrifice, community, heritage and so on, are not powerful constituents of a rapacious global tourism .... In certain cases becoming a tourist destination is part of a reflexive process by which societies and places come to enter the global order.
>
> (Urry, 2002: 142–143)

As we have already begun to see in Chapter 1, the neoliberal ideal of a globalized world typically invokes the image of free-flowing people, capital, ideas, images and texts traversing a shared social, economic, political and cultural space. While the 'global village' is surely in doubt, the increasing interconnectedness of people, regions, nation states and institutions is an enduring and highly consequential mode of operation under global capitalism, encompassing practically all areas of life. As David Held and Anthony McGrew (2000: 4) explain:

> Globalization, simply put, denotes the expanding *scale*, growing magnitude, speeding up and deepening impact of interregional flows and patterns of social interaction. It refers to a shift or transformation in the *scale* of human social organization that links distant communities and expands the reach of power relations across the world's major regions and continents.
>
> (our emphasis)

The key notion or issue here is that of *scale*, but not simply as a matter of quantity or extent, which is what Held and McGrew seem to suggest. Instead, what makes scale a defining feature of global capitalism are the multiple 'levels' at which processes of change, interconnection and (re-)organization are occurring: global/local, national/transnational, regional/continental, rural/urban and so on. From the perspective of human interaction and communication, what is equally significant is the constant transposition of genres, discourses and styles from one level or scale to another – the kind of intertexualities, appropriations and recontextualizations typically characterized by terms like 'niche marketing', 'internationalization' and, of course, 'glocalization'. Most importantly, neither the movements nor the consequences of globalization are evenly 'shared' or freely 'flowing'; they are instead premised on, and constrained by, unequal development, access to scarce resources and divisions of power. Held and McGrew continue:

> But [globalization] should not be read as prefiguring the emergence of a harmonious world society or as a universal process of global integration in which there is a growing convergence of cultures and civilizations. For not only does the awareness of growing interconnectedness create new animosities and conflicts, it can fuel reactionary politics and deep-seated xenophobia. Since a significant segment of the world's population is either untouched directly by globalization or remains largely excluded from its benefits, it is deeply divisive and, consequently, vigorously contested process. *The unevenness of globalization ensures it is far from a universal process experienced uniformly across the entire planet.*
>
> (Ibid.; our emphasis)

It is with this 'unevenness' in mind – the disjunctures and inequalities of global capitalism – that we turn our empirical and analytic lens in this chapter to a site of tourism discourse where textings are being produced by those who are clearly participating in the globalizing flow of language and communication, engaging in the economic, social and cultural exchanges of tourism as a global industry, and arguably benefiting in monetary and symbolic terms from their involvement; however, these same people nonetheless remain resolutely excluded from the driving mechanisms and large-scale gains of globalization. Globalization may not be an equal playing field, but like it or not, we are all players. Here, then, as elsewhere in this book, we are also concerned with sometimes agentful enactments of globalization as glimpsed and accessed through informal, 'vernacular' texts, snippets of spoken or written communication, face-to-face or mediated, which leave a trace of their author's role in making meaning out of globalization and, to whatever extent, 'talk' globalization into existence. In particular, we turn our attention here to specific text types (genres) – trade signs and business cards – their contents, linguistic shape, imagery, materiality and emplacement in their physical environment (what Scollon and Wong Scollon, 2003, refer to as 'geosemiotics'). As will be seen from our discussion, these textual practices form part of a broader 'response' to, or 'repercussion' of, globalization, but are also instances of its production, dissemination and circulation.

On the face of it, trade signs and business cards keep us squarely in the domain of elite, more obviously institutionalized generic practices like inflight magazines. Both are well-recognized and well-established genres of commerce. We ourselves have heard many Europeans and North Americans comment on the way in which every high or main street they walk down seems to look the same thanks to the spread of (multi)national businesses and corporations – a homogenized semiotic landscape of fast-food chains, clothing stores, cosmetic stores, banking institutions and so on (see Figure 2.1). In many respects, these are the

Figure 2.1 Typical British high street

quintessential signs of globalization as people commonly understand it – those global companies and global brands that are Westernizing or Americanizing the world (cf. Garrett et al., 2006). What is often overlooked, however, is that it is not merely the discursive 'content' of these trademarks – the product, the brand – that circulates, but also the practices of trade signage itself. In other words, the genre too is on the move.

Tucked away in the wallets or briefcases of the global elite, business cards are just as likely as inflight magazines to be circulating the globe. Nor is it only people of commerce who take up and perpetuate this particular textual practice. In fact, the business card is a very commonly 'recontextualized' genre – taken up by academics, for example (see Figures 2.2 and 2.3) – with a remarkably stable format: name, institutional affiliation, logo and contact information such as street addresses, telephone number, email addresses and, maybe, a website. For critical discourse analysts, these seemingly innocuous borrowings of corporate genres and other discourse practices (for example, board meetings, quality reviews, customer evaluations) manifest and discursively constitute the increasing reach of commerce into other areas of social life – not least of which is the increasing marketization or managerialization of higher education which Norman Fairclough has been documenting for some time (see Fairclough, 1992, 1993, 2003). We will return to this point a little later.

In spite of the familiarity of trade signs and business cards, and their existing global sway, we want to think about them slightly differently in this chapter, to examine their uptake in a less obviously elite, less

Dr Crispin Thurlow
Associate Professor
thurlow@u.washington.edu
http://faculty.washington.edu/thurlow

Department of Communication
College of Arts & Sciences
UNIVERSITY OF WASHINGTON

Box 353740   206 543-2747 phone
Seattle, WA 98195   206 616-3762 fax
United States of America www.com.washington.edu

Figure 2.2   Crispin's 'business' card

Professor Adam Jaworski

Centre for Language and Communication Research

Cardiff School of English,
Communication and Philosophy

Cardiff University
Humanities Building
Colum Drive
Cardiff CF10 3EU
Wales UK

Tel +44(0)29 2087 4243
Fax +44(0)29 2087 4242
jaworski@cardiff.ac.uk
www.cardiff.ac.uk/encap

Figure 2.3 Adam's 'business' card

obviously institutionalized contexts, and on a somewhat different *scale*. The data we use consists of two ethnographically derived sets of images from Gambia: (a) trade signs in two tourist souvenir markets, Fajara and Brikama; and (b) business cards advertising various tourist services: restaurants, taxi companies, tour guides and so on.[1] The business cards are usually handed to tourists in a variety of service encounters as a reminder of the service provider (for example, taxi company), or when strolling leisurely looking for a place to eat, or while getting into a taxi. These *seemingly* quaint, 'low-tech' discursive practices and strategies on the part of local market-stall holders and informal tourism workers also offer interesting insights into the global language market. With its 'grassroots' orientation, our chapter here (as with Chapter 5) makes a turn towards considering the point of view of the 'tourees' (Van den Berghe, 1994) – the people who are typically thought of as the objects [*sic*] of tourism, the people to be seen. Having said which, these are still textual practices primarily oriented to and designed for tourists.

Before we come to analyse our data, we want to start by foregrounding our discussion with reference to some of the broader issues concerning the linguistic political-economy and global modes of economic production and symbolic exchange. In doing so, we also continue to map a little further the perspective on global mobility we are developing across the book *vis-à-vis* the 'implication' of language in globalizing processes. In particular, and given the site of our data, we want to address the rescaling and resignification of the place-based identities (and textualities) of global capitalism, which in turn come to shape the 'grassroots' discursive practices of tourism as an otherwise elite, privileged mode of global mobility.

New place-identities and tourism reflexivity

A global economy structured around a network of financial flows connected by information networks and communication technologies is what Manuel Castells (2000[1996]) has termed 'network capitalism'. Knowledge and information generated and facilitated by digital information technology play a crucial role in the organization and management of financial markets and separating them from labour markets. The former, says Castells, are global while the latter are local. The rise in the significance of information technologies and the further dislocation of capital from labour have led, among other factors, to a relocation or 'outsourcing' of much of the manufacturing industry from the affluent Western societies to the so-called 'developing world'.[2] David Harvey (1989) uses the term 'flexible accumulation' to refer to this economic regime of greater international mobility for corporations, lowered production costs, increased access to financial markets through sophisticated communication technologies and the exploitation of a virtually unlimited pool of cheap labour which has displaced the traditional, unionized workforce of industrial societies. The dismantling of traditional manufacture-based economies across the Western world has led to the rise of post-industrial, service-based economies and jobs 'characterized in general by the central role played by knowledge, information, affect, and communication' (Hardt and Negri, 2000: 285). In the same vein, money itself has been literally and figuratively *dematerialized* through its decoupling from precious metals, its digitization, its speculation, all of which leads to great volatility and an even greater dependence on the social/symbolic capitals of trust and reputation. Such instability in the representation of monetary value lead to the worldwide financial crisis at the time of writing this book, which has in turn forced a somewhat ironic reappraisal of the neoliberal agenda and the role of national governments in regulating global markets. All of which points again to the more general 'crisis of representation' in advanced capitalism, paving the way for complex cultural and symbolic (including linguistic) signification as the *basis* for the circulation of commodities and capital (Harvey, 1989; Lash and Lury, 2007). We are, as others have observed, living in a highly semioticized world characterized by the privileging of design over substance, of image over reality and of lifestyle over livelihood (see our Introduction; cf. Lash and Urry, 1994; Fairclough, 1999; Baudrillard, 1994; Graddol, 2002).

In his now classic study of life under advanced capitalism, David Harvey (1989) identifies time–space compression as another key feature or condition of contemporary, postmodern life. The acceleration of turnover time in production and consumption of goods, services, entertainment, leisure and sporting habits and so on, has been achieved through recourse to fashion (hence limiting their shelf-life), and the activities involved in 'consumption' have become ever more ephemeral – visiting museums, attending rock concerts, watching multiple TV shows (often simultaneously – channel surfing), playing video games, 'working out' in health clubs and so on Their on-demand, 24-hour accessibility, has speeded up the pace of production, as well as accentuated the whimsical instability of changing fashions, commodities, modes of production, lifestyles, ideologies and social practices. This instantaneity, transience and disposability in commodity production and consumption (for some) has led to the collapse of (many) spatial barriers but not to the loss of significance of space (Lefebvre, 1991 [1974]; Thurlow and Jaworski, 2006, 2010). Our discussion of airline route maps in Chapter 1, for example, showed how the thrill of transcending space is equally grounded in its local, tangible manifestation. As Harvey (1989: 294) notes:

> [h]eightened competition under conditions of crisis has coerced capitalists into paying much closer attention to relative *locational advantages*, precisely because diminishing spatial barriers give capitalists the power to exploit minute spatial differentiations to good effect. Small differences in what the space contains in the way of labour supplies, resources, infrastructures, and the like become of increased significance. Superior command over space becomes an even more important weapon in class struggle.
>
> (our emphasis)

The effects of relative compression of space through time, the extreme fragmentation and uncertainty of boundaries around individual, social, political and cultural spheres has inevitably dislocated and transformed personal and collective identities (cf. Giddens', 1991, notion of the 'tribulations of the self' in Western, consumer-driven societies, at least). Nor is this instability of control over space without opportunity for those less favourably positioned by global capital; the working-class, women, ethnic and sexual minorities and other marginalized groups too have been mobilizing into social and political movements, seeking control over place and the production of new place-identities (Massey, 1994; Brown, 2000). Of course, the powerful typically respond by reasserting their control over space (see Low, 2001; Thurlow and Jaworski, 2010). Nonetheless, the fluidity of space along with the liquidity of social-economic life demands and affords a reconsideration of the relationship between identity and place. This returns us to a concommitant feature of global mobility that John Urry (2002) points to at the very beginning of our chapter – what he labels 'tourism reflexivity' and which he explains further as:

> the set of disciplines, procedures and criteria that enable each (and every?) place to monitor, evaluate and develop its tourism potential within the emerging patterns of global tourism. This reflexivity is concerned with identifying a particular place's location within the contours of geography, history and culture that swirl the globe, and in particular identifying that place's actual and potential material and semiotic resources.
>
> (Urry, 2002: 141–142)

As the single largest international trade and as a global cultural industry, tourism's consumption of place is not only rapacious it is also ubiquitous. And everyone – not just 'the capitalists' (cf. Harvey quoted above) – is potentially and understandably drawn to capitalize on their own 'locational advantages', however small and wherever they may be. One way this is evidenced is in the preservation of tradition and heritage, not least through their (re)invention, commodification, museumification and, we would add, *touristification*. Phaedra Pezzullo's (2007) study of so-called 'toxic tours' reveals some of the interesting opportunities in 'touristification' for generating political and not just economic gain. It is precisely the self-conscious, strategic (re)working of spatial, symbolic and material resources inherent in tourism reflexivity which frames the textual practices we will be looking at in a moment. Any cashing in on local resources, however, also requires that places and people draw on the circulating discourses of tourism and enter into the global political-economy of language – our last theoretical consideration before turning to our textual data.

Language and/as the global marketplace

As we saw in the case of inflight magazines, language clearly has an important role in accessing economic and political resources, organization of forms of production and in the exchange of goods and services (see Bourdieu, 1991; Irvine, 1989). To use just one simple example, authenticating works of art is principally a performative linguistic act and it can affect their value in remarkably dramatic ways. Judith Irvine offers a clear example of this in her analysis of Wolof compliments in Senegal where linguistic objects and performances may in fact gain monetary value and be in their own right exchanged for cash and other goods. The link between language and market exchange is obviously of particular significance in tourism and other service industries which have proliferated in Western, post-industrial societies under globalization, and to some extent, as will be demonstrated below, in other parts of the world.

The general processes of commodification and appropriation of language in the new economic order of flexible accumulation and time–space compression has in the past decade become an object of some interest among sociolinguists and critical discourse analysts (for example, Fairclough, 1999, 2002, 2006; Cameron, 2000b; N. Coupland, 2003a; Pennycook 2007). Broadly speaking, the main focus of this work is on how the reconfiguration of language styles, genres and discourses refashions social practices and social identities. It is here, where the connection with Harvey's (1989) theorizing of new place-identities is most clearly established as the processes he refers to are *par excellence* semiotic or discursive. From the field of sociolinguistics, Monica Heller discusses these processes as part of her work on commodification of language and a shift from work force to word force (see, for example, Heller, 2003a, 2010a, 2010b; Budach et al., 2003). Heller's studies of bilingual areas of francophone Canada demonstrate how the collapse of traditional industries (cod-fishing, mining, logging and so on) in the second half of the 20th century, and their substitution with new information and service-based industries (call centres and tourism) have led to the commodification of language (understood as a measurable skill) and identity, especially in relation to other forms of cultural practice such as dance and music in tourism. In these domains of economic practice based on contact between different linguistic markets through advances in communication technology (call centres) or travel (tourism), linguistic and other symbolic resources become marketable commodities (see also Cameron, 2000a). At the time of the decreasing role of the State in regulating local economies and welfare provision, and the shifting space of national points of reference, ethnolinguistic minorities, however disenfranchised and marginalized they might have been before, are free to engender a new sense of authenticity and community, to invoke new place-identities predicated on the (re)invention of tradition, heritage and the heavy policing of language boundaries. However, due to the new conditions for the commodification of language and other forms of cultural production, language (in the form of language skills, for example, bilingualism) may now be easily separated from 'identity' and used for self-styling and/or the stylizing of others or as commodity resource for members of various groups(Bell, 1999; Cameron, 2000a; N. Coupland, 2007 – see also our introduction to Chapter 1). Heller argues that, in the interest of protecting their cultural capital, francophone elites have claimed the legitimacy to define the boundaries of authenticity with regard to 'who counts as francophone, what counts as bilingualism, and what counts as French' (Budach et al., 2003: 606). These language ideological debates (Blommaert, 1999; Heller, 1999 – and our chapters in Part II) are heavily biased in favour of such notions as language purity and standardization (repressing English borrowing in French and code-switching, for example) and run in parallel to the reproduction of class and power relations based on the division of labour and the establishment of new institutions such as French-language schools. In terms of Pierre Bourdieu (1977, 1990), francophone elites deploy their symbolic capital ('a form of power that is not perceived as power but as legitimate demands for recognition, deference, obedience, or the services of others' (Swartz 1997: 43)) in their bid to release cultural capital locked in the access to and distribution of linguistic resources (French, bilingualism). As Heller argues, the mediating role of language in managing subject positions between commodity and authenticity is typically associated with such struggles over legitimacy, for example,

> attempts on the part of people understanding themselves as francophones to retain the concept of authenticity and community in order to construct collective privileged access regularly encounter resistance from actors who stand to profit from the opening of access that the new conditions provide. These actors include Anglophones who learn French, and francophone immigrants.
>
> (Budach et al., 2003: 607)

Heller's work nicely demonstrates how the *rescaling* of space from 'national' to 'local' or 'regional' has led to a change in the symbolic and economic value of language repertoires of bilingual francophone speakers in Canada.

Of course, the same process may be effected starting from the opposite end, that is, when a linguistic form or repertoire moves across different spaces. This is one of the central issues concerning Jan Blommaert (2003, 2005, 2009) in his attempts to formulate a socio-linguistic theory of globalization. To this end, Blommaert argues that language is too broad and abstract a notion to be used as a starting point in discussion of a 'global sociolinguistics'. Conceiving globalization in terms of (uneven) *flows*, we should instead be concerned with more specific notions of codes, varieties, accents, dialects, styles, discourses, genres and so on, as it is these textual and material manifestations of language that are indeed subject to global and globalizing processes through the agency of social actors. (Here, one has only to think of the locally inflected uptake of instant-messaging and text-messaging styles around the world – see Thurlow and Poff, 2010, for more on this.) Languages no longer map so neatly into nation-states nor are speakers easily ordered into clearly demarcated speech communities (cf Rampton, 2009b).

Blommaert's approach to globalizing linguistic flows is grounded in the work of Immanuel Wallerstein (for example, 1983, 2001) on World System Analysis. The *system* locates nations and regions in terms of three main categories: 'core', 'semi-periphery' and 'periphery'. This division is based on the nations'/regions' political and economic organization, their relative position in the economic hierarchy of the world and the asymmetrical relations of the division of labour across the spectrum. Due to the exploitative relation between the core and peripheral regions, with the former maximizing their profits at the expense of the latter, the system is founded on neocolonial forms of discrimination and control. As Blommaert argues, the differential wealth and status between these strata is responsible for the fact that:

> *[i]nequality, not uniformity, organizes the flows* and the particular nature of such flows across the 'globe'. Consequently, whenever sociolinguistic items travel across the globe, they travel across *structurally different* spaces, and will consequently be picked up differently in different places.
>
> (Blommaert, 2003: 612; original emphasis)

One of the consequences of the movement of semiotic resources and sociolinguistic items through the geographical spaces of 'unequal development' (Harvey, 2006) is that while their form may be preserved, their value, meaning or function are significantly altered: 'Value, meaning, and function are a matter of uptake, they have to be *granted* by others on the basis of the prevailing orders of indexicality, and increasingly also on the basis of their real or potential "market value" as a cultural commodity' (Blommaert, 2003: 72).

Other forms of global linguistic flows follow different fortunes and trajectories. As we noted in Chapter 1, global media have been enormously successful in homogenizing formats, templates and genres (cf. *Cosmopolitan*, *Big Brother*, video games and so on) while allowing their content to be diversified and localized (Machin and Van Leeuwen, 2007). In this regard, one particular linguistic and cultural practice that has caught the imagination of many a sociolinguist writing about globalization is rap and hip-hop (for example, Cutler, 1999, 2009; Pennycook, 2003, 2007; Androutsopoulos, 2007). The significance of this work, not unlike that cited above in relation to Heller's and Blommaert's research, is that it demonstrates how rap and hip-hop has become a global identity resource particularly in the context of youth cultures. In principle, it is in the same way that the inflight magazine serves to construct a 'global player' identity (or brand) for airlines (Chapter 1). However, as Pennycook (2003, 2007) demonstrates, the content, code choice and style of rap and hip-hop lyrics in its many 'regionalized' varieties may be inflected in any number of local ways. The Japanese rap group Rip Slyme, for example, construct their lyrics in what appears as a mixture of Japanese and English, but while on some occasions their English is *mimetic*, that is, echoing both the phonology and lexicon of Afro-American Vernacular English, on others, it is *symbolic* – rooted in Japanese phonology and syntax, it is a form of Japanese-influenced English, or a Japanese performance in English. This complex linguistic play with codes allows Rip Slyme to situate themselves in different spaces of local and translocal identities, which, according to Pennycook, is not in fact located in the code itself, but in the act of performance of the semiotically reconstructed and reconstituted English forms (Kandiah, 1998). Thus, we can see Rip Slyme appropriating a new music genre and code as a celebratory, yet wholly creative and original process straddling dialectically local and global, national and transnational spaces, but never falling short of invoking completely new, refashioned subject positions.

Given these complex 'on-the-ground' textualities and the sometimes unpredictable interplay of core and periphery, Blommaert (2003: 609) suggests that any 'realistic look at globalization' should start simply by asking 'questions about *whose* genres are being globalized, by whom, for whom, when and how?' It is with this in mind that we turn to two genres well-established in the commercial discourse of the global 'core' (that is, trade signs and business cards) with a view to examining the nature of linguistic flows under globalization. As will become apparent shortly, these instances of genre borrowing in Gambia manifest a high degree of creative and strategic appropriation from/within the global language market.

Trade signs and business cards in Gambia

The two souvenir markets providing data for our discussion are located in the coastal, urban area of Gambia in the towns of Brikama and Fajara. They are typical spaces of tourist–host interaction involving economic exchanges accompanied by a high level of symbolic and linguistic exchange such as bartering, providing information about the goods for sale, staging local customs and myths, performing greeting rituals and other forms of small talk between vendors and tourists, as well as the manufacturing and selling of wood carvings, paintings, jewellery, clothes and a host of other objects.

In Figure 2.4, we show one of the two gates to the Fajara market, located next to the Atlantic coast. The recognizably branded (for a local

Figure 2.4 Entrance to Fajara market

beer company) blackboard sign in front of the gate says in capital, handwritten letters:

THE MARKET
HAS TWO SIDES
FRONT AND BACK
SIDES. THEY BOTH
SELL WOOD CAR-
VING, TIE & DYE
AND BATIC

In the absence of any other signposting, the text on the blackboard functions straightfowardly as an indicator of the market's entrance and as an advertisement for its wares. The appearance and style of the sign, like of the market itself, are rather unremarkable. Although some care has gone into the design of the road leading to the market entrance with its semi-circular pockets paved with white beach pebbles, the market is a modest low-rise, covered with corrugated iron roof giving shelter to the market stalls on the inside, arranged in a circle. The writing is clear but its finish is amateurish and ad hoc rather than professional and design-intensive. The linguistic forms indicate some struggle with the control of standardized English spelling/orthography (the repetition of the word 'sides' and the division of the word 'carving' while some empty space is left at the bottom of the board), which suggests that we enter a commercial space organized and run by a 'grassroots' collective of traders rather than a highly institutionalized and regulated organization with a sizeable marketing budget. The seeming swiftness with which the sign has been executed corresponds to the rather makeshift, low-tech presentation of the market stalls inside – none of which is to deny that the sign or the stalls were assembled without care and, no doubt, pride. The market stalls in Brikama (Figure 2.5) have a similar feel of hasty construction, temporary finish, and a chaotic display of the goods, all pointing to the mode of commerce being conducted towards the periphery of the economic and geographical world system.

It is the use of 'low-tech' semiotic and material resources – especially when juxtaposed with the 'high-tech' production of the blackboard itself – that strikes Western tourists as markedly different. Although, in the context of tourism's quest for difference (cf. Favero, 2007; also Chapter 3), what might quickly be derided back home as 'poor English' or 'poor design' can also assume the quality of quaint, charming and/or exotic – as symbolic markers of authenticity. After all, the 'low-tech'

Figure 2.5   Market stalls, Brikama market

nature of the hand-carved wooden statues and hand-made clothing is precisely what gives them their cultural cachet, their symbolic capital.

As in most markets of any sort, the stalls in the Fajara and Brikama markets have assigned identification numbers which appear alongside some optional information, such as the name of the owner or vendor, address, telephone number and so on. A closer look at the markets in Fajara and Brikama reveals a degree of linguistic play in the way the stalls are named and promoted. What was particularly noteworthy for us was the use of the names of large UK department stores and supermarket chains, to name just some of them: Harrods (Figure 2.6), Harvey Nichols, Liberty (Figure 2.7), John Lewis (Figure 2.8), Safeway (Figure 2.9) and Selfridges (Figure 2.10). One of the stalls carried the sign that read, 'Welcome to Lenny Henry' (Figure 2.12; see Lanza and Woldemariam, 2008 on similar 'borrowing' of McDonald's and Starbucks logos in Mekele, Ethiopia).

Gambia is a small nation with a population of approximately 1.2 million, receiving in the range of 120,000 thousand visitors annually, mostly from the UK, its former colonial ruler. Therefore, many if not all of the cultural references used for the self-identification of the market stalls and vendors (cited above) are easily recognized by the mostly

Figure 2.6 'Harrods', Fajara market

British tourists. Harrods, Harvey Nichols and Liberty are 'iconic', luxury department stores in London, with some regional branches in the UK. John Lewis is a well-known, 'mid-range' chain of department stores and Safeway is a well-known chain of supermarkets (from the USA, although no longer present on the UK market). Lenny Henry is a popular Afro-Caribbean British actor and stand up comedian.

Clearly, we see here the appropriation of genres (commercial signage and corporate branding) and other cultural discourses borrowed from one part of the global system (the 'core') to another (the 'periphery'). The agents of the appropriation are relatively poor traders evoking anything but the supposed glamour, wealth and international cachet of these expensive stores and of a television celebrity. While the style, materiality and emplacement of the signs speaks volumes about the global economic inequalities between the UK and Gambia, their instant recognition by most of the tourists makes these relocated signifiers useful vehicles for the marketing of goods which are typically not associated with these brands.

Several of the signs attempt to replicate the logos of the UK stores quite closely. 'Harrods', for example, is a rather accurate approximation of the original lettering and the green colour used by the London

Figure 2.7   'Harvey Nichols' and 'Liberty', Fajara market

department store. It is carved on a solid plank of wood, painted in a mélange of white and black resembling the appearance and texture of a slab of polished granite – a telltale sign of the endurance and reliability of the brand. Other signs are not produced with the same degree of precision. The 'John Lewis' sign is written with a ball point pen on a piece of cut out cardboard and is also accurately located in 'Oxford street', one of London's most famous and, as it happens, most touristic shopping streets. Although it approximates the actual logo of the store, it remains just that: a crude approximation, an echo of the 'real' thing. The 'Liberty' sign meanwhile uses the distinctive, branded font of its London role model, but the vivid blue background and cheap piece of plywood on which it is displayed also distance it from the original. The capital lettering of the 'Harvey Nichols', 'Self riges' and 'Safe way' signs do not even closely resemble the trademarked fonts of their source logos, although the stencilled letters of 'Selfriges' against

Figure 2.8 'John Lewis', Brikama market

Figure 2.9 'Safe way', Fajara market

Figure 2.10 'Self riges', Fajara market

Figure 2.11 Fatima Samba's 'unbranded' stall, Fajara market

Figure 2.12   'Lenny Henry', Brikama market

the yellow background and the painted letters of 'Safeway' against the red background of the metal sheet are reminiscent of the trademarked colours of the two stores, respectively. Though it is less easy to see in this reproduction, the top left corner of Figure 2.4 also shows a John Lewis plastic shopping bag displayed as part of the branding of the stall. Here, the transposition and recontextualization of an inexpensive, disposable item with only utilitarian value in the context of affluent consumer culture of the global core, and its insertion into a commercial space of the global periphery, results in its transformation into a durable, aestheticizing object of considerable symbolic value and marketing potential. It is resemioiticized but by no means totally.

The literacy displayed in the signs is resolutely 'grassroots', in Blommaert's (2005) terms, with their 'unprofessional' finish, cheap materials (torn off pieces of cardboard, recycled and rusting metal sheets, crude bolting, visible repainting over earlier versions) and the non-standard spellings/orthographies ('Self riges' for 'Selfridges'; 'Safe way' for 'Safeway; 'WEL COME' in 'Welcome to Lenny Henry'). It is possible, of course, that these are conscious, playful attempts to avoid copyright infringement – although, as we suggest a little later, this is unlikely.[3] The signs also mix the block-lettered logos with hand-written additional information: 'hand carving · batik stall № 32' (Figure 2.6) provides specific information on the types of souvenirs which localize and differentiate the Gambia Harrods from its London counterpart. 'John Lewis' makes several additional textual references drawing on a variety of commercial, religious and personal discourses: 'Never knowingly undersold' is a long-running slogan of John Lewis; 'BOGOF' ('Buy one get one free'), a common sales promotion technique in many UK retail contexts linking the stall again to an international discourse of commerce; 'Shop call' and 'Phone № 799314' anchor the business in its locality; while 'God over evils' and 'HARD way is the only way' index the vendor as a spiritual, moral person. However quaint these may seem to the Western eye, these marketing strategies are not all that far removed from 'green-washing' and other 'social responsibility' tactics used by the likes of BP and Starbucks. They are also akin to the practices of 'synthetic personalization' (Fairclough, 2001). 'Harvey Nichols', 'Liberty' and 'Selfriges' all have other localizing indexes of their own context: national ('Gambia branch'), personal ('Ya Ida's'; 'Eva and Joanna') and commercial ('A.B.C. Shop stall № 28'; 'No: 36'). These unorthodox – by Western norms – mixings of register, production value and discourse add to the sense of creative entextualization and recontextualization.

Additionally, the signs blend in a degree of humour, good-natured banter and other cross-cultural references. We have already cited the personalizing, quasi-religious aphorisms of the vendor at 'John Lewis' and the witty reference to the national 'branch' of 'Selfriges'. Underneath 'Welcome to Lenny Henry', additional text reads:

Rise up and Shine
Good looking To
LENNY HENRY

The caption alludes to the uplifting spirit of the British actor's performances and, as the vendor explained to us, his apparent physical resemblance to the British actor. The vendor had never actually met or seen Lenny Henry (in real life or on television) but had been assured of his likeness to the comic by some visiting tourists. In a simple way, we are reminded here of another important feature of tourism discourse and of the particular interactional frame of host–tourist encounters. In their search for the 'authentic' or, at least, the different, tourists invariably demand the reassuringly familiar (the home from home) and frequently frame the local with references to home (see Chapters 3 and 5 for more on this tendency). They are also often more than willing to overlook the sometimes obviously co-constructed, staged nature of the 'local culture' and of local identities. As tourists, we often come looking for what we set out to find. And hosts know this only too well; like Lenny Henry, they skilfully, often wittily and always meaningfully style or fashion themselves accordingly. Tourism reflexivity demands that local people too shape and present themselves, their 'culture', their place in the image of the tourist imagination.

Not all market sellers in Gambia make use of these sorts of transnational intertextualities as part of their sales pitch. Figure 2.11, for example, features a sign foregrounding the locality and tangible difference of Gambia in contrast to the UK and other parts of the world, from which most tourists come from:

FATIMA SAMBA
STALL № 5
SEW AND SELL BEST QUALTY
MATERIALS COTTON SILK TIEDIE
AFRICAN EUROPEAN DRESS
HAIR DRESSER WOOD CARVING
ALL AT REASONABLE PRICE

Here, the African-sounding name, Fatima Samba, possibly another pseudonym (like Lenny Henry and possibly the two Christian names in the 'Eva and Joanna' sign of 'Selfriges') indexes the vendor more clearly as a 'local'. Of course, code choice – English – draws on the vendor's multilingualism and positions her simultaneusly as an *international* by likely surpassing most tourists' competence in Mandinka, Wolof or any other indigenous language. Having said which, the linguistic features of this sign, shared with the others discussed above, in terms of its shaky typography, spelling, orthography, lexis (the awkward listing of goods and services) and grammar (absence of the plural marker on 'price'), unavoidably testify to Fatima Samba's economic status *vis-à-vis* most tourists' economic and symbolic capital as 'First World', first-language English speakers.

What is of particular interest here, is the idea of a historically and, specifically colonially, structured 'linguistic corridor' facilitating this sort of language movement – a passageway somewhat removed from the kinds of 'flows' or 'scapes' commonly talked about in globalization studies. One of the legacies of the British colonial rule in Gambia is that English remains its national and official language, which is probably also why so many British tourists choose it as a 'winter sun' destination, and why British cultural and commercial references are freely exploited by Gambian tourism workers in striking up a conversation with British tourists as a 'ticket' to offering tour-guiding services, for example. In this sense, the presence of British tourists in Gambia and the movement of English linguistic and cultural references may be seen as the continuation of the colonial legacy (see our Conclusion for more on the neocolonial trajectories of tourism).

As something of an aside – and stepping beyond our Gambian data for a moment – other similar examples Senegal reveal how French works in a similar way, albeit through a different 'linguistic corridor'. Figures 2.13–2.16 illustrate a parallel phenomenon of naming grocery and souvenir shops targeting predominantly French tourists in Senegal, a former French colony, with the names and logos of French department stores and supermarkets: 'Galerie La Fayette', 'E. Leclerc', 'Auchan', 'Carrefour' and 'Tati'. Here, again, we see appropriations of the source logos and problems with accuracy in the executing of fonts and orthography (for example, 'Galerie La Fayette' for 'Galeries Lafayette'), relatively poor materiality of the signs and their emplacement over shabby-looking, even empty, stores (for example, Figure 2.16). There is also an attempt to appropriate the global discourse of economic enticement of customers by displaying the word 'reduction' (for example, underneath the signs for 'Auchan' and 'Tati'), which is ironic given that West African prices are already clearly 'bargains' for rich-country tourists. Of course, it is also possible that the word 'reduction' appears in the signs for ironic self-styling; it is, after all, a permanent display unlike the seasonal SALES (or SOLDES) signs in other Western contexts.

Such patterns of post-colonial language spread point to an important feature we started out with regarding the language of globalization and/or the globalization of language. Languages (codes, genres, varieties,

Figure 2.13   'Auchan' and 'Carrefour', Senegal

styles, discourses and so on) do not 'flow' freely from place-to-place in a
diffuse and uncontrollable way; instead, their movement is determined
largely by pre-existing social, political and economic conditions of
migration and domination (De Swaan, 2002; also Blommaert, 2005).
Sociolinguistic items are emplaced to do specific 'work', responding to
the strategic needs of the social actors and the expected uptake from
the target recipients, and in response to the particular constraints and
opportunities of place and its location in the global world system. We
have already alluded to the scalar, historical aspects of globalization and
will take them up again shortly, once we have presented the second of
our two 'borrowed' genres.

73

Figure 2.14　'Leclerc', Senegal

Figure 2.15　'Tati', Senegal

Figure 2.16   'Galerie La Fayette', Senegal

From trade signs to business cards

Another genre of global commerce and corporatization that perme-
ates the linguistic landscape of tourism in Gambia is that of business
cards. These seemingly small and insignificant texts are of course
of huge importance in the global economy as part of organiza-
tional needs to manage corporate brands in the areas of so-called
'aesthetics management' or 'identity management' (see Schmitt and
Simonson, 1997). A quick look at any marketing book (for example,
Schultz et al., 2000) shows how much planning detail may go into
the execution of a desirable format: the choice of card (thickness,
texture, finish), size, shape, colour, typeface (flat, embossed, size)
layout, graphics (for example, logo) and contact information (for
example, names, titles, addresses) and so on. Business cards are then
carefully considered and executed *styling* resources for individuals
and institutions, being exchanged, scrutinized and commented on
at moments of interaction and as part of mutual self-presentation
ritual.

The business cards of informal tourism workers in Gambia evidence their uptake of the well-established (in rich countries, at least) corporate discourse of (self-)promotion by the same means. Their entry into, and appropriation of, this language market is, however, by no means a straightforward 'buying in'. Figures 2.17–2.28 provide examples of just some of the cards we collected over a few days spent in various tourist areas. These micro-texts serve as advertisements for goods and service providers in many areas: Lenny Henry's market stall (Figure 2.17), bird-watching (Figure 2.18), taxis (Figures 2.19 and 2.20), tour guides (Figures 2.21 and 2.27) and restaurants (Figures 2.22–2.25). Unusually, Figure 2.28 (below) is a card with contact details for a school, not a typical tourist site. We have elsewhere commented on the enculturation of children and young people into the super-elite markets of tourism (Thurlow and Jaworski, 2006) and, here, in a very different context, we find another example. With nothing to sell, this young person had, it appeared to us, taken up the genre, this mode of social (inter)action, approaching tourists as a way perhaps of reaching out to a world beyond himself. With a crudely torn out scrap of cardboard, the name of his school and his *Hotmail* address, this young person creatively and strategically locates himself in the world and as a citizen of the world.

The first striking feature of our random but reasonably representative collection of business cards is that it comes from the informal sector of the Gambian tourist industry – individuals or small businesses operating without the backing of large, official or transnational tourist operators, who bring most of the package holiday tourists into the country and reap most of the profits. These package tours provide all that the Western 'sun and sand' tourist may need during their stay in Gambia: transportation from place of residence, transfers to luxury hotels, food in hotel restaurants, supermarkets, access to beaches, entertainment and so on. Some tourists do not venture much outside these comfortable enclaves of 'bubble tourism' (Judd, 1999). When they do, they are faced immediately with numerous street vendors (selling fruit, paintings, jewellery and so on), taxi drivers and an assortment of unofficial guides known as 'bumsters' initiating contact with a vast array of business propositions involving walking and chatting, giving directions, birdwatching or having a meal with a family in the village (in exchange for buying dinner ingredients for all). Business cards may be handed over at the time of approach and, when accepted, may be a prelude

Lenny Henry

Shop No 9 Brikama Craft
Mkt Kombo Central W/D
The Gambia
Home 484654   TEL 782850

We know where they are!
ALIEU (ALEX) BARRY
Bird Guide
PMB 733 Serrekunda
The Gambia
MOBILE: 786437

SIZZLA'S TAXi
B.B Hotel Car Park
Car Reg. No. BJL 7525 B
Mob: 783501
Contact the Controller

Figures 2.17–2.19 Business cards

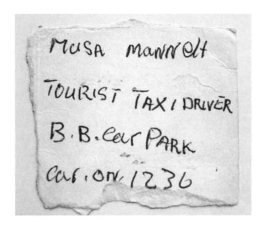

(a)   (b)

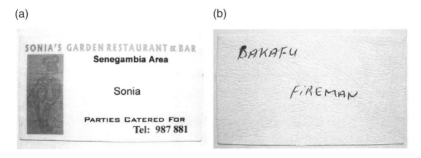

Figures 2.20–2.22   Business cards

78

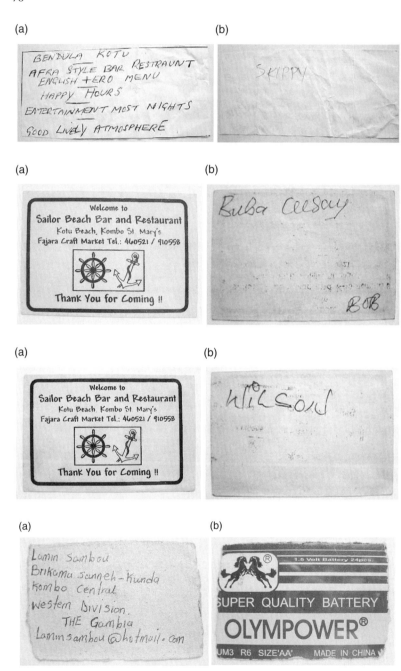

Figures 2.23–2.26 Business cards

(a)   (b)

(a)   (b)

Figures 2.27–2.28   Business cards

to a conversation, initially 'social' and later becoming more 'transactional' (Lawson and Jaworski, 2007). However, as in the case of the market signs, the style, production values and the context of passing business cards in Gambia bear all the semiotic and material hallmarks of global inequality in stark contrast to the Western model which they try to emulate.[4] As with the trade signs, however, the symbolic practices of the business cards tell a more nuanced story about tourism discourse and about the global language market. Once again, there are always 'semiotic opportunities' (Blommaert, 2003: 610) and 'locational advantages' (Harvey, 1989: 294) to be found in the peripheral spaces of globalization.

The cards, which approximate the look and feel of their Western counterparts, are the ones which have been designed on home computers and then ink-jet printed (Figures 2.17–2.19, 2.22a, 2.24a/2.25a). Printed in black and white or colour, they compete for distinctiveness through a range of design features. The Lenny Henry card is rather 'plain' but with the large bold letters used to print his name, a dramatic horizontal line separating the name from clear, highly readable contact details below, this card appears among the most 'professional' looking and unmarked.

However, print quality (that is, patchy, low-resolution saturation, rough edges, 'bleeding' of the characters) all expose the relatively low production values and Lenny Henry's business as a very small fish in a vast ocean of global corporations. The card for the birdwatching tour guide (Figure 2.18; see also Figure 2.22) is more carefully printed with an expensive-looking colour and two photographs – a kingfisher and the guide himself smiling at the viewer, with a pair of binoculars hanging around his neck indexing his professional, expert status; this card is, however, printed on thin, writing paper rather than thick, durable cardboard and the printing often shows through this low-grade paper (see Figures 2.24b and 2.25b).

Apart from Figure 2.18, the only type of figurative graphics used in the cards is computer clip art: a car, two hands in a handshake and a chequered, 'ethnic' frame line around the edges (taxi service; Figure 2.19); a chef (restaurant; Figure 2.22a); a helm and anchor ('Sailor Beach Bar and Restaurant'; Figures 2.24a and 2.25a). Inextricably linked with the monopolistic political-economy of *Microsoft*, clip art is itself a highly ideological, globalizing textual practice (Dillon, 2006). These ready-made, clichéd resources associated with low-tech design in the core regions seem to substitute the expensive, brand-distinctive logos designed for institutions and business in the rich regions of the world, or even in Gambia when operating in more institutionalized contexts. The 'logoization' of these grassroots businesses depends precisely on appropriating widely circulating, generic resources rather than individual, distinctive imagery (cf. Machin, 2004). At the symbolic level, this frames the Gambian business cards as imitators rather than animators of global business practices. And this is a symbolic market that is invariably driven by (or organized around) the inequalities of the economic marketplace. As Thurlow and Aiello (2007) note, global semiotic resources or repertoires are always available for recontextualization and agentful reworking; symbolic values are, however, hierarchically managed and aesthetic agendas typically set by some (usually in the core) and not others (usually in the periphery).

Even greater departures from the received idea of a 'respectable' business card are evident the examples of cards handwritten on pieces of graph paper cut out from a notebook (Figure 2.21) or torn off from discarded, card-board packaging (Figures 2.20, 2.26b–2.28b). These are predominantly the cards used by 'bumsters' with no identifiable infrastructure and institutional support, bearing only their name and address. The visible literacy practices demonstrate little command of the 'received' genre of the global core, as in Figure 2.27a where the shaky writing of the guide's email address is followed by a single line 'Name Edrisa'; in Figure 2.20, where the only contact detail is the reference to the car park where the taxi can be usually found and car registration number (we think), with no directions, phone or email details; or, in Figure 2.21, where the contact details include a particular tourist area.

An interesting linguistic practice adopted by many informal tourism workers in Gambia is the adoption of trade nicknames (see also above), another bid for maximizing their distinctive, memorable branding for tourists – in a similar way that trade signs work. On business cards, nicknames may accompany the full names of their owners ('Alieu (Alex) Barry', 'Ebrima Jadama or Brian') or they may constitute the sole personal self-reference ('Lenny Henry', 'Sizzla's Taxi', 'Name Edrisa'). These personalizing moves are matched by borrowing or inventing catchy taglines or slogans (another interesting appropriation of corporate discourse/styles) aimed at making a lasting impression or synthetically personalizing the appeal: 'We know where they [birds] are!'; 'Contact the controller'; 'Parties catered for'; 'Thank you for coming!!'). The taglines may blend in with more elaborate descriptions of the service as in Figure 2.23a:

BENDULA KOTU
AFRA STYLE BAR RESTRAUNT
ENGLISH + ERO MENU
HAPPY HOURS
ENTERTAINMENT MOST NIGHTS
GOOD LIVELY ATMOSPHERE

An awkwardness of design and execution is often matched by the grammatical or stylistic confusion (for example, 'happy hours', 'parties catered for') including alternative spelling for place names (for example, 'Sanneh-Kunda' for Serrekunda, Figure 2.26a). None of which is to judge the discourse as necessarily 'incorrect' or 'deficient'.

The Gambian business cards seem to have a longer shelf-life than elsewhere. Their well-worn appearance is in some cases a sign of a prolonged waiting for their owners to hand them on to the passing tourists. It would be rather unusual in the Western corporate setting for anyone to pass on a dusty, creased card to a business partner. Indeed, it would be marked as inappropriate and, given their self-promotional function, communicatively incompetent. Some of the Gambian cards are, however, clearly recycled, especially those that have names written on the back: 'Bakafu Fireman'; 'Skippy'; 'Buba Cusay [Ceesay?] Bob'; 'Wilson'). Most of these nicknames belong to bumsters 'employed' to advertise local restaurants and who receive a small commission if a tourist hands in the card and has a meal at the restaurant. These cards then re-enter circulation where in other locations they would be stored or scrapped. The genre – constituted by its format, function and norms of interaction – is thus complexly reworked and recontextualized in ways that are clearly structured by global economic forces and inequalities.

Shopping in the language market: Recontextualization, parody and appropriation

As we noted above with reference to Harvey's work (1989), in a world of time–space compression and flexible accumulation, consumer goods often derive their value less from their material and utilitarian worth, but more from their symbolic and cultural cachet. Wood carvings and other souvenirs in Gambia, guided tours and other services are in large supply and due to the unfavourable rate of exchange between 'weak' local and 'hard' foreign currencies, they are relatively inexpensive for the tourists; nor are they distinctive enough for each vendor to ensure a steady stream of buyers. Competition is stiff and the workers in Gambian tourism industry must resort to discursive practices they associate with the successful economies of the global core – marketing, advertising and branding – and to the appropriation and *recontextualization* (Fairclough, 2003) of successful corporate genres. However, one issue with the disembedding of genres is that this is a sociolinguistic process that is not entirely inconsequential to the meaning of the sociolinguistic item (or genre) being transposed (Bauman and Briggs, 1990, 2009; Silverstein and Urban, 1996). As we saw with reference to Blommaert's work cited above, the movement of semiotic tokens (souvenirs?) across the regions of unequal development may preserve their shape but their value and symbolic meaning can [*sic*] change. Rescaling is thus a matter of magnitude, domain and value – both symbolic and economic.

In the case of Gambian trade signs and business cards, the recontextualization processes are more complicated still. Unlike our own use of business cards (Figures 2.2 and 2.3), Gambian business cards are transposed not from one discourse domain to another (for example, from business to academia) but rather from one *locality* to another. Their meanings may well be shifted through this geographic relocation – some meanings added and some lost – especially for tourists for whom the familiar contexts of use might resonate with suits and ties, boardrooms and conferences, skyscrapers and first-class lounges. Nonetheless, in the context of tourism – a straightforwardly economic or commercial enterprise for most local people – it's business as usual. There is an uncomplicated instrumental value in both the trade signs and the business cards (that is, information exchange, advertising) as well as a skilful symbolic value. What may appear as pretend branding to the tourist is no less strategic, no less effective, branding just because it is carried out by and 'unsuited' Gambian stall-holder.

Having said which, even for the tourist this recontextualization of the genres is not a straightforward one. The valuing and devaluing of literacies, texts and symbolic capitals are, in some ways, a little less linear and clear than Blommaert (2005) appears to suggest. In this regard, Blommaert discusses a handwritten letter sent to him by 'Victoria', a 16-year-old daughter of his friends in Dar es Salam. The letter is written in English, an emblem of elite education, middle-class and relative affluence. In other words, the letter may be regarded as an index of high status and upward mobility in the global periphery of Tanzania. However, despite her best efforts, Victoria fails to fully grasp the mastery of English literacy. In highly normative terms, the short text is marred by severe 'errors' of grammar, punctuation and orthography, narrative style and other literary conventions. Once the letter reaches the core of the world system, therefore, it no longer manages to index the same privileged status as it does at the place of its origin. In other words, the linguistic resources deployed in the letter, characteristic of 'grassroots literacy', typical in the region and sufficient as a display of high rank at source, end up at the bottom of someone else's sociolinguistic hierarchy once relocated.

The kind of exchange Blommaert describes here is surely more unpredictable and not quite so easily mapped onto geographic relocations or economic trajectories. The young woman's letter has clearly not ended up at the bottom of Blommaert's own 'sociolinguistic hierarchy'. While it may not have the 'same privileged status' – or for the same reasons – as it might have had at the moment of production in Tanzania, it has, at the moment of reception, been resemioticized and revalued as nonetheless having status and worth. Of course, we understand the good point Blommaert makes regarding the kinds of very real gate-keeping which usually structures and dictates these exchanges. All the same, the processes of resemioticization and re-evaluation have sur-rounding our Gambian data reveal more discursive complexity. Like most people, (British) tourists moving through the Brikama market place or being handed Lenny Henry's business card are more than capable of or likely to manage a polysemous – and perhaps contradictory – reading of these communicative events. What might mark the business cards or trade signs out for derision or critique 'back home' is precisely what gives them their exotic cachet – their other-worldly curiosity and charm. The 'incorrect' English, the 'poor' design qualities are just as eas-ily festishized as markers of distinction as they are dismissed as markers of deficiency. The value judgments of tourists and the symbolic mar-ketplace of tourism in general are not always that easy to predict. In its pursuit of difference and of the exotic, tourism finds cachet in the most banal, unremarkable, awkward moments – as we see in our next chapter too.

Having said all of this, we admit that these processes of symbolic exchange are never simply mutual or equal. As we saw with Lenny Henry, the metaphor of self-fashioning to characterize a local person's identity works *vis-à-vis* tourists and raises a somewhat more material or political consideration. Any symbolic manoeuvre on the part of local people is, of course, always done with the economy in mind – the dollar one, not the word one. Tourists come not just with their fantasies but also with their money and they are prepared to spend good money to have these fantasies realized. However agentful, cre-ative and strategic hosts' refashioning of global semiotic resources may be, it is always limited and delimited by structurated semiotic (or sociolinguistic) hierarchies. The global semioscape is not an equal play-ing field. While there is always huge potential for speakers or designers to rework semiotic repertoires (symbols, sign systems and meaning-making practices) in circulation, some people's ways of speaking, their design practices and their aesthetic preferences dominate and set 'the standard'. In their study of corporate branding practices of airlines, for example, Thurlow and Aiello (2007) show how the creative variations in aeroplane tailfin designs have tended to follow otherwise unregu-lated 'standards' established by Western European and North American airlines. In the context of tourism, this type of semiotic agenda setting is evidenced in, for example, the fashioning of traditional Zulu craftwork into 'curious' for touristic consumption, which must also be constantly refashioned in accordance with the changing tastes and, indeed, *fashions*

Figure 2.29   Contemporary Zulu beadwork

of Western consumers – as is the case with the Zulu beadwork (see Figure 2.29) nowadays designed for the utilitarian/lifestyle demands of a Westernized market.[5]

The heteroglossic (Bakhtin, 1981) insertions of global brands and genres into the commercial–tourist spaces are also reminiscent of what Marco Jacquemet (2005) refers to in the context of global movements as 'transidiomaticity'. Richard Bauman (2004) meanwhile talks of three types of intertextuality: *generic, reiteration* and *parody*. It is Bauman's framework, in particular, which we think helps most in understanding some of the more specifically discursive work being done with the Gambian trade signs and business cards. Generic intertextuality provides 'orienting frameworks for the production and reception of particular types of text' (Bauman, 2004: 5). It is a resource for the incorporation of one genre to make use of another, for example, how poetry in a prose narrative signals the spiritual, lofty and otherworldly; a fairy tale removes the narrative into an ambiguous or non-existent time and place, while the myth takes the audience back to the moment of creation. It is also, in our case, how global brands and logos add 'glamour' to the mundane if extraordinary trinkets and mementos. Likewise, in the moment of 'chatting up' the tourist, a bumster styles himself as an 'official tourist guide' by handing in a business card (see Figure 2.18). Reiteration (replication), as another intertextual mode, transposes a text from one context to another maintaining the relationship copy–original (cf. Silverstein and Urban, 1996). The reiteration may be attributed to another specific speaker or may be stereotypically attributed to a group of speakers (for example, 'As old people say...') or may be introduced without any specific attribution (see Hill and Hill, 1996). The 'as if' stylizations of the souvenir vendors as members of corporate and cultural elites of the core regions and the clip art logoization of the business cards are fully self-aware but also fully strategic in exploiting these resources for commercial gain.

The third of Bauman's types or modes of intertextuality is parody, 'the ludic or inversive transformation of a prior text or genre' that positions texts as performative acts in an interactive or interpretive frame (Goffman, 1974) organized as a succession of intertextually linked recontextualizations (see also Bauman and Briggs, 1990, 2009). In the moment of tourist–host contact, these recontextualizations of high-prestige but ultimately banal corporate genres and texts opens up new discursive processes, accomplishing new communicative practices involving both production and reception of utterances in ways which are constitutive of new ideological relations between social actors. The display and appropriation of ready-made texts makes them easily recognizable and engaging. As Schechner (1985: 36) states, performance means 'never for the first time'.

With these intertextual possibilities in mind, the global language market – the global semioscape – clearly presents any number of semiotic opportunities as well as limitations. Reinserting familiar genres (and brands) into new contact zones also constitutes intertextual acts of appropriation and performance, which separate the linguistic and other semiotic forms from the identity of their originators or producers (see Heller, above). Humour, irony and pastiche shape *new* identities by creating language forms that have a clear source in two codes but are not recognizable as either (see Pennycook, above). As language displays (Eastman and Stein, 1993), therefore, the trade signs and business cards are good examples of Bakhtinian (1984) *double-voicing*, or stylizations – 'as if' utterances which complicate issues of authorship, ownership and speaker modality, the speaker's inferable relationship to the content and function (N. Coupland, 2001, 2007). In terms of Goffman's (1981) participation framework, the display of 'global' brands (that is, the British store logos) on market stalls in Gambia positions the vendors as the 'principal', 'author' and 'animator' appropriating the first two roles from their powerful institutional 'owners' in Europe. As we suggest, there is also possible ambiguity and disjuncture between the motivations and identity bids in the production of the signs and business cards by West African hosts, and their uptake by the tourists. Bakhtin (1984) discusses two types of double-voicing – *uni-directional* and *vari-directional*. In the former case, the speaker voices a prior style, which she or he endorses or validates. In the latter, the style is discredited or parodied (see also Rampton, 1995). Branding cheap, locally produced souvenirs with the logos of powerful and expensive department stores is a self-reflexive process which aims to add the cultural capital of global brands to the local artefacts. It is humorous but also strategically 'unidirectional' in recognizing the cultural capital of the appropriated brands and imitating them for gain.

However, it is not just about pretending, about simple uptake. There is as much of the 'vari-directional' in the trade signs and business cards. These genre borrowings and their concomitant self-styling are clearly also tongue-in-cheek. Viewed from one angle, it appears that the corporate spaces of the global 'core' have found yet another way to encroach, redefine and appropriate the spaces of 'emerging economies' and 'developing countries' (see the Coca-Cola logo positioned completely *non*-ironically on the empty crates sharing commercial space with 'Tati' in Senegal in Figure 2.13; cf. Gendelman and Aiello, 2010 on the rebranding of urban facades in Eastern Europe; and Chmielewska, 2010). Viewed somewhat differently, those who dwell, and earn their living, in the global periphery do not merely or simply endorse these encroachments from the core. Their responses can be infinitely more agentful, creative and disruptive than, for example, our own use of business cards in academia. In a different time, a different place, it might even be reasonable to suggest that Gambian market traders and informal tourism workers are consummate *culture jammers* – co-opting but also subverting, both strategically and playfully, the dominant semiotic resources and discourses of (Western) consumer capitalism (cf. Lasn, 1999). One 'locational advantage', to use Harvey's term again, of Gambian market places is that through sheer distance and sheer disregard, they fall beyond the reach (or interest) of corporate litigation. (However insignificant, small traders working in *rich* countries often find themselves under attack for copyright infringement.) Drawing from a quite separate fieldtrip, there is something audacious about the *Safestway* shopping mall in Dubai (see Figure 2.30) which unapologetically appropriates and infringes the global brand of Safeway – right down the

Figure 2.30 Safestway store, Dubai, UAE

look-a-like capital-S logo (which we ourselves would probably not have been allowed to reproduce here without 'permission') looking down on one of the major thoroughfares of Dubai. In an age of continuous corporate control and commercial communication (Deleuze, 1990: 174), this has the feeling of something a little more edgy, more political than a shameless money-grab. Perhaps less equivocal, however, is the SAFE WAY stall in Fajara market, Gambia (see Figure 2.10 above). Even as a commercial venture itself, there is a careful shift from pretence to parody, here – a defiant mocking, even. 'Catch me if you can!' Perhaps, in some inverted way, this 'semiotic opportunity' approaches the special kind of culture jamming which Christine Harold (2004: 209) calls 'pranking' – an improvisational (indeed, often 'low-tech') appropriation which exaggerates the practices and topics of corporate discourse in ways which address the *patterns* of commercial power and not simply its content.

Returning to the spaces of place-identity

The creation of symbolic tokens of exchange (money) and expert systems which provide abstract guarantees of expectations across time and space has arguably removed the necessity for the physical presence of social actors at the time of (economic) exchange. This separation (or 'distanciation') of time and space, or the connecting of presence and absence in time and space, has been referred to by Anthony Giddens (1990, 1991) as 'disembedding', or 'the "lifting out" of social relations from local contexts of interaction and their restructuring across indefinite spans of time-space' (Giddens, 1990: 21; see also Fairclough, 2003). However, disembedding does not lead to lack of contact or interaction. Rather, global flows and mobilities create new opportunities for 're-embedding' processes, or 'the re-appropriation or recasting of disembedded social relations so as to pin them down (however partially or transitorily) to local conditions of time and place' (Giddens, 1990: 79). Thus, tourists in Gambia (and elsewhere) are given opportunities to seek pleasure from the social interactions that accompany their economic exchanges with hosts (cf. Granovetter, 1985 on the desire for pleasurable interactions at the workplace). However, while tourists may see these interactions as distinctive, exotic, playful or even exuberant (cf. Chapters 3 and 5) *stylizations* of routine service encounters and other economic exchanges these re-embeddings have far more tangible, material value, for the Gambian tourism workers needing to make a living, support their families and so on. That is not to say that their interactions with tourists are without pleasure and entertainment.

In the interactive and interpretive frame of host–tourist interaction, these intertextual manoeuvres index space as multi-scaled, as simultaneously local and global. On a local scale, they capture the attention of potential buyers/customers, legitimize hosts' initiation of interaction with tourists, create common ground between tourists and hosts by introducing an element of familiarity for tourists in an unfamiliar space, ensure the memorability of the vendor, tourist guide, or taxi driver and infuse tourist experience with humour. But hosts' appropriation of the high status genres is also a globalizing act of claiming the cultural capital not only via the high status of the source texts and their institutional originators, but also through the display of their knowledge about a world beyond their immediate locale. As we have argued in Chapter 1, globalization may be first and foremost a set of tangible social, political and economic reordering, but it is also a discursive resource for styling Self and Other as a particular subject – what we will later refer to as 'new internationals' in our Conclusion. Hence, globalizing brands and logos invokes the play of indexing both tourists and hosts all at once as 'here and there', 'British and Gambian', 'posh and poor'. As such, the mobile find themselves set in place, while the 'sedentary' find themselves on the move.

For tourists, souvenir markets and walking promenades, birdwatching spots and beaches are places to seek the different and the extraordinary. For that reason, the perceived scale of these spaces is local (or national). In seeking to maximize their profits, hosts meanwhile try to engage tourists by framing their distinction with tokens of the familiar and recognizable signposting indexing the very same space as global (or transnational). This mixing of meanings reveals a dynamic reconfiguration of place and what Henri Lefebvre (1991) famously calls the social production of space. To this end, we will finish this chapter where we mean to begin the next, with the following observations by Mimi Sheller and John Urry (2006: 214) about what they call the 'new mobilities paradigm':

> Places are indeed dynamic...Places are like ships, moving around and not necessarily staying in one location.... places themselves are seen as travelling, slow or fast, greater or shorter distances, within networks of human and nonhuman agents. Places are about relationships, about the placing of peoples, materials, images, and the systems of difference that they perform. We understand 'where' we are through 'vision in motion' practised through the alignment of material objects, maps, images, and a moving gaze.

3
Transient Identities, New Mobilities: Holiday Postcards

When people choose specific travel destinations, it is usually because their imaginations have already journeyed there ahead of them. ... [The] imagined possibilities directly influence what travelers encounter, creating a constant and animated dialogue between images in the mind and realities on the ground. These dialogues can be kindled in any number of ways: a co-worker's vacation story, a magazine advertisement, a racy novel, a painting in a museum, a Hollywood film, a postcard. ... Images in the mind are projected onto physical places, which in turn are shaped in ways that most successfully respond to, and further rekindle, the imaginary.

(Kahn, 2003: 307)

... we have to follow the things themselves, for their meanings are inscribed in their forms, their uses, their trajectories. It is only through the analysis of these trajectories that we can interpret the human transactions and calculations that enliven things ... it is the things-in-motion that illuminate their human and social context.

(Appadurai, 1986: 5)

We live in a time of 'new mobilities' (Sheller and Urry, 2006) in which many people experience and talk about their lives in terms of 'dwelling-in-travel' and of being 'on the move' even while 'at home' (Clifford, 1997). Contemporary life is less and less neatly bounded by, or tied to, particular spaces or places and previously disconnected – geographically and historically speaking – cultural practices are increasingly interpenetrated (Harvey, 1989; Appadurai, 1996; Kaplan, 1996;

Clifford, 1997; Bauman, 2000). Needless to say, this is by no means a smooth, monolithic process of change and not everyone senses themselves living in the everywhere and nowhere spaces of a globalizing world. Whilst national borders are coming down for some, national 'fences' – material and metaphoric – are going up for many (Bauman, 1998; Klien, 2002; cf. our Introduction, above). For others, there is also a renewed determination to shore up and to 'purify' their regional, local cultures, for commercial or nationalistic gain (Featherstone, 2002). Nonetheless, it is a well-rehearsed observation in the social sciences that the overall movement and interconnectedness of peoples is more extensive, more intensive than ever before (see Held and McGrew, 2000, for an overview of this literature) and many people experience themselves being interconnected with far-flung people and places through face-to-face or mediatized contact.

It is, therefore, no longer appropriate for researchers to treat people's lives and identities as if they were easily and exclusively pinpointed to specific places. For Mimi Sheller and John Urry (2006; Urry, 2007; cf. Gupta and Ferguson, 1992) the ontological reality of people's new experience of mobility must therefore be met with a revised epistemology – what they call the 'new mobilities paradigm'. This different way of thinking needs to complicate *sedentarist* perspectives (that is, those which treat stability and place as normal, mobility and displacement as abnormal) as well as *nomadic* perspectives (that is, those which over-estimate the extent of placelessness in the way, say, that David Harvey (1990: 278) talks about the 'annihilation of temporal and spatial barriers'). The new mobilities paradigm not only warrants tourism research *per se*, but, more importantly, it also helps direct the methodological thrust of tourism research. In this regard, Sheller and Urry (2006: 217–219) prioritize research that addresses the interactional, ethnographic contexts of mobility; research which, amongst other things, entails listening to people's own accounts of their movements and which attends to the emotions and memories of travelling. Finally, travel research should also consider what Sheller and Urry characterize as 'places of in-between-ness' or 'interspace' – the experience of being simultaneously mobile and immobilized, of 'various kinds of meeting-ness [that] are held in play while on-the-move' (ibid.).

It is with all of this in mind that we turn to our 'on-the-ground' study of holiday postcards as the third example of a 'discourse on the move'. Postcards are, of course, an iconic tourist text with a long history which clearly predates global capitalism.[1] In spite of this – or precisely because of this – postcards also reflect some key cultural and interactional enactments of contemporary globalization. As such, they are instances of both interpersonal communication and global communication. More than this, however, holiday postcards also point us to the kinds of *spatial* relations – the 'new' mobilities – of globalization. In fact, as we mean to show, the indentificational, relational and spatial meanings of postcards work hand-in-glove. And by looking at the actual messages tourists write on their postcards we also come to know a little better the social life of these travelling objects, the 'transient' nature of tourist identities and the interspatiality of their imagined communities of practice. Finally, and following the observation of Scott Lash and Celia Lury in the quote below, we also want to use this opportunity to shift from thinking about tourist texts merely as representations or as straightforward extensions of the tourist, to also viewing them as objects with a life of their own (Lury, 1997; Lash and Lury, 2007).

> With globalization, culture becomes fully industrial. Culture and the culture – or creative – industry shifts from a logic of *representation* to a logic of *things*.
>
> (Lash and Lury, 2007: 181)

It is in this way that we are able to see not only how the social meanings of postcards are inscribed in and by tourist communication, but also how these 'things-in-motion' (Appadurai, quoted above) tell their own stories about travel, about language and about the material-symbolic exchanges of global mobility.

Placing and displacing postcards: Culture on tour

There is no shortage of academic literature about postcards and holiday postcards (see, for example, Mellinger, 1994; Edwards, 1996; Osborne, 2000; Pritchard and Morgan, 2005; Rogan, 2005). As Miriam Kahn (quoted above) reminds us, in tourism – perhaps more so than else-where – the image invariably precedes and, to some extent, precludes, the reality. Peter Osborne (2000: 84) goes as far as to argue that '[w]ith photography and photographic seeing as prime commodity forms in tourism, the photographic image that promotes it is in many instances the very item consumed – the advertisement has become its own commodity'. The imagery of these 'hegemonically-scripted discourses' (Mellinger, 1994: 776) certainly makes important assumptions about the destination and its people, about the experience the tourist is sup-posed to be having, as well as the vision of that experience she or he should be communicating to others back home as part of a nostalgic (re)construction of their travels – what we might call the 'tourist haze'. It is precisely this that makes postcards such an obvious target for our kind of scholarly attention: they constitute a key site of heavily mediated, indirect and usually inadvertent, communication between hosts and tourists (Thurlow et al., 2005) – they are thus resources for intercultural exchange.

Postcard sending is also a cultural practice with a history that connects the colonial heritage of tourism with its neocolonial present (see our Conclusion chapter). In writing about touristic postcards, most academic writers also seem to share a received suspicion towards the genre – a sense of their being, at best, shallow, or at worst, offensive. In this sense, postcards are automatically relegated to the status of 'half-hearted tokens of transparent love', which Zimbabwean poet Kizito Muchemwa speaks of in his poem about the colonial 'tourists' of the past (Thurlow et al., 2005). Perhaps the bad press of postcards derives also from their share in the tourist industry's aggressive commodification of space (Jack and Phipps, 2005: 23) and the mapping of pure and authentic cultures into neat, sanitized, bounded places (Meetham, 2001).

Without trivializing the historically and persistently questionable visual representations on the front of postcards, we want to focus instead on the *language* of postcards, asking: What of the words, which get written on their backs? How might we think of postcards as more nuanced enactments of tourist identities and relations, and of globalization in general? To do this, we need also to think of postcards as material culture and to rethink their discursivity as being more than the representation of place; to think more in terms of cultural objects which travel independently of their senders and which derive their symbolic and social meanings *across space*.

Celia Lury (1997) explains this well. Along with souvenirs, mementos, *objet trouvé* (for example, beach pebbles, tickets) and personal photos, postcards are instances of what she calls 'tripper-objects' (p. 79) – those cultural artefacts in motion 'whose travelling is teleologically determined by their final resting place, as something to be brought [or sent] home ... objects whose meaning appears not as immanent but as arbitrary, imposed from outside the object by external context or final dwelling place'. These tripper-objects distinguish themselves from 'traveller-objects' (note Lury's tourist–traveller dichotomy) such as artworks and handcrafts which 'retain their meaning across contexts and retain an authenticated relation to an original dwelling ... those objects whose ability to travel well is integrally linked to their ability to signify their meaning immanently, most commonly by an indexical reference to their "original" dwelling'.

What we hope this chapter does is to demonstrate empirically the textual enactment of the kinds of broader theoretical ideas proposed by both Sheller and Urry and by Lury, for example, to show what 'inter-spatiality' looks like in practice and to see how tourists themselves 'manage' (that is, cope with and exploit) the liminal, transient nature of tourism. These are both tropes or experiences captured in the almost quintessential postcard shown in Figure 3.1 which also nicely displays a number of the key rhetorical preoccupations in the messages tourists write on the backs of their postcards. Importantly, given the history of this particular discourse on the move, we are also alerted to the fact that these are not exclusively 'globalist' phenomena – not particular to global capitalism. The 'here-and-there' performances of postcard messages do, however, work against overstated 'de-territorialization' claims by show-ing the 'in-between' ways people write space into their travels and the ways in which their identities and relationships are spatialized. By the same token, this sense of the in-between is also a resource by which tourists write themselves into being; in other words, how they are able to perform their identity as tourists and globe-trotters.

Figure 3.1 The transient, in-between identities of tourism

Liminal living: The transience of tourist identities

It's always better on holiday
So much better on holiday
That's why we only work when we need the money

– Franz Ferdinand

The above quote from the Scottish pop group Franz Ferdinand shows someone foregrounding one part of their life in relation to others: it's better to be on holiday than to work; it's better to be a tourist than a worker. Although most people cannot afford the luxury of such a lifestyle, being a global traveller is something that many aspire to in 'modern' society. Holidays have become consumer necessities, and increasingly going on holiday implies international travel. A major feature of going on holiday is the opportunity it affords the tourist to try out new experiences and even alternative identities. Though short and frequently formulaic in nature, postcards provide useful insights not only into what people do on holiday (the enactment of the tourist identity) but especially into the way they represent and justify their tourist identity for their audience back home and for themselves.

The vast amount of work on the tourist in anthropology, sociology and critical tourism studies has concentrated on the nature of the tourist experience (for example, MacCannell, 1999 [1976]; Urry, 2002; Harrison, 2003), tourist–host relations (for example, Smith, 1989 [1977]; Boissevain, 1996a) and taxonomies of tourist types (for example, Cohen, 1972, 1979; see McCabe, 2005, for a critical review). Empirically oriented research on tourist (and host) identity is a relatively recent phenomenon. Interestingly, work in this area has taken up Goffman's performance metaphor as the central analytic concept (for example, Edensor, 1998, 2001; Bærenholdt et al., 2004; Doorne and Ateljevic, 2005). However, one important difference that emerges from the performance-oriented studies of tourist and, say, gender identities is that the former is treated as 'special', enacted only temporarily while on holiday, in ways which are closely linked to enacting ritualized, ceremonial behaviour in the liminal spaces of passage (see Part II). On the other hand, probably due to the influence of Judith Butler's work (for example, 1990, 1993), the enactment of gender is viewed as a mundane, everyday, ordinary sort of performance. While you can only perform being a tourist on holiday, you can never *not* perform a version of maleness or femaleness. It is in these rather simple, analytically convenient terms that we therefore view a difference between 'permanent' and 'transient', or 'central' and 'peripheral' (or 'marginal') identity categories.

John Urry (2002) begins his well-known book *The Tourist Gaze* by accounting for the reasons why he concerns himself with the rather frivolous topic of tourism. He links it with the idea of studying deviance, bizarre and idiosyncratic practices. Of course, he is quick to add that 'the investigation of deviance can reveal interesting and significant aspects of "normal" societies' (p. 2). Nevertheless, the contrast between tourism as a deviance from a 'normal' type of behaviour is set up for the book and repeated frequently in Urry's extended definition of tourism (pp. 2–3). Thus, tourism, as a 'leisure' activity, is contrasted with 'work' (though see below). It involves journeying to destinations 'outside the normal places of residence and work' (p. 3), usually for relatively short periods, with the anticipation of intense, extraordinary sensory experiences. The features of landscape and townscape gazed at by the tourist are separate from tourists' everyday experiences and they are subject to 'different forms of social patterning, with a much greater sensitivity to visual elements of landscape or townscape than normally found in everyday life' (ibid.). These unusual forms of behaviour, involving temporary relocation and suspension of routine behaviour are usually seen as 'restful' and necessary for people's well-being. Tourism in the contemporary world is also a sign of modernity and a status symbol.

The high prestige of tourism may have as many sources and manifestations as there are types of tourism. It may be a mark of self-fulfilment and spiritual growth in the case of individual cultural tourism, a straightforward status symbol linked to spending vast sums of money in 'super-elite' tourism (cf. Bruner, 2005; Thurlow and Jaworski, 2006), or the endurance of hardship and 'roughing it' in backpacker tourism (cf. Richards and Wilson, 2004). There are important hierarchies and divisions in tourism with relatively low and high varieties depending to some extent on one's wealth but also one's habitus (Bourdieu, 1984, 1991, 1993). Such hierarchies are not fixed, and the high cost of a holiday does not uniformly guarantee prestige. For example, cruise holidays, which are associated with the top end of the financial spectrum, continue to project the imagery of passivity and unexciting overindulgence (although, according to *The Guardian* newspaper, cruise companies diversify their offer to attract younger and more active clientele, cf. Harding, 2004).

Tourism has also been likened to a sacred journey or pilgrimage (Graburn, 1989; Urry, 2002: 10–11). In both conceptualizations, the tourist is characterized, like the pilgrim, as leaving the normal place of residence, the familiar, mundane, profane, work- and home-related environment, and entering the temporary, extraordinary, unpredictable, sacred, liminal (or liminoid, Turner, 1969, 1974) zone of leisure, in which everyday social norms of behaviour are suspended and the 'routinized non-routine' (Urry, 2002: 11). Despite its 'abnormality', and due to heightened sensory alertness, orientation to pleasure and recreation, this touristic period, 'though extraordinary, is perhaps more "real" than "real life". Vacation time and tourism are described as "I was really living, living it up ... I've never felt so alive," in contrast to the daily humdrum often termed a "dog's life," since dogs are not thought to "vacation" ' (Graburn, 1989: 26). As the band Franz Ferdinand express it, 'it's always better on holiday'.

What these discussions of tourism emphasize, then, is the fact that in the cyclical succession of life events, of the two alternate states of work time and lesisure time, the former is held to be enduring, stable and mundane, while the latter is presented as transient, unstable and festive. But tourists' transience not only contrasts with their own permanency of status before and after the holidays, or with those who stayed 'back home', but also with the local people who they *may* be coming into contact with during their travels, even if it is only to gaze upon them. Commenting on the relations between tourists and hosts, Boissevain (1996b: 4) states:

> A major factor affecting relations between locals and tourists... is the desire of the latter for a *temporary* change in their life situation. They seek *escape from established routines, from the constraints of time and place*, and the behavioural codes that rule their daily lives. They believe this change will recharge their mental and physical batteries so that they will be better able to cope with the pressures of their daily commitments.
>
> (our emphasis)

Thus becoming a tourist, however briefly, means shedding part of one's 'core' identity and routine behaviour. This involves taking on a new, temporary identity that necessarily incorporates some elements that are perceived to be the opposite of the habitual personality and behaviour. As Victor Turner observed, 'cognitively, nothing underlines irregularity so well as absurdity or paradox. Emotionally, nothing satisfies as much as extravagant or temporarily permitted illicit behaviour' (1969: 176). This process is facilitated by the masking function that anonymity provides. After all, the people visited do not know the normal or 'real' persona of the tourists. Tourists can consequently shed their everyday status (epitomized in shedding ones clothes on the beach) and, temporarily, become 'other' persons and engage in 'extravagant' if not 'illicit' behaviour, typically signalled by donning special 'holiday' clothes. These strange, often garish, occasionally inexplicably scanty costumes unambiguously mark out the wearer as a tourist (see Leach, 1964). Strange dress (or no dress) and weakened inhibitions are often accompanied by behaviour that would be quite unacceptable at home.

Apart from the desirability, prestige and pleasures of the holiday experience, being a tourist brings its own problems. The unpredictability of visiting new places and meeting new people may create uncertainty and anxiety. This may be even greater in the very moments of transition: travel to and from the holiday destination. Following Arnold Van Gennep's (1960 [1909]) work on rites of passage, Nelson Graburn (1989) observes how the moments of parting with family and friends are reminiscent of the rituals accompanying death and dying and, as such, are fraught with tension, special preparations (for example, arranging care for the house, pets, even making a new will) and some sadness of leaving the familiar environment, albeit with the intention of coming back. Equally, returning home creates a similar sense of ambivalence. 'We step back into our past selves like an heir to the estate of a deceased person who has to pick up the threads, for we are *not* ourselves. We are a new person who has gone through re-creation and, if we do not feel renewed, the whole point of tourism has been missed' (Graburn, 1989: 27). For this reason precisely, and despite the quest for a temporary new persona, many tourists do keep in touch with their old or permanent self while they are away, and one of the most popular ways of doing this is by texting or emailing family and friends, keeping travel blogs, or – in a more traditional way – sending postcards back home.

In *The Postcard Century*, Tom Phillips (2000) notes how surprisingly mundane the content of people's postcard messages are. However, as Bjarne Rogan (2005) notes, it is this apparent banality which makes postcards so communicatively salient. The postcard is clearly an important tourist genre (cf. Laakso and Östman, 1999, 2001; Östman, 2004; Kennedy, 2005). It allows tourists an inexpensive and quick display of their tourist identity to those not physically present and who are not local residents. Postcards also seem to embody the transience and ambivalence of the tourist experience and they also point to the interspatiality of travel itself. Postcards are sent as displays of the writers' special status, but also in order to be remembered and awaited for at home; and the postcard may create admiration as much as envy (cf. Graburn, 1989). Russ Belk (1997) specifically considers the ambiguity of the postcard as a 'thinking of you' threshold gift appropriate to the tourist's ritual reintegration into the home community, but which also carries the potential of a status-claim. In other words, postcards may as much show involvement between the sender and addressee, as alienate one from the other. How do the senders of postcards then deal with the ambivalence of their status as 'abnormal' yet attractive? How do they mark discursively not only the desirability of being away from the mundane drudgery of work, but also the longing to be back where they belong? How do they manage their relations with people they love and identify with, but abandoned voluntarily albeit for a limited period only? As has been stated above, different forms of tourism may bestow tourists with prestige in numerous and varied ways, but assuming that one chooses to holiday in a way which is closest to the ideal for the community one routinely identifies with back home, we imagine that displaying one's tourist practice (or the most desirable aspects of it) to the members of one's in-group will normally be associated with approval and cultural cachet.

With these questions in mind, we now turn to an analysis of a corpus of postcard messages with a special focus on tourists' orientations to the 'home' communities which we think illustrates nicely the transient identities and new mobilities of tourism. When we turn to postcards and when we turn them over to look at the messages written on the 'back', we find epistemological and ontological evidence of the interpersonal and spatial relations which reflect and structure tourism discourse. These are also 'banal enactments' of globalization which we see happening in at least four ways: the performative production of tourists' transient identities; the relational maintenance of the imagined tourist community of practice; the strategic but unavoidable management of *here-and-there* spatial relations; and, the commodified (pseudo gift) exchange of objects, places and emotions.

Postcards are by virtue of their open nature at least semi-public documents (Östman, 2004). They often have multiple addressees, such as whole families or co-workers in an office. In the latter case (which we examine here), cards sent to the workplace are often explicitly meant for display to the whole office or department. (See Appendix for more information about the collection of the postcards for this study.) Senders may thus be more conscious of the social identity they are projecting on a postcard than they would be in a private letter or conversation. In this regard, postcards are particularly interesting as projections of tourist identities and constructions of one's self – known to the receiver as a family member or a colleague – as somehow different: this is me – on holiday.

Situating the tourist: Performing here-and-there identities

Before we turn to the backs of our postcards, there are one or two initial observations we would want to make about the *fronts* of the postcards. Perhaps not surprisingly, nearly three quarters of the 600-plus postcards we have looked at for this chapter depicts some kind of landscape – most of which are of a built environment (that is, city, village or town) but also of sea views or rural/wildlife scenes. A few of the postcards (about 4 per cent) shows hotels and maps (see Table 3.1 in the Appendix). The postcard is obviously used to display the location in lieu of a personal photograph (a typical accompaniment of holiday emails and blogs), and the image on the front unambiguously orients the receiver to where the sender is and, more importantly, that the sender is away from home. This, too, is the most obvious performance of 'being away' from home – of 'being here not there' (Recall Figure 3.1 above).

The vast majority of 'fronts' of postcards in our dataset are made up of single or composite photographic images, with at least two thirds further anchoring the image explicitly with a place name (for example, 'Cover-ack'; 'Hong Kong'), sometimes accompanied by a greeting (for example, 'Greetings from Thailand'; 'Groeten uit Katwijk aan Zee'), more elaborate description of place (for example, 'Australia, Koala'; 'Singapore, the statue of Sir Stamford Raffles with background panoramic view of Boat Quay') and an occasional map or national flag. In this way, postcards not only visualize the destinations but also provide a script for the written message – 'look, it's me, here–there'. By turning over the card, however, a somewhat less dislocated sense of identity, relationship and space is revealed. Early evidence of this can be seen in the types of taglines shown in Figures 3.2, 3.3 and 3.4. A version of the *greeting* is the most frequent tagline, but we also find printed messages which more directly embody the ambivalence tourists may feel while writing to their families and friends, for example, 'Hey! Florida is fun! But I miss you!' (Figure 3.2) or, simply, 'Gibraltar. Thinking of You' (Figure 3.3) and 'Une pensée de Normandie' ('a pansy/thought from Normandy'; Figure 3.4).

The short text in Figure 3.2 consists of three distinct speech acts: a greeting, an account of a successful holiday and an assertion of affect for the addressee. As we'll see later, this tagline encapsulates the three key elements present or implied in postcard messages: the greeting, positive

Figure 3.2   Postcard from Florida

self presentation of the tourist and description of holiday activities, and a continued link to home, introduced here by the contrastive conjunction 'but', as a marker of both potential conflict (being 'away' and being 'involved') and its resolution (being 'involved' despite being 'away'). In Figures 3.3 and 3.4, the locating of self in place is achieved by the place name itself, while the phrase 'thinking of you' (French card, literally 'a thought for you') doubles up as a greeting and expression of continued emotional involvement with the addressee. (With the flower shown in the top right-hand corner, the card from Normandy puns on *pensée* as both 'pansy' and 'thought'.) A perfect economical, multifunctional token of small talk on the move. We turn now to the back of our postcards.

In his summary of a corpus linguistic study of a sample of postcard messages sent by British tourists, Chris Kennedy (2005) characterizes the genre as follows:

The overriding presence of positive evaluation is revealed through a wide range of lexical items, including attitudinal epithets, intensifiers and boosters. Negative particles are used with positive meaning and there are few examples of any negative evaluation, which is contrasted with the positive and hence mitigated. Language that expresses specificity is avoided and content is expressed in vague general terms, which emphasise excess, viewed positively. Writers/senders narrate their contact with the tourist environment in terms of general activities but there appears to be little contact with or awareness of local populations at least as expressed in the postcards.

(Ibid.: 244)

What we note in our own data is that the prevailing positive tenor of the postcards is inextricably linked with the senders' placing themselves

Figure 3.3   Postcard from Gibraltar

Figure 3.4 Postcard from Normandy (une pensée de Normandie 'a thought/ pansy from Normandy')

in the destination, with the image on the postcard firmly acting as a metonym of the destination and a point of shared, visual reference between the sender and addressee through comments such as:

(1) The picture says it all [picture of a Malaysian beach with lush green vegetation in the background and only two people on the beach]
(2) It really looks like this [picture of a Florida beach filled with palm trees]
(3) Water – really that blue

The self-referentiality and redundancy of these messages is striking. The 'no need for words' sentiment expressed in extracts (1) and (2) under-scores the phaticity of the messages and draws the reader's attention to the key holiday objective – reaching exotic, beautiful destinations (see extracts 8, 13, 19 and 20). That there is no need to describe them fur-ther is indicated in the semi-dialogic message in (3), responding to the commonly shared assumption that a successful seaside holiday requires the water in the sea to be of a particular shade of blue (or green) as in recall the prototypical postcard in Figure 3.1. A 'witness account' of this particular feature of the landscape is proof enough (though at a high and safe level of generality alluded to in Kennedy's quote above) that the holiday is a successful one.

The positioning of self in the tourist place may be stressed by the use of overt personal and temporal deixis such as first person pronoun 'I' and adverb 'right now' in (4), with both (4) and (5) being indicative of metaphorical ownership of place through the act of gazing, in (5) served by the mention of 'our window' implying privilege and exclusivity:

(4) This is scenery I am looking at right now
(5) This is the view from our window

Homing in on the place, writers get even more specific about their whereabouts, directing the attention of the sender to their hotels, indexed where possible by the postcard images (6–9). The spatial precision in pinpointing tourists' accommodation is often achieved by engaging with the images more directly, making hand-drawn interventions like topographic marks on a map: dots (10), arrows (11) or circles (12) in relevant places, creating single communicative acts through several, multimodal acts. This kind of narrative detail serves not only to situate the tourist but also to legitimate the overall message, to authenticate the travel story being told in much the same way as conversational story-telling (Tannen, 1989).

(6) We are at Bulcock beach which is on this photo
(7) You can just see our hotel in the top right hand of the picture
(8) We are staying in one of these very traditional Villas with a stunning view
(9) Enjoying a well earned rest in one of the beach chalets as shown overleaf
(10) My hotel is on the other side of this dot
(11) The arrow marks our hotel
(12) I have put a circle roughly where we are

The sender may further authenticate his or her emplacement in the desirable scenery by referencing any leisure-oriented activity associated with vacationing, even, or especially, if it is ostensibly 'doing nothing', as in (13) below. Other typical activities involve all sorts of movement – boat trip (14), walking (15), hiking (16), inextricably linked to the constant act of gazing and engaging (17 and 18). Again, all the references to moving through and interacting with tourist spaces (next best thing to being seen doing so) is indicative of the general consumption and 'taking possession' of the destination (cf. Jaworski and Thurlow, 2009a):

(13) We are sitting in the garden of this delightful little pub overlooking a superb view of the countryside
(14) Did a trip up this tributary yesterday in a pea boat like this
(15) Walked up & beyond the waterfalls on the front today
(16) Came over the top of this mountain on Thursday
(17) Yesterday R. and I saw a baboon like this one, she had a baby too
(18) We have passed some barns like the ones in the picture

In several examples, the act of gazing draws in the reader/addressee more explicitly, 'As you can see', (19–21; see also 7, above), suggesting a co-constructed, shared, even solidary stance in the performance of emplacement. Here, the sense of mutuality and interspatiality gets directly invoked by treating the addressee as co-present:

(19) As you can see on the postcard, it's a beautiful and amazing city
(20) As you can see the beaches are beautiful
(21) As you can see from the postcard, we've been to the Pyrenees

The precision and orientation to the visual image demonstrated above may not only be read as encoding pride in being seen to stay in a prestigious hotel in a desirable location and with a 'stunning' view, but also a moment of showing off, enticing admiration or even envy. But at another level, orienting and marking up the image may be a way of drawing the addressee into the picture, literally and figuratively, sharing the tourist gaze and the experience of being 'there'.

Another way of working the dialectic of 'here' and 'there' into postcards is to invoke some kind of comparison or contrast between the travel destination and home. Needless to say, in these cases, the former invariably fares better than the latter, either because of its inherent qualities such as an 'amazing' (22) or imposing view (23), or simply because the place is located anywhere but home (24):

(22) The view from them is amazing compared to Cathays Terrace
(23) a bit higher than the weir on the Taff in Pontcanna Fields!
(24) We've had 'a wild day, 'a cool day', 'a neat day' 'a sizzling day' and yes 'a nice day'. Glad I'm not in Cardiff

On occasion, the contrast is ironically constructed in favour of home, just to emphasize the extreme conditions experienced at the destination. In (25), for example, the sender seems to complain about the hot weather during her holiday by expressing her 'longing' for the moderate climate typical of home. On the other hand, the sender of (26) likens the disappointing weather conditions to those of home, where 'dreadful' weather is taken to be the norm – if the destination does not meet the tourist's expectations, it is just 'as bad' as home:

(25) for the cool green grass of Cardiff!
(26) weather dreadful! (just like Wales)

Whatever the evaluative stance being taken, the writing of references to 'home' into postcard messages bridges the temporary spatial and relational gap between the sender and the addressee by invoking a shared knowledge and experience of place names: 'Cathays Terrace' (22); '[river] Taff' (23); 'Pontcanna Fields' (23); 'Cardiff' (24, 25); 'Wales' (26), topography: 'higher than the weir' (23); landscape: 'green grass' (25); and weather: 'weather dreadful' (26). This relational work, invoking collective identities based on territorial unity and common points of reference, is part of the typical interpretation of tourists' experiences in relation to what they find familiar and knowable. As Scott McCabe (2002: 70) has commented, '[e]ven though tourists are away from home, they are constantly referring their experiences at the destination to life back at home.'

Just as tourists may write into their messages commonly recognizable spatial references, they may also do so with regard to shared (if imagined) desires, aspirations and fantasies:

(27) Nan/Liz/Don't know who the other person is [cartoon picture of backs of three people sitting in deckchairs on a beach]
(28) This is where we stopped for coffee … spot us in the picture … the good old days, eh [reconstructed outdoor shot of a group of people dressed in Victorian costume having coffee]
(29) I think I've found the perfect place for our retirement!! Any takers? [picture from Crete of four elderly women sitting on a pavement in front of a blue door, crocheting]

All of the above examples demonstrate that being away – and the pleasure in being away – is contingent upon a clear sense of home. As such the 'place' of tourism is clearly one of 'in-between-ness'. In fact, throughout the messages we have looked at, we find a lot of discursive effort being directed to establishing the *appearance* of a clearly demarcated 'here', and yet, ironically, this 'here' can only be articulated in a moment when the tourist must imagine him- or herself 'there' and therefore bring 'there', however temporarily, 'here'. So, it seems, we travel to get away from home only to spend much of our time thinking of home.

The interspatial relationships of home: On looking back

Tourists are by definition people who are away from (typically) the family at large, friends and colleagues. Thus, when writing a postcard, it seems important for the sender to underscore the fact that they are also away from their everyday life and, most manifestly, from their work. It is likewise important to reiterate the received touristic wisdom that it is always better to be on holiday than to be at work. What is interesting about the examples of this work–leisure dichotomy in our dataset is that this othering of work necessarily also implies an othering of the collegial recipients. It is here, then, that we can unravel further complexities in the *relational* accomplishments of postcards. Consider the following examples:

(30) No work
(31) I am having a nice holiday from work
(32) Wonderful to be away from it all
(33) Have completely forgotten what a photo copier looks like
(34) Please go on piling up my mail
(35) Having a terrible time. If I have to visit one more picturesque waterfall or look at any more breathtaking scenery, I'll scream. Wish I was at home marking
(36) At least I don't have to think about module description forms or examination papers
(37) not missing the [name of dept.] at all. Ain't that strange
(38) Hope you are missing me more than I am missing work
(39) I'm here. You're working. Ha Ha
(40) happy WORKING!!! (to colleagues)
(41) Hope it's not too horrible there
(42) Hope you're not working too hard

The above extracts seem to epitomize the idea of going on holiday as a complete break from the drudgery of everyday work (it's worth remembering that approximately a third of our dataset comes from post-cards collected from university offices). While extracts (30) to (32) seem to simply 'state the obvious' about holiday time being work-free, (33) to (37) make this contrast more specific, humorous perhaps, by singling out specifically onerous or tedious tasks associated with administrative or academic work: photocopying, reading mail or marking examination papers. This is done in full knowledge that the addressees are not so lucky, that the sender's being on holiday does not absolve his or her colleagues from these duties. This may in fact lead to further injection of humour by mocking one's colleagues about their ill-fate compared to the sender's good fortune (37–40) – a kind of 'sympathetic antipathy' (Malinowski, 1923, in J. Coupland, 2000).

There is much sense here of the senders' complete distancing from their colleagues at work, expressing self-satisfaction – even self-aggrandizement – and a (playful) disregard for one's colleagues back at the office. While these can be interpreted as mocking the addressee(s) at face value, it is hard to imagine that these are the intentions of the senders, risking resentment and scorn upon return to work. Rather, we must interpret these as strategic enactments of solidarity polite-ness, ritualized insults (Labov, 2009[1972]) and taking a playful rather than aggressive stance marked by informal markers of ingroupness such as blatantly false claims and hyperbole (for example, 33, 35), 'special' or 'colloquial' language, for example, representing laughter (39), loud speech (40) or 'non-standard' speech (37). This underlying pragmatic force is confirmed by expressions of concern for the addressees' well-being, as in 'Hope it's not too horrible there' (41), 'Hope you're not working too hard' (42) – albeit marked as ironic by the use of 'too' (see also 54 below).

Just as the performance of space in postcard messages expresses a rela-tional 'in-between-ness', we also start to see how the relational content produces a kind of interspatiality. This is further apparent in references to the tourist's return, which would seem somewhat counter-intuitive given the general investment in performing the wonderfulness of being away from home. In the first instance, the transience of the tourist expe-rience – and, therefore, of the tourist identity – is closely linked to the pre-specified duration of a specific temporally bounded holiday.

(43) We've come away for a few weeks break to the island of Aegina in Greece
(44) We are here for a week. Thoroughly enjoying ourselves
(45) One week in steamboat is drawing to a close

(46) Am really enjoying my week in Tunis
(47) Enjoying a few days rest here
(48) Stayed near the place in the picture for a few days (near Roscoff) before coming down to Quiberon for a short while
(49) In Athens at present
(50) thoroughly enjoying the break and its [sic] nice to have some 'time out'
(51) Coming to the end of a very relaxing holiday

Alongside the attractiveness of the holiday destination, the length of a holidays (for example, 'a few weeks', (43) is another measure of its prestige, with the ultimately desirable lifestyle choice of being permanently on holiday. So why do postcard senders at all mention the brevity, for example, 'one week', (44–46); 'a few days' (47–48); 'for a short while' (48); 'at present' (49); or finiteness of their time 'away', for example, 'Coming to the end' (51)? Our interpretation veers, again, to the idea of senders managing and acknowledging their *transient* status and interstitial existence as tourists, while manifesting the sincerity of their desire to return home renewed but reliably unchanged. The same principle appears to guide the choice of leave-taking formulae in postcard messages:

(52) See you soon
(53) Back on 12th May
(54) See you all TOO soon
(55) Unfortunately I'll be back before you get this card
(56) NO DOUBT I'LL BE BACK BEFORE THIS GETS TO YOU

With their salutations and greetings, middles and endings or leave-takings, postcard messages are reminiscent of complete mini-conversations, albeit *seemingly* one-sided ones. (Compare this with the one-sided vocabularies of guidebook glossaries in Chapter 6.) In this regard, they are not unlike text-messages – a comparison that Rogan (2005) makes in his discussion of early 20th century postcard culture. As in face-to-face conversations, the frequent use of formulaic openings and closings is important for retaining the conventions and use of polite interactions. The leave-taking or closing formulae, stressing imminent future encounters and contact, are particularly important for the smooth resumption of a relationship (Laver, 1981) and for the ritualistic reintegration into 'normal' life (Turner, 1986; Belk, 1997). The symbolic gateway to re-entering the home community is thus opened, albeit with a predictable dose of mock resentment and humour, which we have seen in other examples before, for example, 'See you all TOO soon' (54); 'Unfortunately I'll be back before you get this card' (55).

It is the imminence of the return to one's more permanent or 'central' self which also directs us again to the lack of *immanence* in the tourist identity which is not experienced as an 'indwelling'. While postcards and the tourist identities they help perform may appear to be intrinsic to the destination (for example, the performance of located identities above), the significance of both the postcards and the tourist identities they service is almost totally extrinsic. There is an inherent time–space compression in the selection and inscription of postcards because they are – in those moments – acts of relationship (Jaffe, 1999a) with the recipients. Postcards thus embody a geography of simultaneity (cf. Massey, 2005).

This interspatial-relational nature of postcards is foregrounded even further with explicit comments about the tourist's choice of a location image with the recipient in mind (see Jaffe, 1999a, on the selection of greeting cards).

(57) Thought you'd prefer this to the conventional picture postcard [picture of Belgian chocolates with the caption 'The famous Belgian Pralines' underneath]
(58) When I was in London I saw this card and thought of you
(59) Couldn't resist sending you some Koalas
(60) Best I could do in 'bird' pictures (bottom left) on this visit
(61) I thought You would like the picture of the bag pipes
(62) I thought I would send you a postcard to put on the board in the [name of Dept.] postroom – very architectural

In the same vein, other solidary gestures are sometimes made by mentioning recipients' personal likes, and even dislikes:

(63) If you think this is a terrible card you should see what else was on offer
(64) Sorry I didn't choose a nicer postcard but I liked this one at the time
(65) Inspiring card, eh? But it makes the claim that there is a university here

(66) This is not Munich in the spring I know but when you see a rabbit in an exotic frock what can you do? The card with churches, beer and men with beards had to go. I hope friend rabbit adds a wild touch to your Easter

The selection of the postcard itself – the choice of a landscaped or 'ethnographic' image – therefore has more than just representational significance, which is what many analyses of postcards imply. Postcards evidently also have identificational and relational significance – communicative functions which, in practice, are never separated. Like all textual genres, postcards are a way of acting and *inter*acting discursively (Fairclough, 2003; van Leeuwen, 2005).

Doing tourist: An 'exorbitant' community of practice

There is something about travel [by choice] that continues to captivate us. I suggest that the essence of this something, whether it is sought over the rainbow, at Lourdes, in Disneyland, in the movies, or among the natives of Papua New Guinea, lies chiefly in the *difference* that these places promise from what we regard as ordinary. What matters is that they are regarded as markedly different from the ordinary and in that sense promise to be *extraordinary places* offering the potential for *extraordinary experiences*.

(Belk, 1997: 25; our emphasis)

Difference in the age of globalization, of flows, is always abstract difference.

(Lash and Lury, 2007: 187)

The over-riding formulaicity we see in postcard messages confirms their generic distinctiveness – this is postcard-ese – but it also reveals the enculturation of tourists into the wider community of practice. In other words, we see tourists performatively establishing their identity as tourists by, for example, the very act of sending a postcard, and by the uptake of the postcard's 'wish you were here' style. In doing so, tourists are also in the business of teaching other tourists how to be a tourist and confirming the cultural meanings of travel. By taking up both the genre and the style, tourists also help to shore up the ideologies of tourism discourse, two of the most important of which are the *differentness* and the *extraordinariness* described by Russ Belk in the quote above. Indeed, tourism is not simply a cultural industry; it is a cultural industry of *otherness* (Favero, 2007). And, for the most part, what is produced is a kind of abstract, generalized difference most favoured by global capital and most suited to the consumer lifestyles of the more privileged of 'global citizens' (Lash and Lury, quote above; see also Bauman, 1998; Giddens, 1991; bell hooks, 1992; Jordan and Weedon, 1995). This is 'difference' that is easily commodified and these are commodities that are quickly differentiated. And all the major players in tourism are implicated in this symbolic market, whether it's local people packaging and 'staging' themselves as exotic for tourists (Abram, 1997; MacCannell, 1999[1976]; Bruner, 2005), nation states rebranding their places and people for foreign and domestic consumption (Morgan et al., 2002; Heller, 2009) or tourists yearning for – and paying for – the 'authenticities' or 'genuine fakes' of others (Brown, 1996; Hutnyk, 1996; Dilworth, 2003). In fact, for tourists this is an almost full-time pursuit, which invariably demands a Sisyphean collective performance of the extraordinary, especially when it feels as if anyone can go on holiday and when everyone is a tourist.

Returning to our empirical evidence, we find these ideologies and social meaningsof tourism being evidenced in postcard messages in three interrelated ways: through reciprocal talk about holidays; through talk about 'idle work'; and, for British holiday-makers, exaggerated talk about the weather. These are just some of the common resources tourists use for rehearsing 'being a tourist' and to confirm and cohere the broader community of practice (Lave and Wenger, 1991; Eckert and McConnell-Ginet, 1992, 2003; Wenger, 1998; Holmes and Meyerhoff, 1999). In Penny Eckert and Sally McConnell-Ginet's (2003: 5) definition, communities of practice are 'groups that come together around some mutual interest or concern: families, workplace groups, sports teams, musical groups, classrooms, playground groups, and the like' (2003: 5). While the metaphor of the community (or even better: communities) of practice seems apt for theorizing tourist behaviour, we must stress, yet again, the transient nature of participation, fluctuating membership and the *imagined* scope of (self-)identification of self with other tourists; it is clear that all tourists do not ever 'come together'. But, as with many other types of communities of practice, it is through group participation and interaction, observation and informal socialization that different tourist personae are learnt and enacted. It is also in this sense of fleeting, highly stylized and self-reflexive performances of tourist interactions and exchanges, that Ben Rampton's (2009b; see also Jaworski and Thurlow, 2010a) notion of 'communities of contact' seems apt for capturing the nature of the tourist experience, with one of its central practices being the telling of *exorbitant* travel stories – ones which chronicle the excesses of tourist activities and emotions, and which (safely) dramatize an escape from the rut of everyday life.[2] What follows are the three key discursive resources for 'doing tourist' in postcard messages: reciprocity, idleness, weather.

Reciprocity: Sharing the routines and rituals of tourism

One instance where, in our data, we find the idea of imagining a community of practice most apparent is when tourists not only recognize the temporary nature of the status of their tourist identity but also the fact that the addressee has either already been or will soon be a tourist themselves. Tourists do this partly by demonstrating a more positive second-person orientation and by acknowledge the addressee's status as a fellow traveller.

(67)   How was the States? Nothing like camping in Devon I can assure you
(68)   I hope you had a nice holiday
(69)   Enjoy Portugal
(70)   You were right Margaret it is expensive – never mind

These examples include displaying concern for the addressees' well-being, for example, by using the rhetorical question 'How was the States?' (67), and other forms of well-wishing typically found in leave-takings, for example, 'Enjoy Portugal' (69). All of these examples emphasize the addressees' sense of relational work and identification with the addressee. Furthermore, (70) bestows additional symbolic capital on the addressee by granting her good knowledge of the tourist destination being visited. This kind of reciprocity is important both for maintaining links with the people back home and for mitigating the claim to tourist status made by the sender. It celebrates the ingroupness of the sender and the addressee as travelling moderns. The cost of this reciprocity is for the sender the potential devaluing of her extraordinary experience, which, as suggested by Belk (1999), underlies the need to play up the 'sacred' (the magical side) of tourism as a means of downplaying its routinization, its ordinariness.

Idleness: Busy doing nothing

As mentioned above, being a tourist involves doing extraordinary things that take one away from the places and practices of everyday humdrum life (Urry, 2002) – typically, this is less a matter of cutting oneself off completely from home, as it is of switching off from the routines of 'normal' (working) life. Some of the postcard messages we have looked at highlight hedonistic, lazy aspects of tourist identity, orienting to the expectation of 'switching off' whilst on holiday. Jan-Ola Östman (2004: 425) points out that the act of sending a postcard from holiday 'communicates both that one is lazy, that there is nothing important to do, and sending a postcard is one of the most unimportant things one can do'. The following extract emphasizes the non-working aspect of the holiday:

(71) I could get used to this – lots of lazing by the pool doing absolutely nothing other than sunbathing & swimming. Have been on a boat trip & exploring caves tomorrow. Sian loves the water and is a real water baby.

Once again, the 'I could get used to this' (71) reveals the sender's awareness of the transience of his or her experience. Therefore displaying a 'lazy' streak to his or her personality is not self-threatening, but adopting an accepted tourist persona and prerogative. Besides, the 'textual semantic prosody' (Kennedy, 2005) of tourism and tourist postcards necessarily reframes 'lazy' as a positive, desirable attribute. Alternatively, tourism and holidaymaking can also be construed as 'work'. In modern consumer culture, there is a blurring of leisure and work, where some leisure time can involve strict schedules of timetabled activities and thus assume a work-like quality (cf. Lassen, 2006). The meaning of 'lazy' is clearly site-specific. In a similar vein, postcards sometimes reveal another side to tourism: tourism construed as work, albeit very different work than what we do at home.

(72) Having a very busy fun time – feel as if I've been everywhere. Yesterday Cape Kennedy – today MGM Studios – tomorrow – who knows! The girls are in their element – we had lunch with some of the Disney characters.

(73) Well here I am in San Francisco, having been to LA, Phoenix, Grand Canyon – flew over Grand Canyon in 16 seater plane to Vegas! Hotel in Vegas was right on the strip with a revolving restaurant 850 ft up, wonderful sight. Went to see Ricky Martin in Vegas. Yosemite National Park was wonderful. Looking forward to a rest on the cruise.

Listing all the activities and places visited conforms to the expected way one should fulfil this aspect of a tourist persona on holiday. Tourists are portrayed as being 'busy' and even as needing 'a rest' from their numerous leisure activities (cf. Graburn, 1989), a somewhat disingenuous framing of leisure which might serve to mitigate status anxieties or, more ideologically speaking, bourgeois guilt – an indication of what Pierre Bourdieu (1991) characterizes as the state of 'relaxation in tension', that is:

> the expression of a relation to the market which can only be acquired through prolonged and precocious familiarity with markets that are characterized, even under ordinary circumstances, by a high level of control and by that constantly sustained attention to forms and formalities which defines the 'stylization of life'.
>
> (Bourdieu, 1991: 84)

Consistent with the narratives of everyday life, the detailed logging of activities works rhetorically to authenticate or verify the general story being told (Tannen, 1989; see above also). Conveniently, this type of listing also generates a quantifiable sense of excess. On this note, Kennedy (2005: 236–243) shows from his own corpus of post-card messages the repeated use of excessive subjective appreciation (for example, 'great', 'lovely', 'brilliant'), intensifiers (for example, 'very', 'really', 'truly') and, specifically, quantifying boosters (for example, 'lots of', 'loads of', 'plenty of'). Not coincidentally, these rhetorical moves are akin to the 'discourse of the superlative' we particularly identify in super-elite business and first-class travel marketing (Thurlow and Jaworski, 2006).

There is a fine line that must be carefully monitored between staging the tourist experience as 'work' and maintaining the cachet of not being at work. Tourists must therefore work *together* to suspend their disbelief (that is, nowadays with the availability to all of mass tourism there is little that is truly extraordinary; nor can the experience be too unfamiliar if it is to be recognizable and valued); they must work collaboratively in this production/performance. Which is why the continual relationship between actors (tourists) and their audiences ('folks back home') is so key – they must co-construct the travel story, the show. And wherever you are (here or there), the show must go on. Where does this leave tourists for whom there is little truly extraordinary? Well, to continue the theatrical metaphor, they must ham it up. In other words, they must work to frame whatever they are doing, wherever they are going, as extraordinary; most of this work can be done through comparisons with the ordinariness of home. Of course, the drive for show is what creates the necessity to invoke home constantly – 'home plus' and so on. This is where, for British tourists at least, the weather enters the picture.

Writing about the weather

As the example in Figure 3.1 (not from our original dataset) nicely expresses, part of the stereotypical aspiration of being a (British) tourist is to go somewhere where the weather is reliably good, which is understood to mean warm or hot and sunny. Indeed, 'the weather' (often commodified through the use of this precise phrase; N. Coupland and Ylänne, 2000) is the principal selling point of many holidays, and sunshine or/sunny weather plays a major part in the imagery of tourism. The weather is, then, one of the most readily available and frequently used resources for marking the extraordinary. The following examples from our postcards thus make much of the good weather to underline the sender's tourist identity and his or her temporary distance from home (with its 'worse' weather).

(74) Weather too hot to describe to those not on holiday
(75) Weather here is gorgeous (eat your hearts out you lot)
(76) This is the scenery I am looking at right now. What you can't see is me sipping cold ouzo in a shaded taverna
(77) I'm currently sweating it out on this isolated Greek Island The Island is beautiful and quiet, that is, no English tourists here

These apparent instances of distancing from the addressees tend to be humorous and assume relative closeness and safety in being mildly insulting 'eat your hearts out you lot' (75) just as we have shown in numerous other examples above. Therefore, despite the 'distancing' nature of these examples, they may be similarly treated as tokens of solidarity (positive) politeness or of sympathetic antipathy – a teasing which is possible only because of, and in the service of, intimacy. As such, talk about the weather is 'double-coded' as relational/communal: it exercises the solidarity of a quintessential (British) small-talk topic (N. Coupland and Ylänne, 2000) and it rehearses the shared knowledge of a quintessential (British) tourist trope.

As expected, most of our examples construe holiday weather, including extreme climatic conditions (74), as positive (for an exception see 26 above). The tourist identity entails having pleasurable experiences to report (de Botton, 2002) and any negative experiences are downplayed, dismissed as unexpected aberrations, or omitted altogether. This is consistent with Kennedy's observation above that even the negative aspects of holidays are couched in positive terms, either as part of an (safe) adventure or something to be managed as holiday 'work'.

Trading places: Tourism's playful exchanges

Exchange is interesting because it is the chief means by which useful things move from one person to another; because it is an important way in which people create and maintain social hierarchy.... Exchange is also often *fun*: it can be exhilarating as well as useful, and people get excitement from the exercise of their ingenuity in exchange at least as much because of the symbolic and social aspects as because of the material changes which may result.

(Davis, 1992: 1; our emphasis)

Fun, fun, fun! Tourism must be fun because this is supposedly what makes it extraordinary: freedom from the daily routines, inhibitions and constraints of everyday, working life (Belk, 1997: 27). If this is the central organizing principle or rationale of tourism, it is understandably therefore a major currency of exchange in tourism discourse (see Chapters 4 and 5 too). There are, however, a number of interrelated 'give-and-take' practices that occur within the broader exchange system of tourism; each of which is also manifested in or through the holiday postcard. Together, these different currencies present a system of exchange – an *imagined community of practice* – which is expressed as much in terms of interpersonal, communicative practices as it is in terms of material, commercial ones. What our analysis of postcards also reveals is a *historical* trajectory that situates supposedly postmodern/post-industrial notions of space – the 'new mobilities' – in a *'pre*-post' context. Postcards are clearly not exclusively manifestations of the here-and-now. While the values, meanings and practices of postcard sending have surely changed since the late 19th century, the basic system of exchange seems little altered (cf. Phillips, 2000; Rogan, 2005).

In rethinking exchange like this, we follow Gavin Jack and Alison Phipps' (2005) anthropologically inspired lead in wanting to understand tourism (and, for that matter, globalization) as:

a form of perceptual reciprocity, that engages the senses, the material world, that triggers the emotions and stimulates the intellect and that does so in ways that shift, share and change the balance and nature of power and of social and cultural practices.

(Jack and Phipps, 2005: 24)

However, we part company with Jack and Phipps a moment later in an otherwise excellent chapter of their book, when it seems that they fall prey to the kind of dichotomizing and specious-boundary marking they set out to critique. Specifically, they make an unfortunate – to our mind, at least – mistake by dismissing language in their efforts to 'restore' material culture to its rightful place.[3]

The focus on language and culture during the last three decades, since the (in)famous [*sic*] linguistic and cultural turns and the forays into poststructuralism, has allowed attention to be paid to the processes of cultural construction, the role of language and text in creating culture and to the slippery nature of representation. But all the time, material life continued in almost unnoticed, intimate ways, piling, accumulating, burning, breaking, moulding and shaping, giving and receiving. It is rather like digging in Foucault's earth to find, first and foremost, an artefact, as opposed to power, discourse, process or punishment, and, as this long forgotten thing is carefully dusted down, restored and polished, it begins to show its usefulness again.

(Jack and Phipps, 2005: 30–31)

What this commentary too hurriedly dismisses is the materiality of language itself by regarding language as somehow getting in the way of 'stuff', of smothering it rather than recognizing language as stuff – not necessarily *the* stuff itself, but stuff nonetheless. And language, both written and spoken, is material in more than metaphoric ways; spoken language is sound waves, written language is ink and paper. Both are bodily actions (Thurlow, 2010). This is not to mention the supposedly 'metaphoric' stuff of language as an instrument of control, an institution of consequential power and material circumstance (Cameron, 2009 [1990]; Foucault, 1998 [1976]). It is for this reason precisely that the study of spoken and written texts – the bread-and-butter work of discourse analytic approaches – is as much a study of material culture (the 'biographies of things' – Kopytoff, 1986) as it is a study of symbolic, social life (the biographies of people); it is, in fact, almost always a study of the mutual constitution of both. All of which is perfectly materialized in the holiday postcard that, in ontological and epistemological terms, is simultaneously and indivisibly a linguistic, visual, material, social, historical and spatial practice. This counter-critique aside, we share Jack and Phipps' desire to avoid an overly market-oriented or market-determined approach to tourism. We just prefer to take a more *textured* or discursive approach. It is this which motivates us to elevate the written language of postcard messages for proper consideration, making proper space for textual practices which, as Miriam Kahn has shown in her richly historical and ethnographic account of Tahiti, do so much in the way of *producing* space/place and often in troubling ways (Kahn, 2003; cf. Lefebvre, 1991[1974]).

As exercises in positive self-presentation, postcard messages are said to contain predominantly positive evaluations of destinations, activities and experiences (for example, Alber, 1985; Kennedy, 2005). However, as our analysis above demonstrates, the positive tenor of the messages is often scaled down by simultaneously creating a sense of *closeness* between the sender and addressee. Postcards are essentially phatic, rooted in relationships with the people and places of home. They are evidently all about coming home, which is, of course, the ultimate luxury and privilege of tourism. Therefore, they are free to talk nonchalantly about this home-coming.

Returning to the notion of exchange, Alexandra Jaffe (1999a: 116) summarizes the discursive accomplishments of greeting cards:

> ... when we look at ... the specific contexts of their use, we see that they shuttle ambiguously between pure gift and pure commodity. ... But the fact that the card is not exclusively either gift or commodity is also the source of its unique communicative potential. ... [Senders and receivers] can use these resources to reiterate or perform existing statuses and relationships, or to propose or express new relationships and identities in interaction.

While postcards clearly differ generically in some important ways from greeting cards (they are usually less bound by a written, 'packaged' sentiment or message) they do share many of the same formal and functional characteristics. They are pre-made, multimodal, spatially restricted; they entail brief messages; they are a very familiar cultural practice in the wider discourse community; and, the shopping for and the choosing of a card is also a key act of signifying the 'meaning' of the cards. Importantly, the exchange of postcards positions them as both commodity (that is, common, reproducible and impersonal) and gift (that is, singular, unique and personal). As with greeting cards, the medium is to a large extent the message– irrespective of any image shown on the front or any words written on the back. In other words, postcards in themselves performatively constitute tourism discourse and the identity 'tourist'. (With the growing popularity of electronic postcards and travel blogs, the picture postcard is also resignified as a nostalgic, ironic or traditional performance of 'being a tourist'.) To borrow Jaffe's (1999a: 136) phrase, postcards are 'sites of shared experience' – in and of themselves, but especially when tourists inscribe the range of domestic, personal references we see in our data. Examples of this include: 'Wish I was at home marking' (35); 'Enjoy Portugal' (70); 'The view from them is amazing compared with Cathays Terrace' (22); and 'This is the view from our window' (5).

The holiday postcard is appropriately brief, expressing the temporal 'break' from home and the short-lived freedom from work. Anything longer in the way of a written message would start to feel like work again. Even the postcard which has a clichéd 'Wish You Were Here' tagline can be recast in the context of a particular relationship as interpersonally significant – as intimate, even – through its playful/ironic metacommunicative awareness (like a private joke), but also through the possibility that the sentiment, however corny, is heartfelt (cf. ibid.). This is, after all, material evidence that the tourist was at least thinking about the addressee – even without the added effort of demonstrating the level of thought that went into choosing the card (see Figures 3.2 and 3.3, above). Having said which, genericized, telegram-style statements like the iconic–ironic 'Wish You Were Here' and those messages with an elided first-person pronoun (for example, 'Having a great time') can also afford a little 'rhetorical distance' (ibid.: 130) from what would otherwise be more committed, more literal, more egocentric comments (that is, 'I wish you were here' or 'I'm having a great time'). Even the most impersonal card selected off a rack of hundreds can therefore be personalized through the act of selection, messaging, sending and reception, which discursively turns them into Celia Lury's 'tripper-objects' from the start of the chapter. Besides, all language use is conventionalized and to some degree formulaic (Bakhtin, 1981; Wray, 2002), especially in a standardized genre like postcard writing (see Kennedy, 2005, or our own data here). As we have suggested above, the situated practice of the holiday postcard is also a significant act of spatialization; as such, the meaning resides not merely in the postcard itself or in the intentionality of the sender or recipient, but also in its movement through and across space.

We have said as much several times already, but we remain less convinced of the strong 'de-territorialization' perspective of writers like

Ulrich Beck (2002), Zygmunt Bauman (2000) or David Harvey (1990). This is not to say that we deny the kinds of real global flows which Beck and Arjun Appadurai (1996) describe and the kinds of heightened 'liquidity' that Zygmunt Bauman (2000) writes about; these are undoubtedly tangible and unquestionably have profound social consequences. We also recognize that time–space is substantially and experientially 'compressed' (Harvey, 1990) thanks, in part, to communication technologies and other technologies of travel. Nonetheless, just as it is theoretically and methodologically inaccurate to view spatial relations as unaffected by globalizing forces, it is equally problematic to think of them as being totally undermined or changed. Indeed, what we see in holiday postcards – as we see in all of our 'discourses on the move' – are signs that nationalism and other parochialisms are far from replaced; more often than not, they are only temporarily *displaced* (cf. Sheller and Urry, 2006 on 'reterritorialization'). Besides, as Harvey does acknowledge, 'the forebodings generated out of the sense of social space imploding in upon us' also has the effect of stimulating a renewed concern for 'where we belong' (ibid.: 427; see also Lefebvre, 1991). It is this which returns us to the transience of tourist identities which manifest and account for the kinds of interspatial relations we have been discussing.

'Wish you were here!': Being/becoming a tourist

Postcards – and the messages written on the backs of postcards – can in many ways be compared to the speech act of complimenting. Compliments are thought of as positive verbal acts, offers of verbal tokens of solidarity from the speaker to the addressee (Manes and Wolfson, 1981; Wolfson, 1983). However, despite their general perception as desirable lubricants of social relations and widespread use as a positive politeness strategy – an expression and appreciation of the addressee's needs and values – (Brown and Levinson, 1987), they also pose a threat to the speaker's and addressee's faces (for example, Holmes, 1998a, 1998b). First, they may be seen as acts evaluating the addressee, hence putting the speaker in a one-up position of an authority figure over the addressee. Second, as they place the addressee in a relatively privileged position of somebody exceptionally smart, successful, skilful, pretty and so on, they give a problem to the addressee of whether to accept the compliment and the relatively superior status *vis-à-vis* the speaker (and possibly other people) or whether to turn it down and seek equilibrium of social status appearing to be the 'same' as the speaker's (and others').

The first option creates solidarity with the complimenter in that it expresses agreement (positive politeness strategy) but is potentially distancing by assuming a superior status. The second option is potentially distancing by expressing disagreement but is also solidary by seeking sameness of status (see Pomerantz, 1984, 1998 for discussion). Robert Herbert (1990), following Anita Pomerantz, suggests that (in his sample of South African and American English compliment sequences) the most solidary compliment responses are those which seek a compromise: acceptance of the compliment followed by some form of mitigation or scaling down the form of the compliments. For example:

A: You look very nice today.
B: I'm in such a hurry though.
    (Herbert, 1990: 201)

It appears that postcard messages are similar types of communicative acts. Their primary function is phatic (Malinowski, 1923), hence seeking and maintaining positive social relations between sender and addressee. However, given the positive status (however fleeting) accorded to tourists, senders have a problem to solve: how to play out their privileged status and not alienate their addressee at the same time. The solution appears to be not unlike in Herbert's 'solidary' compliment responses: produce acts with two conflicting messages, for example, to both boast and disparage oneself; to foreground one's good fortune of being on holiday but also stress its passing nature; to mention the addressee(s)'s bad fortune of not being on holiday but also show sympathy and concern for them and acknowledge them as potential tourists.

Another similarity between postcards and compliments is their seeming reciprocity. In Herbert's analysis of American English compliments (among US college students), he noticed that (in his sample) in same-sex compliment–compliment response sequences, American men tend to accept the force of the compliment more often than women, while at the same time exchanging compliments less frequently than women. In contrast, women tend to turn down the force of the compliment more often. Herbert interprets this finding by arguing that men treat compliments more as 'praise' and use them relatively infrequently, possibly to avoid placing the addressee in a situation in which he would be likely to boast (a socially dispreferred act). Women, however, resolve the problem of frequent exchange of compliments, which in their case function more as phatic tokens of solidarity, by denying the force of the compliments.

Herbert argues that the relative face threat associated with the rejection of the force of the compliment is alleviated by the shared expectation of American (college student) women to exchange compliments often. Therefore, the principle of solidarity is fulfilled by the relatively high frequency and reciprocity of compliments, with the egalitarian ethos of women achieved by the rejection of the force of the compliment.

Postcards are sent on the understanding that when role reversal takes place, the addressee will also send a postcard to the sender; 'receiving a postcard reminds the receiver that a gift requires a counter gift' (Östman 2004: 425). Sometimes, the expectation of such reciprocity is overtly marked by mutual requests and promises of postcard exchanges, such as 'here is the promised postcard'. Moreover, as we saw in our examples above, the sender may actually mention the addressee's recent or imminent holidays to create a sense of a shared tourist identity. This is what it means to 'do tourist' and to be a member of the globalizing habitus of tourists (Jaworski and Thurlow, 2010a).

Graburn (1989: 33–34) argues that '[t]ourists almost ritualistically send postcards from faraway places to those whom they wish to impress as well as to those they love. Partly, it is to let the latter know they are well and enjoying themselves, and partly to be remembered and awaited'. It is clear from our sample that postcard-sending constitutes part of the knowledge about and practice of being a tourist. Tourists know that they should send postcards, just as they know they should have a good time on holiday. Arguably, the tourists are using the postcard genre to help construct their tourist identity. The knowledge about being a tourist encompasses knowledge about what to do when on holiday and not only what to write on a postcard but also how to write it.

In sending the cards to friends, family and colleagues, tourists include members of their home community of practice in their holiday experience and acknowledge the knowledge and expectations that these people also have about global travel, even if they are not currently tourists themselves. The tourists also know that sending a postcard serves a dual purpose – to highlight their own tourist identity (and therefore their distance from the home community), but also to confirm their continuing membership of their home community even if they are temporarily absent. Their continued allegiance to home is also exemplified in the lack of mention of contact with host communities (cf. 'we had lunch with some Disney characters' in 72, above) and their explicit desire to avoid other tourists (cf. 'no other English tourists', in 77, above; on tourists resenting other tourists, see also Jaworski and Thurlow, 2009b).

The tourist returns home but is no longer the same person as the one who set off on holiday (Graburn, 1989); the narratives of the transient holiday experiences will be woven into more permanent identities, not only through the postcards sent but also through artefacts and souvenirs purchased (Morgan and Pritchard, 2005b), photographs and videos of the tourist activities, all of which can be used as sources of tourist identification at various times, glimpsing (Goffman, 1974) aspects of the person's temporary identity. These all serve to identify someone who has been a tourist, who belongs to the community of 'new internationals' (see Chapter 5). Thus it would appear that 'home identities' are not diminished by the temporary adoption of a tourist identity. Rather, in claiming the cultural capital of global citizenship through travel on their return, the tourist identity arguably enhances the home identity, by building up a biography as a modern, international, cosmopolitan, travelling citizen. For many, this remains little more than an aspirational identity in which, as Graburn (1989: 34) remarks, 'the next best thing to travelling is to know someone who did'.

Part II

Mobilizing Language Ideologies: The Metalinguistic Production of Tourism Discourse

4
Linguascaping the Exotic: Newspaper Travelogues

> In so far as the restructuring and re-scaling of capitalism is knowledge led, it is also discourse led, for knowledges are produced, circulated and consumed as discourses...Moreover, discourses are dialectically materialized in the 'hardware' and 'software' of organizations, enacted as ways of acting and interacting, and inculcated...as ways of being, as identities.
>
> (Fairclough, 2002: 164)

> Ideologies of language are significant for social as well as linguistic analysis because they are not only about language. Rather, such ideologies envision and enact links of language to group and personal identity, to aesthetics, to morality, and to epistemology. Through such linkages, they often underpin fundamental social institutions.
>
> (Woolard and Schieffelin, 1994: 55–56)

In Part II of this book, we now make an important analytic and conceptual shift from examining touristic *uses* of language (that is, discourse) to looking at *representations* of language (that is, metadiscourse). We continue to examine different tourism genres, but we do so with a specific focus on those genres where language is more or less explicitly thematized – in other words, where there is 'language about language' or metalanguage (cf. Lucy, 1993 Jaworski et al., 2004; Johnson and Ensslin, 2007). Critical discourse analysts, like Norman Fairclough (quoted above), have become increasingly concerned with the role of language in representing, promoting, organizing and reproducing the neoliberal discourses of global (or 'advanced' or 'post-industrial') capitalism. With the shift from manufacture-based to service-based economies,

language and communication become more and more essential to contemporary life, which is increasingly 'textually mediated' (Fairclough,
1999) and *semioticized* (see our Introduction). In economies that rely
on the selling and promotion of ideas, information and lifestyles, it
is words, images and design – the look and sound of things – which
become central. And, as language becomes more important to the
(re)orderings of capital, it is necessarily subjected to even greater intervention and regulation – what Fairclough (1995: 3) elsewhere describes
as the *technologization* of discourse: 'a calculated intervention to shift
discursive practices as part of the engineering of social change.' Language is therefore nowadays being used more than ever as an instrument
for evaluating, controlling and managing not just products and services
but also the people who produce them and who serve. Along much the
same lines, Deborah Cameron (2000) has shown how post-industrial
workers (for example, in call centres) find themselves being policed
into particular ways of speaking according to scripts that are given to
them by managers and the like. This kind of *stylization* is also a form
of 'verbal hygiene' (Cameron, 1995) that entails the imposition of a
sanitized, 'correct' way of speaking complete with is its commodification as a work-related skill. What is more, this sort of 'have a nice day'
MacDonaldization of language is also problematically gendered, rendering certain ways of speaking and certain types of work both the province
and the responsibility of women (see also Heller, 2003a, 2010a).

The strategic deployment of language as a technology of or for control
is manifested clearly in commercial industries such as those Cameron
describes, but also, for example, in the nationalistic language testing of
immigrant communities (for example, Piller, 2001b; Blackledge, 2005;
Shohamy, 2006) and the evaluation of students' 'communication skills'
in education (for example, Jaworski and Sachdev, 2004; Thurlow and
Marwick, 2005). What we would like to show in Part II is how similar processes of stylization, technologization and commodification sit at
the heart of tourism discourse as an enormously powerful global industry. As we noted from the start (again, see our Introduction), tourism
is *de facto* a quintessentially semiotic industry – a site of fierce cultural and symbolic production; it is this which makes it all the more
susceptible to linguistic/discursive intervention and management. To
demonstrate this in the context of global mobility we have selected
three common tourist genres: newspaper travelogues, television holiday
shows and guidebook glossaries. As with the different genres examined
in Part I, these different textual practices reveal the ways in which the
tourism experience and the world at large is prefigured and *scripted* for

tourists. Indeed, it is through their use or reading of these texts that tourists not only learn what to see, to do and to *say* while on vacation, but also what it means to be a tourist or a 'global citizen' – especially because we may expect there to be a significant gap between the stated norm and its uptake.

Our interest in the metadiscourse of tourism extends one step further since, as we suggest, beliefs about language inevitably reveal as much about people's beliefs about the world more generally – beyond the discourse of tourism. In particular, we want to consider the ways tourism metadiscourse can be seen to (re)produce the ideologies of difference and the relations of inequality under globalization. To this end, we mean to show how one 'hidden agenda' of touristic representations of language(s) is to strategically stylize a marked Other and, thus, an unmarked Self through the exaggeration of cultural difference even if, on the surface, speakers/writers appear to be celebrating difference (cf. Jordan and Weedon, 1995; hooks, 1992). Ultimately, the effect is to re-inscribe the privileged position of an *imagined* community of tourists *vis-à-vis* their hosts and 'the rest of the world'. (We return to the notion of the imagined community of practice in Chapter 5; see also Jaworski and Thurlow, 2010.)

In taking this approach, our main theoretical concern here is with the kind of *language ideologies* that give shape and meaning to language itself, but also to tourism and to globalization. As Kathryn Woolard and Bambi Schieffelin observe in the quote above, people's beliefs/talk about language are seldom only about language *per se*, but usually, and mainly, about the *speakers* of language and about shoring up the institutions and histories that structure social life (see also Schieffelin et al., 1998; Blommaert, 1999). So, before turning to the analysis of the newspaper travelogues at the heart of this chapter, we want to give a little more depth to our understanding of the closely related fields of metalanguage and language ideology.

Metalanguage and language ideology

The area of sociolinguistic research known as 'language ideologies', that is, the study of a set of discourses 'on language which represents a coherent set of beliefs about language, a language, a language variety, language use, language structure, etc.' (Watts 2001: 299), has for the past decade produced a number of insightful studies placing language at the centre of various social, cultural and political debates (see, for example, Schieffelin et al., 1998; Blommaert, 1999; Jaffe, 1999b;

Kroskrity, 2000; Johnson and Ensslin, 2007). These studies are usually based on the examination of competing discourses on language in particular countries, locations, communities and so on, in overt texts, written or spoken, evaluating different aspects of language use from a variety of perspectives, such as those of government officials, educators, media organizations, 'ordinary' individuals as well as other self- and other-appointed 'experts', including linguists. The ideologization of language, however, does not only take place through explicit meta-language. Ideas about, beliefs of and attitudes towards language with regard to patterns of prestige and standardness, displays of authority and hegemony, acts of subversion and contestation, orientation to the aesthetic dimension of code and so on may be articulated explicitly or made manifest in *communicative practice*, and they are always linked to specific contexts of use and the speaker's/writer's sociocultural knowledge (see, for example, Woolard and Schieffelin, 1994; Kroskrity, 2004). In this sense, all language use displays some degree of reflexivity (Jakobson, 1960; Bauman and Briggs, 1990, 2009; Lucy, 1993; Silverstein, 2001 [1981]) or meta-level which is inextricably linked with the indexing of specific language forms as ideologically charged with respect to the relative power position and identity of their speakers (or writers; see Coupland and Jaworski, 2004, for an overview).

One example demonstrating language ideological work through code choice in a bilingual setting is Alexandra Jaffe's (2007) study of language representation and use on Corsican radio and television. Jaffe demonstrates how the choice of a minority language (Corsican) and the degree to which it is spoken in media broadcasts indexes audiences as 'Corsican', whether a bounded and homogeneous speech community through hypercorrect, Corsican monolingual, authoritative news radio broadcasts, or a community undergoing a language shift in more relaxed, mixed-language use in light radio entertainment shows. Jaffe also demonstrates how the representation of Corsican–French bilingual education in a TV documentary is achieved, somewhat paradoxically, by the editorial process of *erasing* in the final version of the show most of the French language usage by pupils and teachers to normalize, or authenticate the use of Corsican as an academic register.

In other work of our own (Thurlow, 2006, 2007), we too have examined the nature of metalinguistic and language ideological commentary in the news media; this time, with reference to newspaper reports about young people's new media language (for example, in emails, text messages and online chat). As highly invested 'language workers' themselves, journalists are seen to produce a highly stylized (and consistently negative) portrayal of young people, rooted in a parodic fabrication and exaggeration of young people's otherwise creative, meaningful discursive practices. In effect, this mediatized metadiscourse serves to demonize and commodify youth while constructing and shoring up adult identities and adult authority. Language (and language about language) thus becomes a resource by which young people are othered and disciplined, and also by which difference is 'managed' while appearing to celebrate it with humour and so on (cf. N. Coupland, 1999; Jaworski and J. Coupland, 2005; Jaworski, 2007).

In this chapter, we are concerned with similar ideological processes of indexicality, normalization, commodification and othering in one type of tourism discourse: newspaper travelogues. In the next chapter (see also Jaworski, Thurlow et al., 2003), we examine the uses and representations of languages other than English in tourist destinations featured in British TV holiday shows. There, as here, we follow Deborah Cameron's claim that one of the key tasks of critical analyses of language practice is to reveal how institutions like the broadcast media (cf. Silverstein's 1998 notion of 'centring institutions') produce and reproduce linguistic norms, and then to consider 'how these norms are apprehended, accepted, resisted and subverted by individual actors and what their relation is to the construction of identity' (Cameron, 2009 [1990]: 113). Richard Watts (1999: 84) raises a similar sentiment when he states: 'Since any language ideology is constructed from mythical accounts of language use and language structure, it is important to locate examples of those accounts when observing the social practices of everyday life.'

These mediatized representations of staged encounters and language use in tourism are indicative of the degree to which language has come to be ritualized and commodified in tourism performances – what Jack and Phipps (2005) refer to as the 'languaging and translating' of the tourist landscape (and what we prefer to call *linguascaping*, see also Chapter 6). Just as tourists are used to 'pre-visualizing' their destinations before their holidays (Urry, 2002), the famous landmarks to be visited, local 'types' to be encountered, local food to be sampled, leisure activities to be engaged in and so on, so is the linguistic situation in the destination scrutinized and assessed, even if only through the most banal, rhetorical question of the type: 'Do they speak English there?' Much of the tourist texts consulted before the holiday provide just this information. Most tourist guidebooks published in the UK, for example, include language glossaries, information on local languages, the ability of locals to speak English or, more rarely, other tourist languages, the desirability of tourists speaking some local language, usually limited to a few phatic phrases, and other sorts of 'facts' on the use and ecology of language in the tourist destination (see Chapter 6). Such descriptions, inevitably conceived of as acts of linguistic differentiation are socially constructed and ideologically embedded practices (Gal and Irvine, 1995; Irvine and Gal, 2000, 2009). By the same token, hosts are equally committed to packaging up, displaying and selling their ways of speaking as exotic, authentic markers of cultural difference.

The newspaper travelogue is a well-established and popular genre of tourism writing. In the UK, for example, many weekend editions of newspapers, both those traditionally referred to as 'quality' or 'broadsheet' as well as the 'tabloids', carry travel sections full of stories and accounts of different types of holidays by travelling journalists, assorted 'celebrities' and – increasingly – the reading and travelling public.

In the following analysis of extracts from UK travelogues, we examine how the representations and uses of local languages, communicative practices and the linguistic situation in tourist destinations more broadly are reported as indexes of particular types of people and places. First, we provide examples from a variety of fairly random destinations which nonetheless represent some of the most typical locations reflecting the dominant patterns of British tourism, while in the latter part we shift our attention to a case study of travelogues from one specific location – Switzerland (see Jaworski and Piller, 2008).

We particularly focus on the three semiotic processes of the ideologization of language proposed by Judith Irvine and Susan Gal (2000, 2009; see also Gal and Irvine 1995):

1. *iconization* – attribution of an inherent connection between a linguistic form or linguistic variety and social groups or activities; a transparent and dependable, if stereotypical, representation of the specific and distinctive qualities of the group;
2. *fractal recursivity* – transposition or extrapolation of a meaningful opposition salient at one level of social and linguistic organization onto another level or to another domain, for example, projecting intra-group contrasts onto inter-group contrasts or assuming non-linguistic characteristics about a group based on linguistic judgements;
3. *erasure* – a simplification of the sociolinguistic field through which some sociolinguistic phenomena, and the social actors involved in them, are rendered invisible, for example, imagining a social group or a language as homogeneous by disregarding its internal variation.

Representing language in newspaper travelogues

Newspaper travelogues contain four major types of metalinguistic commentary with regard to the destinations they describe:

(1) naming of site-specific objects and concepts in the local language (for example, indigenous people, dishes, traditions, animals, plants, artefacts, modes of transport and so on);

(2) reporting hosts' speech/code switching (for example, in interaction with the writer in English, or in another language, with the English translation present or absent);

Figure 4.1   Newspaper front page. (*Guardian* travel supplement, 12 January 2002)

(3) metapragmatic comments about local languages and hosts' use
of English;

(4) describing holidays involving foreign language learning.

Like many other newspapers around the world, the weekend editions of
national British papers we draw our examples from – *The Guardian* (published on Saturdays), *The Observer* (published on Sundays and owned by
The Guardian), *The Sunday Times* and *The Telegraph on Sunday* – include
dedicated travel sections, with features, information, interviews and
advertisements on tourism-related themes. All are typically referred to

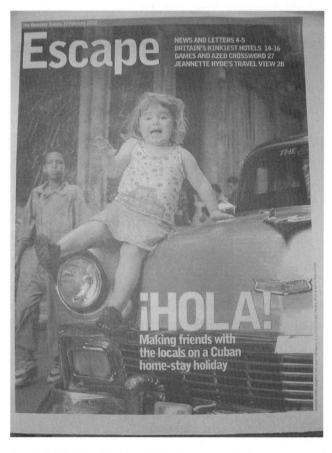

Figure 4.2   ¡Hola! Making friends with the locals on a Cuban home-stay holiday.
(*Observer* travel supplement, 10 February 2002)

as 'broadsheet' or 'quality' papers. They are all associated with different political orientations, *The Guardian* and *The Observer* being known as more liberal and progressive than *The Sunday Times* and *The Telegraph on Sunday* which are associated with a more conservative, right-wing and affluent readership. However, despite these differences, and the former two publications displaying a greater concern with environmental issues (including concern of the effects of tourism on climate change), with their pandering to the pursuit of a consumerist lifestyle and pleasure (with their glossy magazines covering 'style', property, food and drink, culture and so on), all of the newspapers promote high-end, conspicuous consumption and leisure. Even if it only remains aspirational for many readers, as in the case of the TV holiday shows, the overall stance of the newspaper travelogues appears to be far more elitist than that of their broadcast counterparts (Jaworski and Thurlow, 2009b). For example, this is accomplished through such tropes as disdain for 'mass' tourists (and locals); affirmation of and building on celebrity cachet, performative allusions which realize not only the ideologies of elite tourism but also of education and class; appeals to and for exclusivity through favouring quietude and empty spaces (cf. Thurlow and Jaworski, 2010); divulging privileged information framed as 'secrets', 'hot tips' and 'insider information'; positioning of the journalists as knowledgeable 'experts' and purveyors of 'good taste'; endorsement of excess, (self-)indulgence and service; appeals to the spiritual/transcendental experiences and so on. Equally, these tropes allow readers greater scope to fantasise about joining the ranks of the *elite* 'leisure class' (Veblen 1979 [1899]; De Garzia 1964). As we demonstrate in the remaining part of this chapter, linguistic ideologies espoused in the travelogues are premised on an equally elitist stance.

Naming of site-specific objects and concepts in a local language

Our first extract contains several isolated examples from a single travelogue from Buenos Aires. It contains a wide range of Spanish names and referential expressions specific to the city and Argentina more generally which include: place names (extracts 4.1b; 4.1g, below); terms of reference for local people (4.1f); cuisine (4.1b; 4.1c); clothes and accessories (4.1h; 4.1i); means of transport (4.1e); plants (4.1d); music and musical instruments (4.1a); and housing/accommodation (4.1g).

This list of semantic domains is by no means exhaustive and representative of all our data. Other referents may include qualities expressed by adjectives as in the title of one cover story, *Bella Italia* (see Figure 4.3),

Figure 4.3   Bella Italia. All you need to know for the perfect summer holiday. (*Sunday Times* travel supplement, 18 January 2003)

or typographically styled reported speech fragments of interactions between hosts and tourists, as in the following example from a report from an Italian spa: 'I was woken by Bertilla tenderly wiping my brow and loosening my wrappings. "Piano, piano, signorina" '. Other examples will become apparent in some of the extracts cited below. To start, we would like to draw attention to the variable and inconsistent use of metalinguistic markers such as italicization, inverted commas, parenthetical translations, which are typical of the kinds of non-standardized, informal practices of newspaper journalism (for example, the unclear use of quotation marks to report either what was actually said or the gist of what was said; cf. Thurlow, 2006). So, here, we see journalists and sub-editors making different decisions about when to translate something or when to leave it as is, especially true of localities and place names (for example, '*parillas* (barbeque grills)' or 'La Porteña'); when to imply a literal translation or a 'glossing' ('*chinchulines* (intestines)' or 'the *colectivos*, buses that race around the city carving up everybody'); or when to spell the foreign word in its 'standard' format, particularly with regard to the use of diacritics (for example, '*facon*' instead of '*facón*'; see also our discussion of orthography towards the end of the chapter). It is this kind of looseness of translation and orthographic representation which alerts us to the primary metalinguistic function of these foreign terms as exotic 'flavour', as backdrop or, what we would call the tourist *linguascape* – a way of packaging the linguistic reality of the destination for unproblematic and enjoyable consumption of tourists, where language is no longer treated as primarily a means for instrumental communication but as a symbol and index of otherness and difference (cf. Meinhof, 2004). Typically, therefore, foreign and local languages are deployed as (or reduced to) mere backdrop (this theme is further taken up in Chapter 5).

(4.1a) Played by true 'tangueros', tango is dark, dangerous music. Hear Ruben Juarez at Club Homero [...]. Standing with his foot on a chair, his *bandoneon* – the big black German concertina that is the plaintive sound of tango...

(4.1b) El Viejo Bazar, one of a thousand Buenos Aires *parrillas* (barbeque grills).

(4.1c) *matambrito*, 'hunger killer'; *mollejas* (thyroid sweetbreads); *chinchulines* (intestines)

(4.1d) *palo borracho*, 'drunken stick' (plant)

(4.1e) the *colectivos*, buses that race around the city carving up everybody

(4.1f) the locals, *porteños*

(4.1g) I went to his [Ricardo Guiraldes] *estancia*, La Porteña, to see the well where he had jettisoned his earlier books.

(4.1h) *rastra*, a wide belt clanking with silver and gold dollars, chains, horses, flowers, eagles

(4.1i) *facon*, an all-purpose knife, ornamented with cattle and flowers.

(Extract 4.1, Source: Wangford, 2000)

As has been mentioned above, it is not our intention to offer a comprehensive account of all the domains of the open-ended semantic fields prompting travelogue authors to stray from English and invoke snippets of local languages. Rather than carrying out a systematic content analysis of the data, we are more interested in teasing out the underlying motivations and consequences of language representation in the travelogues. However, from our experience of reading these texts, the above examples are quite typical in their scope with references to local food and drink topping the list. It is this area that provides us with a particularly rich source of insights into the language ideological work of the travelogues. Deviating from the expected pattern of English-only texts, the travelogues display linguistic variation in the form of code-switching, or more appropriately code-crossing, connecting the practice of language display to the socio-cultural ideologies of tourism. Here, it is multilingualism and multiculturalism for the relaxed consumption of the Sunday papers readers, feeding their fantasies and desires of foreign travel and feeding their lifestyle identities based on aspirational excess consumption of leisure. The mixing of 'local' languages with English makes these texts polyvocal and polycentric (Blommaert, 2005, 2007) in that they are obviously written with the British, largely monolingual (middle-class) readership in mind, yet orienting to other (imagined) communities with their normative and their indexical orders, norms of code-choice and criteria of appropriateness. Yet, extracted and disembodied from their original communicative spaces, these snippets of foreign languages have their indexical meanings transformed from organizing interactional orders within local communities to indexing these same communities as homogenized, objectified and exoticized. These are instances of fractal recursivity, where contrasts and oppositions between 'our' language and 'theirs' work as dichotomizing and partitioning processes (Gal and Irvine, 2000) indexing a difference between 'us' and 'them', working to establish locally salient (in the context of the travelogue genre) distinct roles and identities for 'locals' and 'tourists'.

Sampling of food has become an essential part of consuming new and exotic places (Franklin, 2003). Be it splashing out on gourmet local delicacies or being 'adventurous' and going 'native' by daringly trying the dishes thought of as less palatable 'back home', food in tourist destinations, just as it is at home, is an essential but also emotional and politicized component of everyday life; a vital source of class distinction (Bourdieu, 1984). Thus, the ubiquity of references to food in the travelogues, and the labelling of local dishes with local names, is a powerful means of creating linguistically a sense of desire or revulsion, admiration or contempt for the destination. The use and mention of foodstuffs is also a recognizable globalist currency (see Harvey, 1989 on global food production; Tomlinson, 1999 on global food culture; also Cook and Crang, 1996). As anthropologists like Mary Douglas (1966) and Claude Leví-Strauss (1970) have commented, food is a key cultural resource for othering, boundary marking – for the production of social order. It comes as no surprise, therefore, to see travelogue authors distancing themselves from the local diet by just providing a list of what is likely to provoke a sense of disgust among the readers (see 4.1c, above). They may employ irony in providing interlingual examples, such as, 'platefuls of *schwein* and *fleisch* (no euphemisms here)'; 'Useful words to know include *inerein* (offal), *lunge* (lung) and *hirm* (brain)' (see, 4.2, below); or they may explicitly combine the labelling of a dish or drink with an explicit commentary on its unsavoury qualities (for example, provoking a 'gagging reflex'; 4.3, below):

> Expect enormous platefuls of *schwein* and *fleisch* (no euphemisms here). You may want to try *schlachtplatter* (slaughter plate). Useful words to know include *inerein* (offal), *lunge* (lung) and *hirm* (brain). Typical Bavarian food can be found in the Hundskugel, the Haxxbauer and the Ratskeller, but the ultimate is probably Zum Durrnbrau, just down the road from the Hofbrauhaus.
>
> (Extract 4.2, Source: Mallalieu, 2002)

> There are about 90 wooden stalls at the market, and at least six of these sell gluhwein at three deutschmarks (90p), with one serving *Eierpunsch*, if you can control your gagging reflex long enough to get the mix of raw egg and wine past your lips, at DM5 (£1.55).
>
> (Extract 4.3, Source: Lazell 2000)

Examples like those quoted in Extracts 4.1–4.3 demonstrate the power of appropriating and recontextualizing local terms not only to create a sense of difference but also othering: positioning travel destinations in a category of stereotyped national diets ('Typical Bavarian food', 4.2; Peckham, 1998; Franklin, 2003) and invoking the names of local dishes for what appears to be little more than their shock value. Friedrich (1989) treats the two tropes used here – metonymy and irony – as key rhetorical devices for the ideological work of maintaining (or changing) a socio-political order and for masking the structures of domination. As our numerous examples below illustrate, language ideological work in the travelogues constantly reiterates the dominant structures of global tourism in privileging the Western/domestic/British tourist over the local 'Other'. And, as Pierre Boudieu (1997) notes, in the nature of these evaluations of (other people's) symbolic capital to 'mis-recognize' the politically and economically (self-)interested nature of the evaluations in the first place.

Reporting hosts' speech/code-switching

Travelogues are predominantly stories of the writers' holidays. One of the key resources for increasing the stylistic and ideological heterogeneity of narratives by 'drawing on the multiplicity of speech events, voices, and points of view' (Bauman and Briggs, 1990: 70) is the use of reported speech. Not only is reported speech a powerful contextualizing device linking the narrated events with the act of narrative but the actual shape of the 'reported' words may create its own illocutionary effects and subject positions. Due to the fact that *reported* speech is largely *constructed* speech (Tannen, 1986), a dramatic recreation of the 'truth', the agency of the author is never fully removed from animating the words of others. Such is also the case with code-switching which, according to Bauman and Briggs (1990: 63, citing Hill, 1985), 'can heighten attention to competing languages and varieties to such an extent that identities, social relations, and the construction of the community itself become open to negotiation'. In more critical discourse analytic terms, the reporting of speech reveals important authorial assertions about the social actors being represented. Norman Fairclough (2003) distinguishes between direct reporting (Susan said, 'I'll be there soon.'), indirect reporting (Susan said she'd be there soon.), free indirect reporting (He sat patiently by the window. Susan would be there soon.) and narrative reporting of speech acts (Susan had made a promise to be there soon.) Each degree of modalized reporting indexes a different claim to truth, a different incorporation of social actors into the text, and, thus, a different level of dialogicality between the *authorial* (and authoritative) voice and the voices of others. Fairclough concludes that the relative dialogicality (or monologicality) of texts indexes degrees of openness to, acceptance of or recognition of social difference. Importantly, for our purposes, metalinguistic framings of reported speech reveal some of the telling ways in which (cultural) difference is addressed, displayed and contained (or 'packaged') in tourism discourse.

In the following extract, the voice of an Italian host ('the Princess') is introduced through reported speech together with an instance of code-switching:

> The Princess had different ideas. 'You must go to Taormina today,' she told us over breakfast. 'If you don't go today, it will be the Italian bank holiday and there will be *tanto confusione* [*sic*].'
>
> (Extract 4.4, Source: Boase, 2002)

Whether the Princess had actually uttered these words or not is highly debatable given what we know about the speakers' and writers' liberties with representing past events through reported speech (cf. Tannen, 1986, cited above). As Tomasso Milani points out to us in a personal communication, the Italian phrase used in 4.4 should in fact say '*tanta confusione'*, which suggests that the author misremembered or indeed made up the Princess' words altogether. Minor details of grammatical gender are either not known or not relevant to the narrative purpose, even though detail ordinarily serves as a key authenticating function in story telling (Tannen, 1986). However, the largely inexplicable (or not self-evidently motivated) shift from the monologic to a more dialogic style changes the footing of the text (Goffman, 1981) and introduces a host's voice to the story about the planned trip to a nearby city (Taormina). The contextualization of the Princess' words with the phrase 'she told us over breakfast' with the metonymic identification of the setting through reference to a shared activity (having breakfast) places the exchange 'there and then' dramatizing the decision-making process of the author's next tourist exploit. In addition, the Princess' code-switch to Italian indexes her Italianness legitimating the author's travelling experience, while affording the reader the impression of authenticity reinforced by the high likelihood of the comprehension of the Italian phrase (despite its apparent 'mistake') due to its relatively close affinity to English via shared Latinate roots for cognate words such as 'tantamount' and 'confusion'. Alternatively, the author may have simply assumed her 'elite' readers' capacity for the recognition of occasional foreign phrases based on their broader literary practices or schooling. Thus, the use of Italian creates an exotic linguascape on the one hand and forms a basis for a shared elite (highly educated, middle-class) identity of the writer and target readership. Language snippets (reported soundbites) serve primarily as authenticating detail.

Metapragmatic comments about local languages and hosts' English

Newspaper travelogues abound in metapragmatic comments about local languages and their speakers. Examples in our data can be grouped under the following headings:

> lesser spoken languages;
> foreign language soundscapes;
> hosts' use of and proficiency in English;
> identifying local languages as 'problematic';
> identifying local languages as 'unproblematic'.

More than one category of metapragmatic comments may occur in one stretch of discourse. For example, the following extract invokes a reference to the peculiarity of Malti as a 'unique blend of Arabic,

Italian and Spanish', and the ability of hosts in Malta to speak 'excellent English':

> The locals are a friendly tolerant lot, and save you struggling with Malti (their unique blend of Arabic, Italian and Spanish) by speaking excellent English. They also drive on the left, use bright-red post-boxes and seem to know London as a Camden cabbie.
>
> (Extract 4.5, Source: Green, 2002)

As we point out elsewhere in this book (Chapters 1, 2 and 6), the dominant ideology of the discourses of tourism and much of the tourism discourse scholarship is premised on privileging 'big', expansive, former colonial languages such French, Spanish, Italian, Portuguese and German. Travelogue authors display their knowledge of these languages more than any others – smaller or genetically further removed from English. It is also possible that, other things being equal, the European and other destinations in which these languages are predominantly spoken are, alongside English-speaking destinations, more frequently visited by travel writers and British tourists than other-language destinations. Therefore, the visibility of powerful (European) languages is increased while less spoken languages become at best objects of exoticizing metapragmatic comments with emphasis on their uniqueness and, therefore, apparent insurmountability. In Extract 4.5, there is a fleeting neocolonial 'leakage', we think, in the characterization of the 'locals' as a 'friendly tolerant *lot*' which, to our mind, invokes a somewhat patronizing association with 'natives' and/or the 'hoards'.[1] It is this derisive stance that also establishes the key of the statement as a whole.

Such delimitation of languages is certainly manifestation of the travelogue authors' language ideologies that 'locate linguistic phenomena as part of, and evidence for, what they believe to be systematic behavioural, aesthetic, affective, and moral contrasts among the social groups indexed' (Irvine and Gal, 2000: 37). Just as the reported speech of the Princess' words (including an untranslated phrase in Italian in 4.4) indexes her foreignness but assumes comprehension on the part of the reader, a degree of affinity and 'sameness' (that is, the reference to Malti as a language to be struggled with in 4.5) similarly renders the Maltese as distant and potentially difficult to handle. Interestingly, this threat is offset by an assurance that the Maltese are in fact 'tolerant' and 'friendly' due to their high competence in English (and knowledge of various aspects of British social life) – the high prestige, expansive, post-colonial language that happens also to be the dominant language of the intended readership of the travelogue. In this case, the linguistic ideology of (British) tourism and the linguistic market (Bourdieu, 1991) of tourist relations is closely linked with the global political economy (Friedrich, 1989; Irvine, 1989) through the implication that, for the Maltese, to make a living out of tourism is premised on their ability to speak English to the tourists, rather than for the tourists to require any extensive knowledge of Malti.

Just to indicate how pervasive the ideological work of recursivity is in linking hosts' ability to speak English to their 'friendliness', we cite three other, random examples expressing similar sentiments, albeit Extracts 4.7 and 4.8 below rely on the inverted expression of the same belief:

> The city centre is traffic free, but the rest of Ljubljana is not much busier. It is probably the most *laid-back* city in Europe, and the *safest*, and the most *visitor friendly* (*almost everyone speaks English*).
>
> (Extract 4.6, our emphasis, Source: Mallalieu, 2005)

> Our destination was San Romano, about 10km off the main road that snakes through the valley and a two-hour drive from Florence airport. Forewarned that although it passed the accessibility test and is a thriving if sleepy hamlet, it contains only one tiny shop and no bar, we stopped off at the municipal centre of Borgo a Mozzano to buy provisions from the old-fashioned little shop on the main street. *The staff speak no English*, like most people in the valley, *but* they are *cheerful, patient, very friendly* and seem genuinely pleased to see you again.
>
> (Extract 4.7, our emphasis, Source: Henry 2001)

> For a start, nobody said hello. I mean, everybody was very *friendly* – they smiled, waved and greeted me. *They just didn't say hello in English*. They said 'sabai di'. In Lao.
>
> (Extract 4.8, our emphasis, Source: Thomas, 2003)

All of these extracts manifest their authors' preoccupation with the hosts' speaking (or not speaking) English and the projection of this ability onto their personality and behaviour towards the tourists (*recursivity*). It also gives some an opportunity to display their phrasebook knowledge of some of the genetically more distant languages (in relation to English), as in Extract 4.8. Such forays into code-crossing (Rampton, 1995, 1998, 2009a) throughout the travelogues demonstrate another aspect of the writers' knowledge and first-hand experience of the destinations. (We return to this point in Chapter 5.) Also telling here is the collocation of, and association between, the stylized host behaviours/identities and the tourist/writer's explicit evaluation. Thus, across the three extracts, we learn that speaking (excellent) English equals 'friendly', 'very friendly', 'tolerant', 'laid back', 'the safest', 'visitor friendly' and genuine (as in 'genuinely pleased to see you'). The ideological framing thus implies that *not* speaking English (or *not* saying 'hello' in English) is unfriendly, unsafe, intolerant, uncheerful, insincere and so on.

Some references to the hosts' use of English are more overtly ironic and scathing, as in the following extract from a travelogue from Lesotho:

> Trekking guides have to speak some English, though don't expect long, enlightening conversations on the economic situation in Lesotho – you probably won't get much more than the names of villages, headmen and mountain peaks.
>
> (Extract 4.9, Source: Sykes, 2001)

What this extract selfishly concentrates on is the trekking guides' apparent lack of refined language skills indexing them as unsophisticated – unable to discuss complex topics (Gal and Irvine's *iconization*). In the process, the author *erases* a whole swathe of sociolinguistic information about the guides who, given the linguistic situation in Lesotho are more than likely to work through two or three languages (that is, Southern Sotho and English as official languages, Xhosa and Zulu also spoken), their English being in its own right a facilitator and marker of global flows and internationalism (as well as a post-colonial legacy). However tongue-in-cheek, this condescending remark epitomizes Paolo Favero's (2007) description of the tendency for 'tourist ways of seeing' to eclipse the social-politics of destinations; in this case, for example, that 50 per cent of the population of Lesotho lives below the poverty line, there is an HIV infection rate of 30 per cent, and a life expectancy rate of 40 years old (CIA World Fact Book, 2008). Whatever this journalist's impression, Lesotho also happens to have one of the highest literacy rates in Africa – higher than Egypt and almost equal to that of South Africa (ibid.). It is hard not to be impatient with moments of Eurocentric, touristic arrogance, even if it is common knowledge that tourism representations are frequently so skewed and problematic (cf. Morgan and Pritchard, 1998).

The aesthetic dimension of language ideology is frequently made manifest in the travelogues as part of the evaluative comments about foreign linguascapes – especially in their representation as soundscapes. As Extracts 4.10 and 4.11 below suggest, they can be either favourable or not.

More than once I've sat at trestle tables where nobody bothered with knives or forks, the air full of the sound of *people talking, calling out, laughing*, the scene lit by the flames from the open fires. My relationship with the island [Madeira] may have begun as a holiday romance: it developed into a long-lasting affection.

(Extract 4.10, our emphasis, Source: Langley, 2002)

Mantua deserves more than a few hours to explore the town's treasures and the 16th-century Palazzo del Te, an imposing country house on the outskirts. For us, the visit was spoiled by *gaggles* of school children. Italians are *noisy by nature* and so are children. Combine the two and *bedlam reigns*. We shall just have to go back at a quieter time.

(Extract 4.11, our emphasis, Source: Fenn, 2001)

In these two contrasting accounts of Madeira and Mantua, linguistic and paralinguistic features (laughter, volume) are at the centre of evoking desirable and undesirable – unbearable, even – descriptions of place, respectively. In Extract 4.10, the romantic and romanticized image of Madeira is invoked by a relaxed, unpretentious, cosy and warm atmosphere complemented by an agreeable soundscape of 'people talking, calling out, laughing'. Extract 4.11, meanwhile, construes the local soundscape as undesirable as it apparently spoils the normative ideal of the authentic/luxury tourist experience as a quiet and solitary (or uncrowded) activity (Thurlow and Jaworski, 2010). Just as earlier we saw local languages (and other cultural markers like 'weird' food) being framed as anthropological curiosities (in an old-fashioned sense), the kind of commentary in Extract 4.11 manifests a very conventional geography, one predicated on and privileging the built environment (plazas and buildings) rather than the people living their lives in these spaces.

The disturbance of silence as a mark of distinction and sophistication (in the act of appreciating a historical monument) is therefore construed as 'noisy' and incomprehensible ('gaggles'). Noisy behaviour and incomprehensible language are indexes of an uncultivated, somehow deranged *national* demeanour.

As above, local languages (or scripts) are typically used by travelogue writers as indexes of *difference*, which almost whimsically can be construed as hindering their tourist pursuits (Extract 4.12), or not (Extract 4.13).

> There's also a tangle of bus routes – cheap, but language difficulties make the network hard to use.
>
> (Extract 4.12, Source: Bleach, 2001)

> Station signs are often in Cyrillic only, so you'll need to transliterate – which soon becomes second nature.
>
> (Extract 4.13, Source: Stewart, 2001)

Language learning

It may be quite encouraging to linguists, generally presumed to be enthusiastic language learners and polyglots, to see that once in a while newspaper travel sections offer information about language

Figure 4.4 Prêt à parler. Can you learn a language in eight hours? (*Sunday Times* travel supplement, 18 January 2003)

learning, alongside numerous other lifestyle, activity-based holidays (see Figure 4.4). The following is a typical example:

Parlare Italiano

Euro Academy, with bases in Siena, Florence and Rome, combines language tuition with special-interest courses such as cookery, wine, art history, and Italian cinema. The courses are suitable for all levels and age groups, including intensive courses for business travellers. The tuition can be taken one-on-one or in groups, and home-stay accommodation is available.

(Extract 4.14, Source: Barrell, 2001)

The information is short and factual, positioning language learning on a par with other Italy-themed courses, which, understandably, appear more for 'popular' interest than academic. Of course, we cannot judge what the uptake of the language (or other skills-learning) holidays is (though see Yarymowich, 2005), but the general tenor of the information suggests the idea of learning Italian to be 'fun' – a rather familiar trope in other genres of tourism discourse that constructs holiday language courses or informal learning as 'fun' (see also Chapters 5 and, especially, 6). A similar sentiment is shared by Alison Phipps (2007: 183) who argues that holiday language learning is 'a quest for... recreation... for forms of rest, for time that represents a break from habituated daily action'. Yet, to our mind, Phipps takes an unfortunately moral high ground in arguing that tourist language learning invalidates, to some extent, Zygmunt Bauman's (2000) conceptualization of post-industrial life as *liquid modernity*; for Phipps, tourists learning a foreign language are involved in acts of 'kinetic resistance' (after Cronin, 2000: 116):

resistance to English as a dominant language; resistance to easy consumption through the *slow learning* of language; resistance to alienation, through the imagination and enactment of courtesy and charity, through the commitment that grows from intercultural speaking and listening to the social miracle of conversation.

(Phipps, 2007: 184; our emphasis)

Although we do appreciate that Phipps speaks here from the position of her own, personal experience as a scholar and holiday language learner, we doubt that similar ideologies of language, based on quasi-religious metaphorization and imagery, are indeed prevalent in the minds of the majority of the promoters, operators and consumers of tourism. Indeed, newspaper travelogues appear most of the time to frame language learning as little more than a simple ('liquid') formula for fun. In a *Sunday Times* cover story 'Learn the lingo' (Figure 4.5), three journalists set out on one to two week courses in France, Italy and Spain to learn French, Italian and Spanish (Crump, Green and Bowman, 2005). Their individual reports provide humorous and self-mocking accounts of their efforts, mixed success and continued commitments to study their chosen languages back home. Although there are echoes in their stories of the Phipps/Cronin 'kinetic resistance', the sub-editors' caption under the collage photo of the three journalists surrounded by textbooks and dictionaries (Figure 4.6) subverts the centrality of language learning to the holiday experience. It says: 'Total immersion: Vincent, ... Richard and Katie perhaps enjoyed the food, drink and culture more than the linguistic effort'. Again, at least from the vantage point of the travel section editorial policy, the dominance of English seems to remain unchallenged. We return to these issues later in Chapter 6; for now, however, we want to turn to one specific tourist destination in order to think through tourist linguascaping a little differently.

Linguascaping Switzerland

> INTERLACKEN [*sic*]: From back and front of our hotel sounds most unsabbatical greet our ears on this Sunday morning of July 5th [1863], – the dull, heavy roll of the wooden ball as it struck down the skittles, and the animated voices of Swiss idlers before our windows ... At eleven o'clock the majority of the Club, indeed all who were not overcome by a state of 'sunny somnolence', went to church.... How refreshing it is after wandering for days amongst foreigners to meet again with fellow countrymen and join them in prayer for dear old England, in the familiar language of home.
>
> (Morrell, 1863: 59–60)

Arguably the birthplace of modern tourism, Switzerland (and Interlaken, in particular) has been organizing and promoting itself since the 1850s as the quintessential tourist destination. It was between 26 June and 15 July in 1863 that Thomas Cook ran the first ever organized tour of Switzerland for the 'Junior Alpine Club'. The quote above is taken from the journal Miss Jemima Morrell was charged with keeping on behalf of the group. Nearly a century and a half later, and given the kind of newspaper travelogue commentary we have been looking at here, what is striking is how recognizable Miss Morrell's linguascaping

Figure 4.5 Learn the lingo. (*Sunday Times* 'Learn the Lingo' cover, 9 January 2005)

Figure 4.6 The 'learn the lingo' article. (*Sunday Times* 'Learn the Lingo' story, 9 January 2005)

is: her surprise at the 'animated' Swiss voices outside her hotel window on a Sunday, to the reassuring comforts of the English language after spending 'days amongst *foreigners*'. Given its history, Switzerland presents itself as an interesting site (or text) for exploring the neocolonial trajectories of tourism (a theme we take up again in Chapter 5). For our purposes, it presents a particularly interesting case study for language ideological issues (cf. Watts, 1999).

In this next section, we focus on similar travelogue data selected from 23 *Guardian* and *Sunday Times* travel 'reports' about Switzerland. 'Swiss' travelogues provide an interesting case study because of the country's 'elite' and 'first world' status, on one hand, and (British) tourists' playground since the beginning of mass tourism, on the other. The country's complex sociolinguistic situation also offers fertile ground for observation and metalinguistic commentary in newspaper travelogues.

The predominant interest of travelogues focusing on Switzerland is with winter holidays in the Alps, particularly reporting and giving advice on winter sports (mainly skiing), food and drink, accommodation and transport. Four articles differ (slightly) from this pattern: one article features a report on a 'walk' across the Bernese Alps during summertime; two articles choose urban rather than Alpine locations (Zürich and Lucerne). Another article stands out as it is a feature on Romansch in the canton of Graubünden (Milnes, 2001, which, for reasons of space, we do not reproduce here; for the full text and discussion, see Jaworski and Piller, 2008).

Various countries and regions around the world have developed specific genres of tourism for which they are known internationally – with more and more places finding more and more creative ways to exploit their 'uniqueness' in a bid to enter the global tourism market (Urry, 2002). Probably most famously, the UK seems to have morphed into an over-sized 'heritage site' attracting international tourists seeking 'history' and 'tradition'. Although not exclusively, France is typically associated with romantic (Paris) and gastronomic tourism, Italy with cultural tourism and Thailand with backpacking or sex tourism (see Morgan et al., 2002, on 'destination branding'). As reflected in our data, in the context of the British media representations of tourism, and probably conforming to the stereotype and also patterns of actual British tourist behaviour, Switzerland appears to be associated predominantly with Alpine, winter sports holidays. Today, British tourists are among the top five source countries for tourists to Switzerland. One consequence of the traditionally very strong presence of British tourists and British institutions in Swiss tourism is the ubiquity of English in Swiss tourism contexts (see Piller, 2007, for an overview). Although English is not an official language in Switzerland, it is often dubbed the fifth national language (Watts and Murray, 2001). The most widely known sociolinguistic characteristic of Switzerland, however, is its diglossia in the German-speaking region (that is, Standard German and Swiss German dialects) and its official quadrilingualism (Watts, 2001): German, French, Italian and Romansch.

Exotic linguascape – Romansch

Not unlike in travel stories about other destinations, where relatively lesser spoken languages are used (cf. Extract 4.5), tourism writing about Switzerland often mentions Romansch, the smallest of its national languages, spoken as a first language by approximately 0.5 per cent – a percentage significantly smaller than the combination of other minority languages spoken in Switzerland (for example, Spanish and Turkish) and just about equal to English L1 speakers (Watts, 1999).

> If Switzerland is the Greta Garbo of European states (its federal slogan should be 'We want to be alone'), then the Engandine must be its most isolated outpost. Nearly four hours by train from Zurich airport, and 1,650 metres above sea level, it's a collection of medieval villages and small farming communities stretched out across a vast Alpine valley.
>
> Romansch, that curios hybrid of French, German and Latin, is the central language of this canton. To add to the sense of seclusion, the Engandine remains one of the least developed corners of the country, free of the high-rise developments and commercial glitz that so characterise the usual ski-resort scene. St Moritz is its notable exception.
>
> (Extract 4.15, Source: Kennedy, 2002)

Romansch in Extract 4.15 is described as a 'curious hybrid', not unlike the designation of Malti in Extract 4.5 as a 'unique blend'. Judgements such as these hinge on an ideology or mythology of linguistic purity; a case can be fairly easily mounted for English (especially in the form of World Englishes) as a hybrid, although not 'mixed', language – as is true for most languages. The distinction is, as always, a matter of standardization, history and power. The mixture of languages making up Romansch is transposed to the idea of the whole region being a 'collection' of random and somewhat insignificant if quirky-sounding 'medieval villages and small farming communities' (Gall and Irvine's *recursivity*). The remoteness (ideological *discreteness*, Irvine 1989) of Romansch is also matched by the remoteness of the whole region (*recursivity*, again), St Moritz being dismissed as an 'exception' to the relative underdevelopment of the canton, it is a region in Engadin (which is in fact a region in the canton of Graubünden).

Multilingual linguascape – German, French and Italian

Despite Switzerland's multilingualism as a nation consisting of several distinct linguistic areas, the majority of its population is said to remain monolingual. For example, quoting Dürmüller (2001), Demont-Heinrich (2005: 73) claims that 'a majority of its citizens, with the exception of the speakers of what some have called the 'small' languages of Italian and Romansch, are in fact monolingual'. It is the peculiar tension between *state* multilingualism and individual monolingualism that remains one of the defining features of the Swiss ethnolinguistic identity (Watts, 2001; Demont-Heinrich, 2005). British press travelogues featuring Switzerland draw on this fact by slipping in the display of the rather predictable snippets of German, French and Italian words and phrases. As in other publications of this type, they predominantly draw from the semantic domains of food, drink and other aspects of the locale (cf. above). In our sample, we have found several examples of this sort of language play, reproduced in Extracts 4.16–4.19 below, mostly but not exclusively dealing with the culinary semantic field.

Specialties here include warm chicken salad with wild mushrooms, *pot au feu* and pancakes with berries.

. . .

Situated in a tiny hamlet of little *mazot* huts, Zum See has its own formal terrace with Matterhorn views, but in busy periods – which seems like every day in springtime – extra tables (sometimes simply comprising slates on oil drums) are sited in sunny corners amid the huts. Max Menning is an accomplished cook, and his home-made pasta is superb. Many people phone ahead on their mobiles to reserve slices of *Apfelstrudel* and other confectioneries. Max's wife, Greti, exudes a serene calm as the ambience gets ever more frenetic.

(Extract 4.16, Source: Scott 2001)

For rustic Alpine atmosphere: really, almost anywhere that sells *vin chaud* or schnapps will do – provided the view's good. Last season, our favourite was the very rudimentary Holzerbar, at the side of the Tschuggen piste in Grindelwald.

Sure, the gluhwein was good enough, but what really mattered was the weather, the scenery (care of the north face of the Eiger) and the skiing: the Tschuggen is one of the best high-speed carving tracks we know.

(Extract 4.17, Source: Anonymous 2005)

On the slopes by the Klein Matterhorn, it was even better – long, flattering stretches of dry powder reaching down to Plan Maison, above Cervinia, over the invisible frontier in Italy. We lunched off *capaletti* and *tagaliatelle ai funghi porcini* and skied down, no passports needed, enjoying the sunshine from the south and the enthusiasm of Italians up for Sunday from the Aosta Valley.

(Extract 4.18, Source: Bray 2000)

German-speaking Lucerne is a smooth, near-silent 50-minute train ride from the airport at Zürich...

The name (spelt Luzern in German) probably derives from the Celtic *lozzeria*, meaning 'a settlement on marshy ground', but the town dates its origins from the mid-eighth century, when its Benedictine monastery is believed to have come under the control of the Alsatian Abbey of Murbach. Lucerne's ecclesiastical past keeps watch over the modern town from its many spires and bell-towers, and the verdigris-laden onion domes of the Jesuit Church, where several of this year's spiritually-inclined concerts will take place.

You might also try a little lip-smacking walnut schnapps...

Many venues will also warm guests with a Kaffee fertig: a coffee laced with schnapps.

(Extract 4.19, Source: Brown 2006)

The high concentration of the German, French and Italian used in the above examples, alongside the overt comments about languages spoken in particular towns or areas (see Extract 4.19) index Switzerland as a foreign(-language) *and* multilingual tourist destination. Of course, here and in several other of our examples (4.1–4.4), this sort of code representation and/or code-crossing performs also several other functions: (1) they authenticate travel destinations by adding additional local 'flavour' to the creation of the sense of place in the travelogue description; (2) they legitimate the author's role as 'expert', bone fide reporter, 'engaged' rather than disinterested, passive tourist and a well-educated, 'elite' traveller; (3) they also style the reader as an engaged, well-educated and 'elite' consumer of the mediated destination, especially if they are capable of recognizing, pronouncing or translating the 'foreign' words without further explanation. We return in just a moment to the variable use of italicization as a typographic marker for 'foreign language'.

Safe linguascape – English

Much of the ideologized commentary about the 'foreign' (cf. Miss Morrell's comments above) languages of Switzerland is, of course, back-grounded by the ethnocentric perspectives of the British writers and by dominant ideologies of the English language. Writers' attitudes towards other languages are inevitably rooted in their beliefs or assumptions about English. As Alastair Pennycook (1998: 33) remarks:

> Discourses of the Other adhere to English both because of the history of co-articulations and because of the relationship between English and the discourses of the Self (discourses about English) and between the discourses of the Self and the discourses of the Other.

In our 'Swiss' data, by far the most frequent language to represent interactions between tourists (writers) and local people is English. Whether English was the original language of the interaction, which is most likely, or whether it is an unacknowledged translation is never clear. As has been mentioned, most features in our sample present the attractions of winter/skiing holidays, with only occasional mention of non-Alpine resorts. The Swiss people represented in these stories are quite limited in type, mostly (named or unnamed) tourism operators such as owners or managers of restaurants, hotels, skiing businesses, guides and so on. One of them – a named 'igloo supervisor' – in Extract 4.20 below appears in dialogue with the author of the article:

> 'Now,' said Rahel Zürcher, the igloo supervisor, as she gave me my 8 am cup of tea, 'do you want to catch the railway back down the mountain, or shall we go sledging?' Of course, we took the less sensible option.

Other English-speaking Swiss (and foreign) people encountered in our data are other Swiss and international, always English-speaking tourists. In Extract 4.21, the two tourists are a Swiss male skier, and an Italian female train passenger. They are both 'othered' through the author's mild ridicule of their attire, taste and intellect. However, as they are members of the privileged 'leisure class' (Veblen, 1979 [1899]; MacCannell, 1999[1976]), the damage of such prejudicial language, in our view, is relatively minor.

(Extract 4.20, Source: Newson, 2006)

'This is where the jet set come in', Gerhard told me.

Gerhard was a middle-aged gent decked out in one of those stretch-Lycra tracksuits that tends to accentuate every bulge in the human body (and that led me to wonder: why do the taciturn, uber-controlled Swiss go in for these cartoonish super-hero outfits?). As we stood there talking, a Gulfstream jet made its approach towards the nearby runway.

'It's probably Naomi Campbell,' Gerhard said, with a mischievous smile. 'It's only a 15-minute drive from the airport to St Moritz, so all the *beau monde* land here.'

'And how far is it by skis?' 'Another 13km.'

I paid the equivalent of three quid for a train ticket to Zuoz, and stood for most of the way back, gazing out at the terrain I'd covered earlier that day. By rail, the journey took 20 minutes. A seat finally opened up and I flopped into it – right next to a chic Italian woman in regulation electric-red parka and overpriced eyewear.

'You look happy,' she said.

'That's because I'm not skiing any more,' I said, then explained that it had taken me five unstinting hours to haul myself from Zuoz to St. Moritz. 'Five hours by skis?' she said, aghast. 'You must be insane. The train is so much faster.'

'Really?' I said.

(Extract 4.21, continuing from Extract 4.15,
Source: Kennedy 2002)

The English spoken by the authors, hosts and other tourists in these and other extracts creates a sense of cosmopolitanism of Switzerland. The unproblematic use of English as a lingua franca indexes the tourists and hosts as international, globalized, well-educated and wealthy; an interpretation consistent with the self-image of the elite, middle-class UK readership that we associate with these newspapers. It is somewhat ironic that English-speaking hosts in poor countries do not engender the same degree of prestige bestowed by them on the travelogue writers – recall our example from Lesotho (Extract 4.9).

The topics of the conversations and of the descriptive parts of many extracts are also frequently focused on 'global' topics such as 'designer' brands, royalty, 'celebrity', elite lifestyle – also very much a part of the 'Swiss brand'. In Extract 4.20 above, this is achieved through the mention of the approaching Gulfstream jet, Naomi Campbell and St Moritz as an apparent magnet for 'the *beau monde*' in general. In other articles, readers are exposed to typical lists of available 'designer' shops located in various towns and resorts, for example, 'Prada, Gucci, Louis Vuitton, Dolce & Gabbana and Bulgari are only the start of it' (Newsom, 2003 – see Appendix). These signifiers of extreme luxury lifestyle, 'iconic' media personality and the crossing into French (in the predominantly Roman-sch/German speaking area) reinforce the status of Switzerland generally and St Moritz in particular as a *glamorous* and *elite* tourist destination. We are reminded also that travel writers are only marginally independent of commerce and that travelogues function as 'advertising features' – more so even than movie reviews. Most travel writers are also subsidized or sponsored by local tourism agencies.

English-speaking hosts and tourists are not the only resource used in these travelogues to create a sense of familiarity with Switzerland for the British readers. Continuing the recognizable trope of high-profile portrayal of the Swiss ski resorts, the authors repeatedly mention other 'celebrities' frequenting their slopes, exclusive hotels, bars and discos such as British royals and an assorted list of mostly British and some 'international' celebrities: Prince Charles (and his family), the Duchess of York (with princesses Beatrice and Eugenie), George Clooney, Claudia Schiffer and many others. As a sure sign of Switzerland being interna-tionalized, albeit from a decidedly 'Anglo' perspective, references to the British presence in Switzerland past and present are common. For exam-ple, Extract 4.22 plays on a commonly acknowledged 'appropriation' of Switzerland by British tourists going back to the Victorian era:

It was the English who began the vogue for Swiss tourism, my guide Gabby tells me as we strike out on a bracing hike around the lake, and Lucerne's popularity snowballed after a long stay by Queen Victoria in 1868.

The strong presence and 'Anglicization' of Switzerland appears to continue today, not surprisingly drawing on the imagery of traditional British upper-class lifestyle.

(Extract 4.22, Source: Brown, 2006)

Other recent developments include the acquisition (six years ago) of the Hotel de la Paix by Stephen Purdew, the owner of the famous Champney's health spa chain. Purdew has spent over £1 million furnishing the hotel in English country style. He's named the rooms after counties, fitted tartan carpets and en suite whirlpool tubs. In typically tricky Champéry style, it's a corporate-bookings-only operation. The owner insists it is a labour of love rather than a serious business venture.

(Extract 4.23, Source: Mills 2005)

Overall, the newspapers create an image of a safe English linguascape through easy English conversations with locals and other English speakers, being surrounded by international, commercial signage and more localized but resolutely English linguistic landscape, for example, '... The Pipe, a snowboarders' hang out, which advertises "groovy music, chillin' sport videos and wild party nights" ' (Bray, 2000 – see Appendix) and Anglo-themed hotels (see Extract 4.23). To invoke Gal and Irvine's (1995) terminology again, all of these metadiscursive representations ideologize language by recursively transposing the international status of English (and French) to represent Switzerland as cosmopolitan and globalized, and by erasing local languages from the scene creating a sense of Switzerland as an 'easy' winter holiday destination.

Linguascaping the exotic

A brief exploration of the linguistic knowledge about Switzerland that is produced and reproduced in British newspaper travelogues leads us to make three observations: the smallest national language, Romansch, appears to receive a great deal of attention in the travelogues as it serves to exoticize and romanticize parts of Switzerland as 'different', 'rural' and 'underdeveloped'. The 'larger' national languages of Switzerland – German, French, Italian – are also exoticized but to a relatively lesser degree and through one linguistic practice only, namely the use of local terms for local cuisine, landmarks or cultural events – a practice that can be observed relative to Romansh, too, of course (see Jaworski and Piller, 2008, for examples). All these practices serve to render Switzerland linguistically 'special' and 'foreign'. These linguistic observations are not complete and they *erase* much of the complexity of the Swiss language ecology, for example, the presence of immigrant languages spoken in Switzerland, especially in the tourist sector, for example, Croatian, Portuguese, Serbian or Spanish. We also came across little or no use of Swiss German dialects.

Thus our data offer us an insight into the language ideological work with regard to what count as touristically legitimate languages of Switzerland. While English is unproblematically legitimated as the default code available to (British) tourists for communication in Switzerland, the country's official languages tend to be invoked largely as symbolic indexes of difference, and possibly elite lifestyles (another desirable marker of difference). As a 'small' language, Romansch indexes just that – relative smallness, quaintness and charm of the rural regions, while immigrant and other community languages are completely disregarded from view.

In sum, as we have seen throughout this chapter, and as will be discussed in greater detail in Chapter 6, tourism as a practice carries with it its own form of linguistic technologization and commodification, which may take the form of more or less overt comments or representations. Categorical in nature, they are far from being consistent, as each travel writer will relay on a different set of personal experiences and impressionistic judgements. For example, Italian is represented as part of a host's repertoire in a code-switched utterance in 4.4, but as annoying racket in 4.11, and Malti (a 'blend' of other languages) is dismissed as too difficult to bother with on holiday (4.5). English is naturalized as the international lingua franca spoken by 'everyone' – everyone who matters, to the tourist that is – and if they don't, suspicion of unfriendliness and uncooperativity creeps in and needs to be denied (cf. 4.5–4.9). And, where 'foreign' languages may be useful, it is mostly so in orienting the tourists to 'spicing up' hedonistic pleasure or spectacular revulsion of consumption (cf. 4.2–4.3, 4.17–4.19).

Returning to the orthographic and typographic variation of the 'foreign' language forms in our extracts, we need to comment on the meaning potential and sociolinguistic status of these forms. The following list brings together all the relevant examples from the extracts reproducing them following original spelling, punctuation and typeface:

'tangueros' (4.1a)
bandoneon (4.1a)
parrillas (4.1b)

matambrito (4.1c)
mollejas (4.1c)
chinchulines (4.1c)
palo borracho (4.1d)
the *colectivos* (4.1e)
porteños (4.1f)
estancia (4.1g)
rastra (4.1h)
facon (4.1i)
schwein and *fleisch* (4.2)
schlachtplatter (4.2)
inerein (4.2)
lunge (4.2)
gluhwein (4.3; 4.17)
Eierpunsch (4.3)
tanto confusione (4.4)
'sabai di' (4.8)
pot au feu (4.16)
mazot (4.16)
Apfelstrudel (4.16)
vin chaud (4.17)
schnapps (4.17; 4.19)
capaletti (4.18)
tagaliatelle ai funghi porcini (4.18)
Kaffee fertig (4.19)

Even in a small sample such as this, we can see intriguing variation in the use of italics and quotation marks, while some words and phrases are left in unmarked typography. Other orthographic peculiarities include losing the umlaut in both occurrences of 'glühwein' but preserving the tilda on the 'porteños', and – as expected – the Laotian greeting 'sabai di' has been Romanized rather than reproduced in an abugida script. A similar example is found in one issue of *The Guardian* travel section (3 February 2001), where the Italian word '*la passeggiata*' appears in three different features, each following different typographic and orthographic conventions: with or without italicization and with or without the definite article:

la passeggiata (MacLeod, 2001)
passeggiata (Nicholson, 2001)
passeggiata (Fenn, 2001)

Further, while most of the words and phrases above are translated or glossed into English, some are not (see extracts above). This variability does not seem to wholly depend on the degree of integration of the apparent borrowing into the English lexicon. For example, while 'schnapps' and 'gluhwein' [*sic*] remain untranslated due to their relatively transparent meaning to an average English reader, 'mazot huts' will be understood probably by only a minority of skiers who are familiar with this sort of accommodation in the Swiss Alps.

The degree of editorial uncertainty in the representation of 'foreign' words and phrases in travelogues demonstrates some affinity with different areas of non-standard orthography, where variation, creativity and respellings are common (for example, Preston, 1985; Sebba, 1998; Androtsopoulous, 2000; Jaffe, 2000). Although all of the examples in our extracts are associated with 'standard' (foreign) languages, their variable orthography and inconsistent usage undermines their status and is cause for 'demotion' (Preston, 2000) as legitimate codes. Due to the editorial control of typographic and orthographic design, the recontextualization of host languages into (British) travelogues and variable respellings are symbolic of difference (distinction) or sameness (unity) (Jaffe and Walton, 2000: 506) between the host populations and newspaper writers and readers. Certainly, some of the differences may be due to authors' own lack of awareness of host languages, and as we learn from Rampton (1995, 1998, 2009a), code-crossing is frequently marked by suspension of linguistic and pragmatic norms of the 'legitimate' users, hence 'mistakes' and metacommunicative comments (for example, glossing) are common. However, this precisely points to the fact that host languages are used here in a playful frame invoking social personas of travel-writers as detached rather than involved with the local populations, on occasion exoticizing travel destinations with foreign-sounding linguascapes while at the same time blending and homogenizing linguistic difference visually for easy consumption and unobtrusive visual scanning of would-be-tourists/readers.

5
Language Crossing and Identity Play: Television Holiday Shows

> The Other in *our* geography is a source of disgust; the Other in *their* geography is a source of pleasure. In *our* place the Other is pollution; in *their* place the other is romantic, beautiful, and exotic.
>
> (Bruner, 2005 [1996]: 194)

> I miss Holiday type programmes. It was great escapism, especially at this miserable time of year. The more exotic, far flung or expensive the destination the better, as far as I'm concerned – wonderful armchair travel.
>
> (Post on the *Digital Spy Forum*, October 2007)

Television travel (or holiday) shows have always been hugely popular in the UK – a wonderful, escapist form of armchair travel says the one viewer quoted above. According to their own publicity, both the BBC's *Holiday* and ITV's *Wish You Were Here?*, which each ran for over 30 years, boasted weekly ratings of well over four or five million viewers.[1] While for some tourists, holiday shows form an important part of their pre-holiday preparations providing information and tips about holiday destinations, the shows also offer major entertainment on primetime TV for a much wider audience (Hanefors and Mossberg, 2000). The basic format of the shows we looked at for this chapter always followed an introduction by a lead presenter and then three or four 'episodes' where other presenters or guest celebrities try out different holidays in a variety of locations. Although most local people featured in these particular shows used English to communicate with the travelling 'journalists', regardless of the official status of English in the destination, it was not uncommon for the presenters to initiate interaction with the hosts in their native language, or to quote 'foreign' language phrases in their commentaries and narratives. Occasionally, the presenters also elicited words or phrases in the host language from the hosts – in much the same way that we saw journalists doing in Chapter 4. As with newspaper travelogues, one of the primary functions served by the use of local languages is for linguascaping the tourist experience. There are, however, other functions – other sociolinguistic considerations – that we want to bring to light in this chapter.

Before we turn to a discussion of the functions of local languages, we want to first comment on their use in tourism discourse as a form of performance, and to consider their particular functioning in terms of what Erving Goffman calls the 'theatrical frame' (1974: Chapter 5), that is, strips of behaviour which are produced and interpreted as, or by analogy to, a rather narrowly conceived stage performance. (Performance as metaphor has, of course, become a central point of discussion in critical tourism studies, taking its cue from the early work of Dean MacCannell, 1999 [1976]; see also Crang, 1997; and Edensor, 2001). In this sense, performance involves one or more performers engaged in a make-believe interaction (or monologue in the case of just one performer) and an audience, where performers and an audience are likely to be separated spatially (the former, traditionally, performing on a stage viewed by the audience from an auditorium). Of particular importance to our data here, however, Goffman recognizes how an audience operates in a dual role. On the one hand, every member of the audience engages in the act of buying a ticket, taking a seat in the auditorium, spending real time in the theatre, taking part in the non-performance activities such as having a drink during intermission and so on, that is, every member of the audience is a 'theatregoer'. On the other hand, every member of the audience also collaborates as an onlooker in the 'unreality onstage' (Goffman, 1974: 130) – or what, in dramaturgical terms, is known as the suspension of disbelief. In other words, the audience is an essential constituent or co-creator of the performance since it is only through the audience that the performance is itself ratified.

Goffman (1974) also notes how participants' activities may fall out of the ongoing frame. This may take place in moments of disattention to specific actions or participants and usually results in changing patterns of alignment, or footing, among participants (Goffman, 1981). In 'real-life' conversation (that is, that which is perhaps less overtly, self-consciously staged), this may be achieved linguistically, for example, by adopting a vocative form of address to turn one's attention to a new participant, although this is usually achieved through non-verbal means such as facial expressions, body orientation and gaze (cf. Levinson, 1988). In performance (at least in its most canonical form discussed with all the caveats above), or the theatrical frame, the audience, despite its status as a group of accepted onlookers, is such a disattended participant by the actor-in-character. Although it is also true that the specific status of the audience as ratified eavesdroppers is 'maximally facilitated' and, to continue, 'theatrical audiences have only restricted rights to reply to the show they watch and are allowed only a restricted role. But, unlike the onlookers at excavation sites, they do have *some* expectations in this regard' (Goffman, 1974: 226).

> Examples of new positions that may be taken up by audiences are those brought about by the special role of chorus, 'orator,' or other mediating, editorialising functions that can easily be built into the performance. The mediator – a specialised viewer who also partic- ipates as a staged character – can comment on whole aspects of the production, treating as an object of direct attention what the projected characters have to treat as something in which they are immersed. He is a footnote that talks.
>
> (Goffman, 1974: 226–227)

Other examples of such mediations between the performance and the audience mentioned by Goffman are prologues and epilogues, subtitles in silent films, other slightly out-of-frame stage voices such as soliloquy in which the actor allows the audience to 'hear' his or her thoughts, and different forms of direct address, which is used to comment on or explain a twist in the plot, elaborate on a moral issue or summarize what has happened so far. In unstaged interaction, an out-of-frame activity may involve asides and collusion, as 'individuals can turn from their companions and give fleeting vent to their 'real' feelings, through ges- ture and *sotto voce* comment (Goffman, 1974: 233). Goffman's example of such 'electronic collusion' in the case of TV shows is the case of an announcer's voiceover in a quiz show 'telling the folks in TV land what the answer was while the contestant manfully strained at pretending to strain at recalling it' (ibid.).

Following Goffman's work on the theatrical frame and out-of-frame activities, we treat the TV holiday shows as instances of scripted per- formances, with the TV audiences being the accepted onlookers whose right to participate in and respond to the staged activities is necessar- ily minimal, but whose role in ratifying the shows is hugely important. In simple economic terms, known as the 'ratings game', without the viewers' mass participation, the shows would be scrapped by the TV stations producing them (as was indeed the case in 2003 and 2006). And, as we hope to demonstrate in this chapter, the use and representation of host languages serves as an important aspect of the show makers' realignment with the viewers. This, in turn, offers us further insight into the ideologies of tourism, the commodification of language in tourism and the nature of intercultural exchange under globalization.

On display: The functions of local languages in TV holiday shows

In an initial analysis of the primary functions of languages other than English in our TV holiday shows, we identified four main categories:

1. expert talk (for example, guided tours, explanations, instructions)
2. service encounters (for example, purchasing foodstuff in shops or markets)
3. phatic communion (for example, exchanging greetings, thanking – often as part of a service encounter)
4. naming and translating (for example, providing labels for local concepts, artefacts or dishes, translating local place names)[2]

These functions are performed by the presenters and/or hosts either when the two parties are shown interacting with one another, or by either party when no face-to-face interaction is present, for example, in numerous voiceovers by the presenters or when racing commentary is heard during a visit to a race course. Of course, most communicative utterances perform multiple functions, and we found such overlaps in our data. As such, it was not always possible to isolate communicative intent. In looking to code our data, therefore, interactions were categorized in terms of their *primary* functional orientation, while allowing coding in terms of more than one function to retain something of the multifunctionality of exchanges where relevant. Nonetheless, these general functions represent the typical ways in which local languages come to be put on display in the context of tourism.

Expert talk

We define talk as 'expert' when a host is portrayed in the role of an authority or guide and shown explaining a process, system or local custom to the presenter, who is portrayed in the role of learner, listening and perhaps asking questions. Expert talk appears to be the most common function of local language use by hosts in the shows. The majority of these instances take place in English (in our sample, almost as much as 90 per cent of all instances of expert talk). After all, this is British television, English is its unmarked linguistic code, and it is important for the viewers to understand what is going on. In fact, what is surprising is that, in these highly scripted and edited shows, there is any room left for languages other than English, which is precisely what makes us wonder what viewers are expected to make of the snippets of 'foreign' languages they do get to hear. Consider Extract 5.1, for example, featuring Vera, a hotel owner in Tuscany. Once again, we see 'exotic' food being produced (or staged) as a quintessential marker of otherness in much the same way that our travelogue data did in Chapter 4. It seems that this pastoral trope of the 'Italian mama' making pasta is a popular tourist fantasy (see also Figure 5.1). In this case, the presenter, Mary Nightingale, introduces Vera to the audience in an English voiceover and the latter continues in Italian a highly edited demonstration of the preparation of her homemade pasta:

Mary Nightingale in Tuscany, Italy

1	Nightingale:	(voiceover) I found all the hotels <u>very</u> comfortable
2		and what's nice is they're all so individual and they
3		feel so (.) Italian (1) this farmhouse has been in the
4		family for generations (.) Vera is the <u>boss</u> (.) and the
5		chief pasta maker
6	Vera:	(cut to Vera's kitchen where she is making pasta
7		watched by the presenter)
8		quest'e' la pasta queste sono (.) l'impasto (.)
		this is the pasta these are (.) the mixture (.)
9		mangiala cruda mangiala cruda
		eat it raw eat it raw
10	Nightingale:	(picks up a single strand of raw pasta, moves away 11
		from Vera, raises the piece of pasta to the camera)
12		there's a piece of Vera's tagliatelle (.) isn't that
13		absolutely beautiful (.) it's perfect
14	Vera:	(looks baffled at Nightingale's interest in the piece of
15		pasta)

(Extract 5.1, Source: *Wish You Were Here?*, ITV, 26 February 2001)[3]

In the voiceover, Vera is clearly cast in the role of a cooking expert (lines 4–5), followed by a kitchen scene where she shares her knowledge and experience of pasta-making. In her very short turn, she is shown

Figure 5.1 'Vera, the chief pasta maker' – Take #2

commenting on what she is doing in a way that is reminiscent of typical TV cooking shows. Likewise, in this extract, Vera comments on the high quality of her cooking, recommending it with confidence accorded to her by her expert status and fluency in her native language.

However, very quickly, at the end of her turn, *she* becomes an onlooker. The presenter's (Nightingale) evaluation of Vera's pasta is directed at the viewer, as is evidenced by both her non-verbal orientation (lines 10–11) and verbal commentary (lines 12–13): she looks at the camera away from Vera and speaks in English. In this moment, Vera loses her 'expert' status being left just watching the presenter and her crew (unseen by the audience) filming the rest of the scene. Vera becomes sidelined and forms a mere backdrop to the presenter's continued demonstration of the charms of Italian living. Here, Vera is noticeably caught off guard; we see her looking confused when she realizes that Nightingale is no longer listening to her but holding up her ethnic fetish (the strip of pasta) for the camera while talking to the viewers 'back home'.

Already in this extract, then, we see both the performance frame of the TV holiday shows, in which the presenter tells the story of her holiday and enacts some 'live' interactions with hosts, but also the disattention to this performance frame and the enactment of a second stream of 'out-of-frame activity' (Goffman, 1974: 210). In Extract 5.1 above, this is achieved by Mary Nightingale's disattending verbally and non-verbally to Vera, depriving her of the full *participation status* (Goffman, 1974: 224). Vera's role in lines 10–13 gains what Goffman calls the 'toy status, namely, the existence of some object, human or not, that is treated as if in frame, an object to address, act to or comment on, but which is in fact out of frame (disattendable) in regard to its capacity to hear and talk' (ibid.).

From an analytic point of view, we face a dilemma here. Why do the show makers bother to introduce Vera as an 'expert' only to sideline her immediately? Given the constraints of the show, they are unlikely to treat her as some kind of superfluous decoration or a participant to be simply ignored. What we would suggest, then, is that Vera acts as a 'vehicle' for injecting some local (linguistic) flavour authenticating the touristic experience of the presenter and viewer (see also below). This is a perfect example of what Dean MacCannell (1999 [1976], 1984) has famously called 'staged authenticity' and 'reconstructed ethnicity'.

As we demonstrate throughout our analysis, this out-of-frame activity of orienting to the audience becomes more consequential to the achievement of the main goal of the holiday shows, that is, creating involvement with the audience. Even more importantly, it is also crucial in understanding the metalinguistic function of the 'foreign' languages in these encounters. In Extract 5.1, Nightingale's overt orientation to the viewers starts in lines 1–3 with her voice overlaying images of Tuscan countryside ('they feel so Italian') and the hotel in which she is staying. The extract then shifts back to the performance frame (lines 6–9), in which Vera is centrally positioned as the expert in pasta-making explaining the process to the presenter (and by extension to the viewers). Finally, Nightingale steps out of the performance frame (lines 10–13) by literally turning her back on Vera and orienting herself towards the camera and the audience. (What cannot be conveyed by the transcript alone are the proxemics of this reorientation to the TV viewers which, in lay or 'social' terms, are plain rude.) Clearly misjudging or misunderstanding her televisual role as human scenery, not unlike many other hosts in the extracts we have analysed, Vera is thereby doubly disempowered: first by being cast involuntarily in- and out-of-frame by the presenter, but also by being seen to afford the presenter undue benefit of the doubt in terms of conversational relevance (Grice, 1975), having taken Nightingale's interest in her work at face value. We find a similar sense of interpersonal disconnect being played out in some of the service encounters we also identified.

Service encounters

Service encounters (for example, Ventola, 1987; Aston, 1988) are the next most common category of function identified in our TV show data – a typical communicative event in tourism. Presenters are shown interacting with people such as local shopkeepers, market stall-holders, waiters and hotel staff. In the following extract, Jilly Goolden and her teenage daughter, Verity, go shopping for food at a market in France.

Jilly Goolden and daughter Verity in France

1	JG:	now what do you fancy?
2	VG:	(to vendor) je voudrais un kilo de tomates
		I'd like a kilo of tomatoes
3	Vendor 1:	un kilo merci
		a kilo thank you
		[ ]
4	JG:	let's go and get cheese
5	Vendor 1:	merci
		thank you
6	JG:	merci
		thank you
7	JG:	loads of lovely French cheeses now (.)
		[
8	VG:	smells gorgeous
9	JG:	what sort of cheese do you fancy?
10		(vendor hands over cheese)
11	JG:	merci
		thank you
12	Vendor 2:	voilà
		here you are.

(Extract 5.2, Source: *Holiday 2000*, BBC1, 28 November 2000)

In this extract, the presenter and her daughter are shown to interact as clients with the local vendors in service encounters, using brief, for- mulaic phrases in French – precisely the kind of linguistic material promoted in guidebook glossaries (see Chapter 6). Interaction is min- imal and the vendors appear as anonymous and fleetingly encountered servers or helpers on the tourists' journey across the country. The edited nature of the extract, which involves two service encounters in which goods are selected, accepted and paid for, lasts only 13 seconds. This makes the exchanges look even more brief but also more efficient and successful; use of the host language is made to look effortless and no real obstacle to buying food. Additionally, French adds local flavour and authenticity to this episode, even though it does not go beyond the most stereotypical foreign language textbook or tourist phrasebook repertoire.

A similar encounter, in which the desirability of the 'authentic' expe- rience of buying local produce using a local language, and succeeding, is demonstrated in Extract 5.3, where Mary Nightingale tries out her Italian in a Tuscan delicatessen.

Mary Nightingale in Italy

```
1  Nightingale:   (voiceover) the hotels provide packed lunches for
2                  around seven pounds but I think it's much more fun
3                  to go to a local shop (walks into a shop)
4  Nightingale:   (to shop assistant) er prosciutto
                                       ham
5  Assistant:     prosciutto (.) prosciutto della casa
                  ham (.) our speciality ham
                  [
6  Nightingale:              (hesitantly) si (nods) si ah (.) (voiceover)
                             yes        yes
7                            isn't that gorgeous.
```
(Extract 5.3, Source: *Wish You Were Here?*, ITV, 26 February 2001)

Again, the use of the host language and the interaction with the local shopkeeper are minimal. The presenter's use of Italian invites the shop assistant to use Italian in return, albeit in a simple repetition of the order (line 5). However, in a hesitant attempt at Italian (line 6), the presenter tries hard to maintain the travel frame in a combination of the most rudimentary linguistic skill articulating the repetition of a singular *si* 'yes', followed by the 'safe' or communicatively less entropic strategy of expressing sociability through non-verbal nodding. This is followed by a sudden switch to English voiceover, in which, not unlike at the end of Extract 5.1, the presenter (Nightingale) acknowledges the superior quality of local produce for the benefit of the viewing public and not of the shopkeeper. Rather like 'tanto confusione' (Extract 4.4), there is no Italian here that would be unrecognizable or inaccessible to many British viewers; much of it has the quality of the kind of 'mock Italian' (cf. Hill, 2001[1998]) one might hear in a stand-up routine.

Phatic communion

The third most common function of talk in these shows is phatic communion – exchanges of 'mere sociabilities' and apparently 'purposeless expressions' (Malinowski, 1923: 150; J. Coupland, 2000). This again is a type of interaction that tourists might typically be expected to engage in with hosts. Naturally, and as we have already indicated, many of the interactions in our corpus are multifunctional; our next example is no exception, where playful banter is seen woven into a service encounter.

Craig Doyle in Italy

```
 1  Doyle:     (voiceover) the Italians are passionate about food and no one
 2             more so than Massimo one of Siena's larger than life grocers
 3  Massimo:   grande grande=
                large large
 4  Doyle:     =grande
                large
 5  Massimo:   questo è pesto pesto genovese (.) guarda (picks up a packet
 6             of pasta)
                this is pesto pesto from Genoa (.) look
                                            [
 7  Doyle:                                   si si pesto fresh tomatoes si=
                                              yes yes pesto              yes
 8             =so I need these as well yeah (picks up a tray of
 9             blackberries)
10  Massimo:   avanti
                let's go on
11  Doyle:     oh yeah
12  Massimo:   tomatoes dried si chiamano ciliegini (shows Doyle some
13             dried tomatoes)
                they're called cherry tomatoes
14  Doyle:     (points over M's shoulder) look at that out there (M looks
15             away briefly and D pops a tomato in his mouth with a look
16             of mock guilt-cum-innocence)
```

17 Doyle: (cut to D paying) grazie grazie (.)
            thank you thank you
18 Massimo: a posto cosi?
            anything else?
19 Doyle: ciche ciche cento
20 Massimo: no (.) ciche ciche ciu (.) ciao a presto (they shake hands)
            bye see you soon
                        [
21 Doyle: ciao grazie
                        bye thank you
22 Doyle: (cut to Doyle walking out of shop; voiceover) thank you
23   Massimo.
            (Extract 5.4, Source: *Holiday 2001*, BBC1, 30 January 2001)

Although Doyle's primary goal in this scene is to buy food for the meal he is going to cook later in the show, the playful use of Italian and non-verbal behaviour by the presenter and the shopkeeper make it a fairly sociable occasion. They are not just buying and selling, respectively, but apparently having fun. Massimo is cast as an affable caricature of an Italian who is stereotypically 'passionate about food' (lines 1–2). The playful and therefore phatic nature of this encounter is emphasized by Doyle's Italian–English code-mixing (line 7), mocking repetition of Massimo's utterances (lines 4, 7) and his uninhibited phonetic approximation of Italian regardless of whether it is 'correct' or not (line 19).

Massimo's role in this extract could be also construed as that of an 'expert' explaining and recommending his goods (for example, lines 5, 12), but the jocular tenor of the interaction makes the propositional content of his talk secondary. For this reason, the Italian in this extract, as the host languages in Extracts 5.1–5.3, remains untranslated by the show makers. What Massimo and Doyle say in Italian is not greatly relevant, and in Doyle's case not always 'correct' (line 19). In this moment, Doyle appears to be attempting to repeat a price given to him by Massimo but which has been edited out. The first part of Massimo's response (line 20) may be a teasing comment on Doyle's inability to articulate the Italian figure. From the pragmatic point of view, the main aim of this scene is to demonstrate to the viewers the 'ludic' potential of the local language – a sense of pleasurable, but somewhat derisory, play. Admittedly, many of the Italian expressions used in Extract 5.4 (as with the French expressions in Extract 5.2) may again be fairly easily recognizable to British viewers (for example, *grande*, lines 3, 4; *avanti*, line 10; *grazie,* lines 17 and 21, and *ciao,* lines 20 and 21), but these are largely politeness formulae anyway which do not carry much semantic weight.

In the next extract, Ingrid Tarrant's exchange with a waiter, who brings her a drink to the poolside, is even more revealing in demonstrating the presenter-tourist's skeletal proficiency in the phatic use of the host language (Swahili):

Ingrid Tarrant in Kenya
(IT on poolside, waiter brings her an exotic looking drink)

1	Waiter:	jambo
		hello
2	IT:	jambo
		hello
3	Waiter:	our special (.) welcome
		[
4	IT:	oh asante sana (voiceover) cheers Chris
		thank you very much.

(Extract 5.5, Source: *Wish You Were Here?*, ITV, 26 March 2001)

Here, phatic communion, again embedded in a service encounter, is made manifest by the presenter's use of the most basic greeting and thanking formulae in Swahili. In this way, the viewing audience is reassured that a close encounter with a host, even in a most unfamiliar location, requires little more than a couple of routine, courtesy phrases to cope with a simple service transaction. As such, the ludic quality emerges once more in the knowledge that, in such status-unequal interactions, no talk is strictly necessary – let alone in the potentially more effortful 'foreign' language.

The use of host languages for phatic communion in the holiday shows does, of course, transcend the mutual displays of civility between tourists and hosts. When we consider the occurrence of such exchanges with the primary orientation to the audience, they become demonstrations of yet another characteristic unique to the travel destinations: 'local language'. For example, the interplay of host and audience orientation in Extract 5.6 makes it clear that the exchange of the Fijian greeting *bula* between the presenter, John Savident, and a local shopkeeper, is used only to invoke the sound of host language as part of the presenter's elaboration of his point about how 'friendly' Fijian people are.

John Savident in Fiji
(Savident apparently wandering through a market place)

1 Savident: away from the hotel the town of Nandi [*sic*] is just ten
2   minutes away (.) Fiji is such a friendly place and you're
3   always greeted with a big smile (cut to a woman smiling)
4   and a call of BULA: the local greeting (to a street vendor)
5   bula:
6 Vendor: bula bula John (Savident continues walking past her stall,
7   **laughs to her) how are you? bula bula la la la.**
          (Extract 5.6, Source: *Wish You Were Here?*, ITV, 22 January 2001)

In this example, both the presenter's and the local's use of Fijian is limited to a single greeting formula, mixed by the vendor with the English greeting 'how are you?' (lines 5–7). Note that it is the host again, as in Extract 5.5, who switches to English, which subverts her role as a 'local' limited to speaking the local language. Interestingly, in an almost imperceptible televisual faux-pas, the vendor greets the presenter by his first name, which clearly indicates the rehearsed nature of this scripted encounter and suggests that the interaction is set up for the sole purpose of staging friendliness with the addition of the authentic feature: the Fijian greeting – that other typical tourist speech act (Jaworski, 2009).

Naming and translating

The Fijian location provides an example of the fourth main category of local language use – naming and translating. As we saw in Chapter 4, the naming of things (especially food and 'cultural artefacts') is a common rhetorical strategy in travelogues. In this function, the local language is used to denote such things as local artefacts, dishes or place names. Extract 5.7 shows John Savident in the same piece providing as above names or labels for traditional housing and dress.

John Savident in Fiji

1 Savident: (looks at camera) and just a shell's throw from the beach (.)
2   your very own bure (points to a bungalow; 'ethnic' music
3   plays in the background'; cut to a camera pan of the inside)
4   (1) (voiceover) a traditional thatched Fijian bungalow
5   (3) (shot of room in a bungalow) (walks on the beach) do
6   you like my sarong by the way? (.) here they're called (.)
7   sulu.
          (Extract 5.7, Source: *Wish You Were Here?*, ITV, 22 January 2001)

The above extract operates wholly as a direct address to the audience. The visual imagery of the bungalow and Savident walking on the beach is accompanied by the sound of 'ethnic' drumming music. Together with the mention of the two Fijian words (lines 2 and 7), unlikely to be remembered by viewers, this scene creates an authentic and exoticized vision of the destination. But there is a paradox here. Apart from using 'strange' words, the same local concepts are also labelled with two more easily recognizable terms: 'thatched bungalow' and 'sarong', and these acts of naming also render the exotic more familiar, adding to the show's construction of a holiday destination as simultaneously adventuresome and safe. Once again, it seems that these snippets of local language are deployed as narrative detail (Tannen, 1989) for authenticating not only the staging of culture but also the general veracity of the presenter's story as a whole.

Extract 5.8 shows the presenter learning some useful phrases in Korean – translation equivalents of a toasting formula – with the help of a resident couple. Here the act of translating and invoking a local phrase is jointly performed by the presenter (Doyle) and one of his hosts, Kevin.

Craig Doyle in South Korea

1 Doyle:	so I met BBC correspondent Kevin ((Kim)) and his
2	girlfriend ((Mirren)) in one of the street bars where he
3	introduced me to the local tipple soju which <u>will</u> be my
4	reply next time I'm offered a glass
5 Kevin:	in the UK you say cheers in Korea you say geon-bae
6 Doyle:	geon-bae
7 Kevin:	geon-bae geon-bae.

(Extract 5.8, Source: *Holiday 2001*, BBC1, 20 February 2001)

Sharing the toasting formula is an easily recognizable, phatic accompaniment to drinking in a linguistically mixed group and viewers are likely to find such behaviour unremarkable and possibly, even, familiar from their own experience. The use of a host language here, again, has the dual function of exoticizing the destination while depicting a customary social situation.

At this point, and before we move on, we would like to note our intention *not* to promote an unduly sinister or one-sided agenda for the presenters. First, of course, they are themselves one of many agents in the production of these shows, along with directors, editors, scriptwriters and so on. What is more, as we discuss in some detail elsewhere, there is undoubtedly a complex, complicitous relationship between tourists and hosts. As such, it is possible to some extent to view presenters and local people in the holiday shows as being engaged in a kind of 'commercial' relationship. As Penelope Harvey (1992) notes from her own research, local people are rightly capable of exploiting the power of the media and it is not always possible to second-guess their 'political consciousness'. Nevertheless, as long as show makers and presenters hold ultimate editorial control, it is their ideological frames that will continue to dominate the programmes' patterns of representation.

Having a go: Metacommentary about host languages

One aspect of the direct address of the audience that merits separate discussion is that of metalinguistic and metapragmatic comments (henceforth 'metacomments') on the use and mention of host languages. So far our discussion of overt orientation to the audience has focused on the presenters' use of voiceover (for example, Extracts 5.1, 5.3, 5.4, 5.5), body posture and direction of gaze (for example, Extracts 5.1, 5.7), as well as editing of video footage to produce a quick succession of unconnected exchanges (for example, Extracts 5.2, 5.4).

A close examination of some data extracts containing metacomments on host languages confirms that there is often an ulterior motive in their use in these shows, one that goes beyond the functions we have discussed so far, and that extends our initial discussion of language ideology in Chapter 4. In fact, expert talk, service encounters, phatic communion and naming/translating in host languages should be primarily considered in terms of their viewer-orientation. We have alluded to some of these functions above. In this section, we specify them in more detail according to the following overlapping themes: *having 'fun'*, *out-grouping of hosts* and *creating a linguascape of the travel destination*.

As we have already begun to show (see also Chapter 3), the unquestionable and unsurprising message coming from all the holiday shows is that holidays are 'fun'. Even if the educational aspect of travel is included in the show (usually in very small doses), it is subordinate to the consumerist and hedonistic goals realized through attention to the tourist's comfort, efficiency of service, the pleasures of eating and drinking, shopping and generally engaging in all sorts of *fun* activities. In most of our examples (with the notable exception of Extract 5.12 below), the presenters are also shown having fun with host languages. It may not be everyone's idea of fun, but the message to the viewers is that managing simple interactions in host languages is not only possible but also pleasurable. Consider the following example, in which the presenter tries out a phrase she has presumably learnt from her phrase book (or her producer).

Lisa Riley in Spain

1 Riley:	(voiceover) it's well worth taking a wander up the side
2	streets off the square (camera on LR and friend) where you
3	can find traditional tapas bars just like this one (points to
4	bar) ((shall we take a look)) (walks to bar) hola me puedes
5	dar la carta por favor?

               hello can you
     give me the menu please?

6 Barman: (hands over menu) ((unclear))
7 Riley: gracias (to camera, cheerfully) been learning that all day
       thank you
8   (giggles).
    (Extract 5.9, Source: *Wish You Were Here?*, ITV, 22 January 2001)

Although the presenter's comment in line 7 gives the impression of the host language as being 'difficult', her cheerful tone and the giggling suggest a degree of pleasure in using Spanish, and succeeding in achieving the transactional goal of the utterance (requesting and receiving the menu). Arguably, Riley uses an otherwise inappropriate, familiar address-form (that is, second-person *tú* rather than third person *Usted*), which may again betray the prior, off-screen interaction needed to stage the scene as a spontaneous encounter. Nevertheless, picking up a formula in a foreign language is construed as an enjoyable accomplishment, which despite its rote learning and limited scope gives the speaker a sense of fluency in L2 (Coulmas, 1981).

Given our underlying interest in language ideology, an important function of metalanguage is of course making judgements or expressing attitudes towards the speakers of different accents, dialects or languages, with a view to drawing social boundaries between 'self' and 'other', reinforcing similarities and differences, respectively. In our analyses thus far, we have also pointed to the inclusion and exclusion by presenters of local people from the performance frame. Indeed, the idea of 'othering' of local people in tourist destinations is not new (for overviews see, for example, Morgan and Pritchard, 1998). Having said that, in the context of the holiday shows hosts are usually portrayed superficially and tokenistically (Jaworski, Ylänne-McEwen et al., 2003), their primary message remains that the holiday destinations are 'safe' and so are their 'friendly' hosts (cf. Galasiński and Jaworski, 2003; Thurlow et al., 2005).

Linguistically, the out-grouping of hosts in the holiday shows is achieved through metacomments drawing the viewers' attention to the fact that host languages are incomprehensible and that they require translation – not unlike the characterizations of Malti and Romansch in Chapter 4.

Kate Silverton in Spain
(KS sitting at a beach bar)

1	KS:	(receives a drink from the barman) oh gracias what do you
		thank you
2		recommend I have for lunch now?
3	Barman:	sardinas al espeto
		barbecued sardines
4	KS:	(cut to grilled sardines on a skewer; soft voiceover) that's
5		barbecued sardines to you and I (to barman) is that what
6		everybody does on the beach?
7	Barman:	mainly yeah (.) there's about a hundred of these beach bars
8		and they all do that
9	KS:	and they're called?
10	Barman:	chiringuitos there's friendly atmosphere on the beach nice
11		restaurant fresh air from the sea
12	KS:	I think I'll have the (.) sardines
13	Barman:	(to chef off camera) UN ESPETO POR FAVOR
		one barbecued sardines, please
14	Chef:	(off camera) HASTA
		coming right up.

(Extract 5.10, Source: *Holiday 2000*, BBC1, 21 November 2000)

Following the barman's naming of a local dish, the presenter uses voiceover to translate the name of the dish (lines 4–5), which, as noted before, explicitly shifts the orientation of the presenter to the viewers. Additionally, the soft voice creates an aura of confidential, secretive communication as if to exclude the host from this communication (which obviously is the case). Besides, the presenter's comment 'to you and I' (line 5), overtly separates the barman, and by implication all other hosts, from the community of actual and implied (British) tourists. (In this particular case, our impression is that the barman happens to be a fluent English speaker.) This example is not unique. The following extract includes a similar use of translation and an in-grouping/out-grouping comment.

Lisa Riley in Spain

```
1 Riley:   (voiceover) there's more to Marbella than sun glitz and
2          glamour (.) take a short stroll up from the main street and
3          you'll find the old town (2) this beautiful quarter is
4          centred around the Plaza de Naranjos (camera on sign)
5          orange square to you and me.
```
            (Extract 5.11, Source: *Wish You Were Here?*, ITV, 22 January 2001)

Although the last two examples suggest some difficulty in understanding local place names or reading local menus, they are resolved positively by the presenter-tourists finding out their meanings (even though if it is only the approximate meaning as evidenced in Extract 5.11, line 5 – *naranjos* translating as 'orange trees', not 'oranges' or the colour orange). Again, there is a ludic promise of coping with, but also playing with, host languages and, by implication, local people and culture more generally.

In the next extract, however, the incomprehensibility of the host language is posed as a more serious problem.

Kevin Duala in Italy

```
1 Duala:   (voiceover) but Turin hasn't needed to chase the tourist lira
2          (.) it was a wealthy city especially in 1861 when Turin
3          became the first capital of the new united Italy (.) Palazzo
4          Real was the official residence of their first king (shot of
5          Palazzo Real's decorative ceiling, cut to a group of tourists
6          with a guide speaking Italian, cut to KD speaking to camera
7          with mock horror intonation and facial expression) the entire
8          tour is in Italian but you've got to book on the tour to get in
9          (1) (glances at guide) I can't understand a word (to
10         camera) no capito (gesticulates 'no')
                   *I don't understand.*
```
            (Extract 5.12, *Holiday 2001*, BBC1, 23 January 2001)

In Extract 5.12, the guide's talk (untranscribed here, see line 6) is portrayed as truly 'incomprehensible', as the presenter's metapragmatic comments (lines 8–9) reveal that his competence in Italian does not go beyond the level of phrasebook (or movie) expressions such as *no capito.* The presenter's paralinguistic and non-verbal behaviour also communicates an aura of disbelief at how tourists can be made to do something as useless as joining a guided tour in a language they do not understand. The relational aspect of this example, such as seeking sympathy with the viewers, emphasizes the sense of solidarity and in-groupness among the tourists (the presenter and the implied tourists at home) in the face of somewhat irrational and unaccommodating hosts.

What is also really apparent from Extract 5.12, is how the use of Italian by the expert host is presented as meaningless babble; it is in this way that the 'foreign' language is thereby rendered an untranslated linguascape. In fact, one of the most successful ways in which out-grouping is achieved in these holiday travel shows is through the general disattention to the languages of hosts and their relegation to mere backdrop – or, in theatrical terms, scenery. Even in Extract 5.10 above, for example, both the presenter's and the local person's use of Spanish politeness formulae (lines 1, 14) and the naming of a local dish (lines 3, 10) again also serve to create a linguascape.

Although British holiday shows position English as the international medium of communication, host languages are used frequently to authenticate or stage holiday destinations in the same way as, for example, the shots of local people and scenery, sampling, descriptions and evaluations of local food and drink, references to the places' history and customs. In this sense, host languages create linguascapes, together with other uses of the soundtrack, for example, when 'ethnic' music is played (cf. Extract 5.7), or when in an episode from Egypt, a wall covered with the hieroglyphics in an ancient tomb is accompanied by the soundtrack from *Raiders of the Lost Ark*. In the following extract, French is used phatically between the presenter and a group of local people (lines 5–7), but the subsequent voiceover by the presenter (lines 7–8) again reframes it as linguascape.

Craig Doyle in Mauritius

```
1 Doyle:  (to camera; walks along the buffet table with chefs preparing
2         and serving dinner) so what we have tonight is Indian food
3         with a little twist of Mauritian we've got tuna kebabs there
4         and a bit of roast deer leg with spices being sliced we've got
5         some pancakes being made (.) and lots of spices and
6         coconut being sprinkled on (to the chefs behind the serving
7         table) bonsoir
```

> *good evening*
> 8 Chefs: (various voices; softly) bonsoir
> 9 Doyle: bonsoir (cut to Mauritian landscape; voiceover) yes don't let
> 10   the fried rice and fish curry let you forget that this <u>is</u> a
> 11   French speaking island.
>   (Extract 5.13, Source: *Holiday 2000*, BBC1, 14 November 2000)

The greeting exchange in French is clearly initiated by Doyle (line 7) for the benefit of the viewers to 'warn' them that the apparent familiarity of the cuisine associated with the Indian subcontinent, and its widespread use of English, does not bring the promise of English being a 'safe' medium of communication in Mauritius.

Importantly, this use of sound-bursts (by analogy to snapshots) to create an aural backdrop or linguascape begins to reveal a far more multi-sensory tourist landscape – something, which, as we noted earlier, has traditionally been overlooked in theoretical discussions of tourism (see Franklin and Crang, 2001). In the remaining part of the chapter, we develop this analysis further, dividing discussion into two parts: first, we review and elaborate on the significance of the use of host languages in the holiday shows and in the domain of tourism in general; second, we offer a somewhat more ideological critique of the TV shows in the light of a broader sociolinguistic framework of discursive style and language 'crossing' (Rampton, 1995, 2009a).

Linguascaping the exotic in tourism

In all of the above examples, whether presenters' explicit metacomments are present or not, the performance frame, in which the presenters narrate their experiences and engage with the hosts, appears to be

HAGAR the HORRIBLE .

Figure 5.2 Reproduced by permission of King Features Syndicate

subservient to their orientation to the TV audience. Performing phrase-book dialogues, offering translations, providing local terminology and so on, not only make host languages accessible but also help the viewers to familiarize themselves with the destination as a whole. At the same time, the use of host languages serves to create a more 'authentic' atmo-sphere in the holiday shows and thus contributes to the entertainment aspect of the shows. To repeat a point we made earlier in Chapter 3, tourism discourse is also committed to the production (and exaggera-tion) of difference – especially the kind of 'difference' that can be easily commodified for the purpose of economic and symbolic exchange. All the major players in tourism are implicated in this market, whether it's local people packaging and 'staging' themselves as exotic for tourists, nation states rebranding their places and people for foreign and domes-tic consumption or tourists yearning and paying for the 'authenticities' or 'genuine fakes' of others. In fact, for tourists this is an almost full-time pursuit that invariably demands a Sisyphean collective performance of the extraordinary, especially when it feels as if anyone can go on holiday and when everyone is a tourist. Local languages lend themselves readily to this production of difference.

In some cases, using host languages constitutes just another form of 'fun' activity on a par with trying different local culinary speciali-ties or learning new skills such as sailing, horse-riding, skiing and so on. Although host languages are sometimes portrayed as being diffi-cult to learn, or impossible to understand, trying them out in different situations is seen to be enjoyable.

Overall, in the TV travel shows examined in this study, the use of local languages is quite limited. Certainly, this could partly be explained by the short duration of the coverage of any one destination, which is commonly in the order of three to six minutes (Rice, 2001); it may also be due to the linguistic profile of viewers. The functions for which local languages are used in these shows are also limited, centring around expert talk, service encounter talk, phatic communion and nam-ing/translating – all types of interaction that a tourist might expect to have on holiday.

As we have discussed them, as a genre holiday shows are inher-ently instances of performance – as such, we have here a restaging of already staged tourist sites. It is also important to remember that TV holiday shows, although providing viewers with information about par-ticular travel destinations, are broadcast at peak family viewing times and hence also have the function of entertainment. It is this underly-ing viewer orientation in production values that persists in the use and representation of local languages. Doug Hammond, Executive Producer of *Wish You Were Here?*, has been quoted as saying, 'If the audience is not entertained, there will be no audience' (Rice, 2001: 7). Arguably, in this sense, TV travel shows constitute a cultural product, which is designed to be consumed regardless of whether viewers actually intend to travel to the destinations covered. However, as Rice (2001: 6) reminds us, it is also true to say that the shows 'play a crucial role in both influencing us about our holiday choices and showing us aspects of life in other countries'. Representations of local people and their language(s) are therefore important considerations in revealing their ideological bases in terms of intercultural/international communication (cf. Bruner, 2005; Favero, 2007).

In addition, the frame of the TV screen is also indicative of the ideological frame surrounding tourism more generally. John Urry suggests that the 'frame' through which tourists experience their holidays, 'the hotel window, the car windscreen or the window of the coach...can now be experienced in one's own living room' (Urry, 2002: 90–91). According to Urry, Maxine Feifer's (1985) so-called 'post-tourist' 'does not have to leave his or her house to see many of the typical objects of the tourist gaze' (2002[1990]: 90). Moreover, in the TV travel shows, the tourist destinations are mediated through a consistently Anglophone lens, made safe and accessible by being translated – thus Michael Cronin's (2000: 95) observation that, for speakers of powerful languages, 'the Other is always already translated'. Generally, hosts in the tourist destinations are shown to speak English and, when the presenters do use other languages, it tends to be to enhance the entertainment level for the television viewer rather than to serve any other communicative need. As such, the ethos of the shows positions English as a global language and British (native) speakers of English as global, or at least globe-trotting, citizens – the same ones we encountered in the inflight magazines from Chapter 1. Local languages, meanwhile, are reduced to the status of rubber-stamp phrases from guidebook glossaries (see Chapter 6), co-opted for the staging and authenticating of unproblematized, exoticized linguascapes. This is the aural equivalent of precisely the kinds of 'mediatized motifs' and 'key exoticisms' which Tim Edensor (2001: 67) highlights in his discussion of visual performance in tourism; as he suggests, 'through the use of such "scenography" the tourist gaze is directed away from extraneous chaotic elements, reducing visual and functional forms to a few images'. Extending the concerns of Ed Bruner, quoted at the start of this chapter, here is how Paolo Favero (2007: 71–72) sums up the problem with the 'touristic ways of seeing':

With their focus on limitless spectacularized and 'fictionalized' details of foreign cultures, landscapes and peoples, on difference, beauty and the extraordinary, such ways of seeing seem to leave out of the picture (quite literally!) other visions...What is made invisible is therefore not the result of randomness but rather of the specific political and ideological context in which these particular technologies of representation (and travel) are used.

Crossing and an imagined community of 'new internationals'

We have already suggested that by using a variety of languages in holiday shows, presenters can demystify holiday destinations and reassure the implied tourists that language is not necessarily an obstacle to successful travel. Host languages add exotic flavour to the destination and can be used with relative ease to get things done (for example, facilitating service encounters, as in Extracts 5.2, 5.3) or to have fun with, or to poke fun at, local people (for example, while socializing, in Extract 5.8). And, in the worst possible scenario, if a host language *is* a problem, it and its speakers, can simply be ignored (Extract 5.12). There is, however, also a relational aspect involved here. The presenters in the shows are cast in a kind of two-fold tourist role: both as tourists in their own right (thus 'presenter-tourist') and as role-models or proxies for 'viewer-tourists' – a kind of Every Tourist or 'tourist-tourist'. Through participating in various holiday activities, the presenters' main allegiance is to the viewers, not hosts, and all that we see them do in the shows, including 'conversing' in host languages, is geared towards creating a sense of involvement with and for the viewers – what in media psychology would be referred to as a parasocial relationship (Rubin et al., 1985).

In her study of the use of 'mock Spanish' by Anglo-Americans in the United States, for example, Jane Hill (2001[1998]; 2008) demonstrates how apparently jocular incorporations and ungrammatical approximations of other languages are employed by non-native speakers as an important identity resource. Following Elanor Ochs' (1990) earlier notion of 'direct indexicality' (that is, the production of non-referential meanings), Hill argues that playful, flippant snatches of, in her case, Spanish-language materials, serve to elevate the identities (or 'Whiteness') of Anglo-Americans. To our mind, therefore, and extending our earlier discussion about out-grouping/in-grouping, much the same argument may be made for the use of phrasebook expressions by presenter-tourists and the general linguascaping of tourist destinations; in this case, however, it is the elevation and constitution of a Britishness which is at stake.

In fact, we would like to argue that TV holiday shows' main aim is to create for the viewers a sense of belonging to an *imagined* community of (international-British) *tourists* (cf. Anderson, 1983), and that this is achieved largely through the presenters' specific exploitation of the sociolinguistic resource known as 'crossing' (see Rampton, 1995; 1998; 1999), which is the use of a language (or variety) of a group of which the speaker cannot legitimately claim membership.

As far as our data are concerned, all uses of host languages by the holiday show presenters fit many of Ben Rampton's defining characteristics of, and explanations for, crossing. In these terms, therefore, our data may be recontextualized in the following ways:

- crossing occurs or results in liminal or liminoid (Turner, 1977) moments and activities, that is, when routine expectations about the flow of events is suspended – holidays (represented in our data as 'holiday shows') are a liminal/liminoid activity *par excellence* in taking tourists to a world beyond the ordinary world (Selwyn, 1996; Urry, 2002); they usually involve the suspension of everyday norms of behaviour (dress, cf. Extract 7, eating and drinking habits, cf. Extract 8; daily routine, sexual behaviour, communicative patterns and so on);
- crossing occurs in the context of ritual and performance art – holiday shows are media performances staged for mass audiences ('high performance' in Coupland's, 2007, terms); they involve scripted, fairly routine and self-reflexive accounts of the experiences of travel;
- crossing occurs at peripheral stages of interaction requiring negotiation of participants' status – most interactional code-crossing in the holiday shows involves greeting, parting and other politeness formulae in service encounters or in phatic communion; even though status roles in these encounters are seldom ambiguous, crossing may be used as a means for the presenter to assert or reclaim status;
- crossing occurs in games, which suspend everyday rules and constraints of interaction – playful interactions with hosts in a host language require the adoption of new rules and lengthy preparation (cf. 'been learning that all day', Extract 5.9, line 7);
- in contrast to in-group code-switching, which is largely unexceptional and unremarkable to the social actors in everyday situations, out-group code-crossing 'is much more likely to be "flagged" (for

example, "marked by pauses, hesitation phenomena, repetition and metalinguistic commentary", Romaine, 1988: 141)' (Rampton, 1995: 282) – instances of host language use in the holiday shows are frequently brought to such prominence, especially through meta-comments (cf. Extracts 5.9–5.12);

- due to its de-routinization and the effect of incongruity that crossing may have on some participants, it requires extra inferential work – the uses of host languages transcend their propositional meaning, their main inferential value lying in invoking the images of authenticity and exoticization on the one hand, and familiarity and trust in a holiday destination on the other;
- crossers' proficiency (spoken or listening) in the semantico-referential dimension of the out-group language may be quite minimal – in the holiday shows presenters often display minimal knowledge of host languages (cf. 'no capito', Extract 5.12, line 10);
- minimal significance of the propositional content in code-crossing finds compensation in the greater significance of the expressive meaning, which may be augmented, for example, by music – holiday shows use host languages alongside music and other incidental noises to create the kind of linguascapes described above (see Extract 5.7, lines 2 and 7).

If our characterization of host language use by the holiday show presenters as crossing is right, this has certain consequences for how we characterize the orientation of the presenters to their hosts (into whose languages they cross) and the TV audience (for whom they do the crossing). In this sense, our examples of crossing also evoke Allan Bell's (1999, 2009 [1997]) notion of 'referee design', by which he means style-shifting in the direction of linguistic forms associated with a group different from that of the speaker *and* addressee. What is more, this group is often also absent from the communicative situation. One especially pertinent example discussed by Bell is the use of a Māori song *Pōkarekare Ana* in two Air New Zealand TV commercials. In one of the commercials, the song provides most of the sound and verbal track as background to the rich and varied visual imagery including Māori people as the exponents of the New Zealand nation, middle-class Pakeha New Zealanders (that is, of European descent) in the context of international travel (for example, at airports), New Zealand scenery and birdlife. With a voiceover in English, the song is performed in Māori, which is a non-native and an out-group language to both the performers (including the opera singer Kiri te Kanawa) and the target audience for the TV commercial (middle-class Pakeha New Zealanders). Māori therefore functions in the TV commercial as a symbol of New Zealand national uniqueness and identity, but paradoxically, the cultural imagery and linguistic association is that with a marginalized, othered ethnic minority with whom the performers of the song (and implicitly the makers of the ad) and the target audience do not identify.

We find a number of analogies between the use of Māori in the Air New Zealand adverts analysed by Bell and the use of host languages in our holiday shows. As we have already emphasized, the interactions with hosts (in English or host languages) are presenters' performances for the target audience of largely monolingual TV audience in Britain. This renders hosts the absent reference group in Bell's sense. They become a snapshot, part of the tourist's narrative about their travels, places seen, people met and activities performed. This is where tourist gaze becomes *tourist haze*: the remembering and the telling of tourist narratives after the trip has ended. Just as tourist stories are predominately aimed at 'the folks back home' (see Chapter 3), when British TV presenters report from a 'foreign' country, they report back to the British viewers – both as audience and as 'fellow nationals'.

The use of host languages, together with the imagery of hosts and the scenery of the destination produces short, condensed representations of a destination's 'essence', and gives an impression of its accessibility, but the presenters embrace the identities of the hosts only playfully, in short, 'as if' moments never claiming a new national identity. This point is also consistent with Rampton's view of the way crossing among British, 'multi-ethnic' adolescents affects locally construed identities in talk:

> First, the intimate association with liminality meant that crossing never actually claimed that the speaker was 'really' black or Asian – it didn't... imply that the crosser could move unproblematically in and out of the friends' heritage language in any new kind of open bicultural code-switching. Second, crossing's location in the liminoid margins of interactional and institutional space implied that in the social structures which were dominant and which adolescents finally treated as *normal*, the boundaries round ethnicity were relatively fixed.
>
> (Rampton, 1998: 299)

By appropriating host languages, the presenters in the holiday shows never claim to be 'really' French, Italian, Kenyan or Fijian. On the contrary, more often than not, they emphasize their difference from their hosts. For example, by often sending themselves up as incompetent host language speakers they position themselves firmly as *British* tourists. Different from the hosts and similar to the (implied) tourists in front of TV screens, their ultimate aim is to create a sense of community of (British–international) tourists with their viewers. Through these shows, and venturing into host languages, they reassure their compatriots about the safety of foreign travel in these destinations: they can remain British even outside of Britain, finding 'home away from home'. Using host languages may be useful and fun, but only the low-level proficiency required on holiday does not threaten anyone to having to become 'someone else'. Just as Rampton talks about crossing creating new cross-ethnic patterns of identification, we regard crossing in the holiday shows as creating new cross-national or *inter*-national allegiances, which allow one to maintain a preferred national identity while momentarily venturing outside of one's own national boundary. Even if one ends up in Italy, France, Kenya or Fiji becoming Italian, French, Kenyan or Fijian is no more than an optional pretend play. As with the inflight magazines (Chapter 1) and, to some extent, the holiday postcards (Chapter 3), this 'new international' identity is predicated simultaneously on the transcendence of and on the cultivation (or 'turfing' – Wray et al., 2003) of nationality.

In this chapter, and returning to Goffman, we have primarily been concerned with the theatrical scripting of tourism both in terms of the everyday performances of host–tourist interaction and the more stylized, deliberate stagings of the tourism industry. In the holiday travel shows, presenters are clearly both performer and casting director; where they inevitably cast themselves in the lead role and local people are invariably cast as either chorus/extras or understudies. Together with the show makers (for example, directors, editors, script-writers), it is the presenters who get to change and choose participant alignments and status. Local people have little control over their own subject-positioning or footing, and the ground is constantly changed for them as they are shifted from participant to object and back again. In Goffman's (1981) terms, theirs is truly 'subordinated communication' – in an interactional sense and also in a sociopolitical sense. Within the framework of critical language awareness, what is even more noteworthy is the underlying promotion of the presenter-tourist as a kind of tourist role-model, effectively saying, 'here's how we celebrity Brits do tourism; these are the places to go, these are the things to do, these are the ways to be a tourist'. As viewer-tourists, we are thereby encouraged to subscribe to the kind of scripted performances shown us by presenter-tourists, and we are also invited to improvise and play at the expense of local people.

While the staging of encounters in tourism is by no means new to academic perspectives, what we are looking to do here is to approach this issue from the perspective of sociolinguistics and discourse analysis. In particular, what our analysis shows is how language comes to be ritualized and commodified in the service of tourism as a global cultural industry. By referring to linguascapes and linguascaping, however, we mean also to reveal the very particular deployment and devaluing of local languages as both backdrop and ludic resource. The underlying message this sends to viewers about the value of learning foreign languages is, at best, ambiguous and, at worst, deleterious. Ultimately, it is in this way that as powerful ideological mediators TV holiday shows and their style-setting presenters promote a regime of touristic and intercultural truth about local languages which construct subjectivities for hosts and identities for viewers (cf. Foucault, 1980; Mellinger, 1994). Specifically, host languages are appropriated as a primary identity resource by which visitors may construct themselves as tourists. Furthermore, it is through their playful, transient crossings into local languages that they further position themselves as 'cosmopolitans' – not in the sense of their being culturally engaged with or embracing of local people (cf. Hannerz, 1996), but rather with respect to their appeals to the elite cachet of global citizenship. These are people freely traversing national boundaries but staying firmly rooted in their mutual identification as (British) nationals. In Naomi Klein's (2002) terms, and again following the double standard described by Ed Bruner at the start of this chapter, these 'new internationals' are invited to enjoy globalization as a series of windows rather than fences.

6
The Commodification of Local Linguacultures: Guidebook Glossaries

> 'Tut, tut! Miss Lucy! I hope we shall soon emancipate you from *Baedeker*. He does but touch the surface of things. As to the true Italy – he does not even dream of it. The true Italy is only to be found by patient observation.'...Tears of indignation came to Lucy's eyes partly because Miss Lavish had jilted her, partly because she had taken her *Baedeker*. How could she find her way home? How could she find her way about in Santa Croce?

Set during the time of the archetypal Grand Tour, these well-known extracts from E.M. Forster's 1922 novel *A Room with a View* highlight the ambivalence of disdain and dependence with which many tourists have come to regard the travel guide.[1] On the one hand, guidebooks cannot possibly compare with the untold diversity and richness of the 'true' destination which only the most committed, experienced insider can properly know. To carry a guidebook, therefore, marks one out as a dabbling amateur rather than a discerning connoisseur. On the other hand, the guidebook is a practical necessity for newcomers, reassuringly orienting them to significant geographic and cultural landmarks. In this sense, the guidebook merely invites visitors to take responsibility for their own ignorance and to assist them in their preparations and explorations. However, it is usually when, as in Figure 6.1, guidebooks promise more than this basic introduction that they lay themselves open to stronger critique. In these instances, readers are wrongly encouraged to see the guidebook as something more comprehensive, more authoritative than a simple snapshot, or a rough introduction, to a place and its people. Likewise, visitors are persuaded that the place and its people can indeed be fully 'understood' and truly 'known'. The artefacts, rituals and meanings of any culture are, needless to say, never

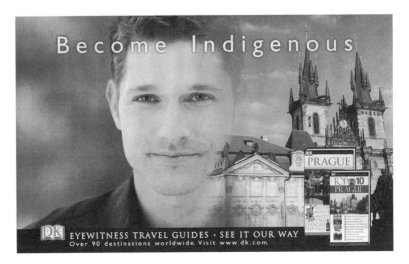

Figure 6.1   Going beyond itself: An advertisement for the DK Eyewitness travel guide to Prague

quite so easily documented or revealed, even though anthropologists and other professional tourists have at times fooled themselves into believing otherwise.[2]

Perhaps the most widely recognized example of a touristic textual genre – or 'discourse on the move' – the travel guidebook is in itself an iconic, genre-defining feature of tourism. Whether it is the authoritative tone of *Baedeker*, the picture-book-cum-encyclopaedic style of *Eyewitness*, or the 'alternative', off-the-beaten-track ethos of *Lonely Planet* and *Rough Guides*, guidebooks have long since usurped the importance of the local, mother-tongue guide or the commercial tour guide. As Cronin (2000: 86) notes:

> The guide book translates the foreign culture into the mother tongue of the traveller. The traveller no longer had to rely on the oral translation of the guide/interpreter as the guide book provided the written translation. The Murray and Baedecker guides thus facilitated the transition from heteronymous dependency on the oral interpreter to an autonomous mode of travelling grounded in literacy.

In fact, scholars often comment on the way the emergence and rise of the guidebook has paralleled changes in tourism more generally and especially the growth of 20th-century mass tourism (see, for example,

MacCannell, 1999 [1976]; Edensor, 2001). By the same token, Gavin Jack and Alison Phipps (2003) discuss how, as part of these changes, guidebooks have also come to resemble less-and-less the instructional and educational style of, say, Victorian travel guides; many contemporary, mass-tourist guidebooks are a great deal more informative and entertaining. As guidebooks like the *Eyewitness* series take on the appearance of colourful, richly detailed coffee-table books, they also become ideal texts for the 'post-touristic' experience described by John Urry (2002) – that virtual, mediatized touring of the world which happens from the comfort of the post-industrial home.

Certainly, patterns of change in the format and function of guidebooks are increasingly evident; for example, in the growing use of online versions of print guidebooks (for example, <travel.roughguides.com> and *Eyewitness'* 'e-guides' <uk.dk.com>) or cases where traditional guidebooks have been transformed into very different online travel resources such as *Lonely Planet's Thorn Tree Forum* <thorntree.lonelyplanet.com>.[3] In fact, tourists nowadays – especially self-styled 'travellers' – are increasingly turning to alternative, web-based resources, side-stepping the centralized authority of commercial guidebooks altogether and relying instead on organizations such as *Virtual Tourist* <www.virtualtourist.com> and on creating and networking their own travel blogs (see, for example, *BootsnAll* <http://blogs.bootsnall.com>).

In spite of these changes, however, the guidebook still constitutes one of the most established and recognizable of tourism genres. Its distinctiveness is, for example, evidenced by spoof publications such as *Molvania: A Land Untouched by Modern Dentistry – A Jetlag Travel Guide* (Cilauro et al., 2004) that premise their intended humour precisely on widespread familiarity with the standardized format and style of commercial guidebooks. Although the order and prioritizing of content may vary, travel guides almost always contain a stock repertoire of practical information on how to get to the destination country, entry formalities, historical and geographical background, social and cultural activities and local flora and fauna. They may feature a list of the country's 'top ten' sights to see and recommend particular itineraries, following a region-by-region approach to visiting the country. Other regular features in guidebooks include various tips for travellers, such as how to bargain, hotel and restaurant listings, information on food and drink and what to do in an emergency. Each of these 'communicative stages' (van Leeuwen, 2005) works to establish the recognizable generic format of guidebooks; in other words, they make a guidebook a guidebook. Almost without exception, there is also likely to be a section on the local language(s) spoken along with a phrasebook-type glossary. It is these glossaries that we make the focus of our final chapter.

There is certainly no shortage of scholarly literature on guidebooks *per se*. Scholars in a range of disciplines have been concerned for a while with describing and understanding the role guidebooks play in shaping the tourist experience (see, for example, Lew, 1991; Koshar, 1998; Gilbert, 1999; McGregor, 2000; Jack and Phipps, 2003; Nishimura et al., 2006). For the most part, these studies take as their central focus the ability of guidebooks to powerfully direct and shape the tourist imagination, and, for this reason, what typically concerns scholars is the problematic (mis)representation of local people and local cultures. Indeed, part of what lays guidebooks open to criticism is their often explicit claim to be 'telling it how it is' and to being a comprehensive 'take' on a destination – be it a city, a region, a country, a continent or even the whole world (see Extracts 6.1–6.4). In looking at a range of different guidebooks ourselves (see Appendix and Figure 6.2 for method and analytic procedures), our intention has been to look specifically at guidebook glossaries – their content and the way they are framed metadiscursively elsewhere in the guidebook and by the publishers who produce the guidebooks in the first place. In this regard, we wanted to start simply by finding out what publishers intend by including such potted language 'lessons' and, along these lines, whether and how they believe readers actually make use of them. This insider perspective offers us a little further insight to the following types of pragmatic context readily available from the guidebooks themselves:

> The editors of Insight Guides provide practical advice and general understanding about a destination's history, culture and people.
> (Extract 6.1, Source: *Insight Guide, Mexico*, p. 2)

> This guide helps you to get the most from your visit to New Zealand.
> (Extract 6.2, Source: DK Eyewitness, *New Zealand*, p. 6)

> The Thomas Cook Traveller to Mexico comes from the world's leading travel experts and has everything you need to plan the perfect trip.
> (Extract 6.3, Source: *Thomas Cook, Mexico*, back cover)

> The main aim is still to make it possible for adventurous travellers to get out there – to explore and better understand the world.
> (Extract 6.4, Source: *Lonely Planet*, all destinations, foreword)

Guidebooks such as those quoted in Extracts 6.1–6.4 are typical in making varying degrees of commitment to their readers, from offering practical advice, to detailing everything that's needed for the perfect trip, to promising a better understanding of the world. Ultimately, however, their common objective is to digest into a manageable book an otherwise limitless range of information about the destination, and, in order to do this, editors must obviously make numerous decisions about what to include and what to exclude. As such, and even though they seldom draw attention to this fact, guidebooks are inherently ideological. Theirs can only ever be one particular representation of the destination and one that unavoidably privileges certain versions of social, cultural, political and historical reality over others. It is their singular judgment of what makes for a perfect trip on which we are encouraged to rely – their idea about what preparations are needed, about how to make the most of the travel experience and how, along the way, to 'better understand the world'. It is with this general intent that guidebook glossaries too are framed.

Turning to language: Guidebook glossaries

In their discussion of the performative and agentive functions of guidebooks, Gavin Jack and Alison Phipps (2003: 288) make the following observation: 'Linguistically then, as well as materially, the travel guide is a kind of ontological security blanket for survival in the unknown.' We certainly share their sense that guidebooks serve to prepare and secure tourists while also reproducing certain ideologies of tourism. However, Jack and Phipps appear not to be concerned with the literal 'languaging' (their term) of guidebooks as much as with the interesting ways guidebooks are 'languaged' into the discourse of tourist encounters. In a similar way, Andrew McGregor's (2000) interviews with tourists about their use of these texts attempt a more situated, quasi-ethnographic understanding of guidebooks. Surprisingly, however, McGregor too makes not a single reference to the language sections of guidebooks – in spite of being specifically concerned to discuss the host–tourist intercultural interactions engendered (or not) by guidebooks. (A similar, more recent study by Sachiko Nishimura and colleagues, 2006, likewise fails to consider language.) In our own examination of guidebooks, therefore, we have sought to take a step back from the actual host–tourist encounter and to consider how this encounter is imagined (or pre-figured) through the (re)presentation of local languages in the phrase-book sections of guidebooks. To be clear, we are well aware that tourists are not unthinking, unreflexive dupes or that local people are suckers; this counter-critique has been well rehearsed (for two good

examples see Harrison, 2003; McCabe, 2005). Indeed our own ethnographically oriented work (Jaworski et al., forthcoming) reveals something of the complicated nature of the host–tourist relationship and of
the multiple, contradictory practices of tourists themselves. Nonetheless, in taking a *critical* perspective in our analysis, we cannot fail to
notice – and remark on – the questionable language ideologies of tourist
texts. And they are questionable not only because, to our 'expert' eye,
language is represented 'incorrectly', but rather because they consistently produce such a lop-sided image of the host–tourist relationship
and about the identities of both tourists and hosts. When this is also
done under the pretext of promoting intercultural exchange and global
understanding, we believe our critique is all the more warranted with
empirical evidence derived from the analysis of multiple genres and
multiple instances of each genre. It is this textual patterning that offers
us a clearer sense of the structuring, not necessarily totalizing, power
of these texts and the 'orders of discourse' of which they are a part
(cf. Fairclough, 2003).

In guidebook glossaries we once again witness language coming to
the foreground of the tourist landscape. Far from being travel with the
sound turned off (see Cronin, 2000), tourists are explicitly encouraged
to speak, to participate in the 'babble' of the linguascape (see Chapter 5).
In this case especially, guidebook glossaries shift us towards an analysis
of a more 'embodied' discourse on the move in the sense that these
are texts that tourists literally carry with them and that fulfil their purpose – or realize their meaning – only in their actual use. In principle at
least, these textualized practices invite the tourist to engage bodily and
actively with local people. Accordingly, this chapter mirrors the kind
of embodied practice of the postcards we examined in Chapter 3. Like
postcards, guidebooks are texts that tourists (potentially) are invited to
annotate, to reinterpret and to make their own. It is at this point also
that, although still mediated, tourists can move into closer interaction
with local people. While all tourism is mediated – semioticized – some
practices undoubtedly entail increasing degrees of direct (for example, face-to-face) interaction. In some respects, this understanding of
guidebooks runs counter to the usual critique presented in tourism
literature which dismisses their 'top ten', 'six-easy-steps' ethos as oppres-
sively directive and prescriptive. In relative terms, however, these are
more open, active texts that invite greater involvement and, potentially,
multiple reading positions. We return to the ideologies of host–tourist
contact implied in these texts below.

Speaking for themselves, publishers appear to be fairly practical and
realistic about the purpose of including a language section in their

guidebooks, as shown in Extracts 6.5 and 6.6. In this case, the glossary is meant to serve as general background information and for essential and practical assistance, for example, 'how to shout "Help!" in an emergency'. (Of course, this begs the question, 'Who or what defines "essential"?') As such, the glossary, like the guidebook as a whole, is a risk-management resource – a trope which recurs in tourism discourse (Jack and Phipps, 2005; Phipps, 2007) and which is consistent within the 'risk society' in general (Beck, 1992).

> We know from the very substantial sales of our DK Eyewitness Travel Phrase Books that many travellers want some reference material on the language of the country they are visiting. Therefore we put a 2–4 page phrase book into most of our guidebooks, as a basic reference.
>
> (Extract 6.5, DK representative)

> On a practical level, it gives readers the essentials (and a bit more) that they'll need when travelling in a country where English is not a first language. This might be information on where to catch a bus, how to book a room, or how to shout 'Help!' in an emergency. And in the event that they don't attempt to speak the language, they can at least show the written phrase to someone.
>
> (Extract 6.6, LP representative)

For other publishers, the rationale for including a glossary is somewhat loftier. As one guidebook representative (IG) put it, this is a 'politeness issue'. Another informant (Extract 6.7) construes the glossaries as of 'cultural importance', emphasizing their usefulness for tourists in getting interpersonally involved [sic] with local people rather than offering a 'merely' transactional form of engagement.

> We just figure that every traveller should be aware of the cultural importance of language and we offer them the opportunity to experience travel in a richer and more fulfilling way...we have a strong desire to encourage people to engage through language with the local people they have contact with while travelling.
>
> (Extract 6.7, LP representative)

Here the concept of personal enrichment – another common trope in tourism discourse – and the acquisition of cultural capital are evoked through the suggestion that a 'richer' and 'more fulfilling' experience may be achieved through contact with hosts. The promise of a more meaningful engagement with local people sits, of course, at the heart of tourism's mythologies (see Harrison, 2003); it is certainly a key discursive theme which runs through each of the genres we have looked at in this book. What might constitute a 'meaningful' engagement for any one tourist, however, is not easily ascertained, nor is it possible to know if this could reasonably be achieved through the kind of vocabulary on offer in the glossaries themselves. It is also never clear if the desire for engagement – or the same kind of engagement – should be assumed on the part of hosts. (We return to this point in a moment.) It is the same touristic conceit, however, which accounts for the marketing of Lonely Planet's more recently published, and significantly titled, *Small Talk* guides, which, in the case of Eastern Europe, promise: 'All the basics you need for short trips and city escapes. Chat [*sic*], eat, shop and celebrate your way through the wonders of Eastern Europe.'[4]

When asked about how and when readers used guidebook glossaries, some publishers report receiving feedback from readers, which suggests they find them 'very useful' and, in some cases, would like more extended phrases. Other publishers, however, are less confident and admit that they do not track this kind of user information. The only time readers mention language sections, it seems, is when they write to point out 'translation mistakes'. There are also mundane, practical considerations that help account for any textual practice. In the case of guidebook glossaries, for example, publishers evidently know that the use and value of their language sections varies depending on the destination where, for example, it may be very easy or very difficult to find people who speak English. As our informant from Insight Guides told us, 'Further afield [than Europe] they become useful again, for example to tell the rickshaw driver to stop, or ask how much the rickshaw ride will cost'. In fact all the publishers we spoke to were fairly clear about what they were willing and able to achieve as in the following extracts:

> Because the phrase books in our guides are fairly short, we focus on the essential words and phrases which we think the holiday-maker is most likely to need.
>
> (Extract 6.8, DK representative)

> While language chapters are fairly basic (compared to a phrasebook), it's a simple way of getting people started on the right track and hopefully leads to a desire for more.
>
> (Extract 6.9, LP representative)

Often, the tendency in tourism studies is to reduce tourists to types (see Cohen, 1985, for the most well-known example of this), to speak of them as a homogenous group rather than acknowledging the ways they differ. Certainly, this is how tourists find themselves represented and addressed by the industry itself. It occurs to us, however, that few assumptions can be made about when, if and how tourists might actually make use of guidebook glossaries. In talking about this ourselves as authors, we realize that we have somewhat different tourist styles; for example, where one of us always enjoys spending time learning key phrases as a mark of respect, another prefers never to 'play' with the local language also as a mark of respect. Any decision to engage with the local language is clearly a matter of personal as well as ideological preference and, therefore, of variation.

It is for this reason, of course, that it is important to avoid making overly confident assumptions about either the extent to which guidebooks shape the tourist experience or the manner in which (different) tourists make use of them. Sarah Quinlan (2005) offers a very useful review of the academic literature, which shows the kinds of varied responses tourists give when interviewed about the way they use guidebooks. Nonetheless, and as we explain above, the primary motive behind the kind of critical discourse analytic work we are interested in lies in exposing the particular 'regimes of truth' established by texts, which is to say the consistently and often unquestioningly repeated stories they tell about tourism and its place in the world. Like inflight magazines, television holiday shows and newspaper travelogues, guidebooks are *potentially* very influential if only in terms of their ubiquity and popularity. (Much more so than academic monographs.) When, however, we also discover that, on closer inspection, these texts promote a remarkably uniform, one-sided version of the tourist experience, the question of their ideological impact surely warrants greater comment and perhaps even concern, regardless of what the publishers say or think they are doing.

Folk-linguistic characterizations of local languages

The objectives of critical discourse analysis – our chief analytic frame in this book – are in some respects akin to those of research on folk linguistics and metalanguage (for example, Lucy, 1993; Jaworski et al., 2004; Preston, 2004; Thurlow, 2006); in different ways, they are all concerned with the way that 'language about language' reflects people's attitudes and beliefs, and helps constitute ideologies of difference. In this regard, the intention is less to evaluate the validity or accuracy of folk-linguistic discourse, as it is to critique those metalinguistic claims to authority by which social/power relations come to be organized and normalized (Cameron, 1995; Thurlow, 2007, 2010). Indeed, all metadiscourse, regardless of its linguistic validity, is always a site of constant bureaucratic and interpersonal struggle. Invariably also, the promotion or denigration of certain languages and ways of speaking serves as a means of rehearsing or reproducing the wider social and economic order (cf. Bourdieu, 1991). It is in this way precisely that we see how general metadiscursive comments in guidebooks (re-)encode a number of beliefs about the nature, function and politics of language. More importantly, though, they also offer important insights into the way that host–tourist exchanges are framed and promoted more generally.

In this regard, we can start with the following example, an observation about 'Chinese languages' in Extract 6.10, which represents the kind of language myths (cf. Bauer and Trudgill, 1998) lay people often recognize and like to rehearse. It deals with an 'unusual' aspect of Cantonese phonology, unusual in the sense of its being apparently in stark contrast to English:

> Chinese languages are rich in homonyms (i.e. words that sound alike) and much of their superstitious beliefs, poetry and humour is based on this wealth. The Cantonese word for 'silk', for example, sounds the same as the words for 'lion', 'private', 'poem', 'corpse' and 'teacher'. What distinguish the meaning of each word are changes in a speaker's pitch or 'tone' and the context of the word within the sentence.
>
> (Extract 6.10, LP, Hong Kong, p. 372)

Manifesting the 'some languages are harder than others' myth, this bit of background information (see also Extracts 6.11–6.13, below) focuses on the apparent confusion the tourist may face when interpreting or producing Cantonese words. However, while it is obviously true that tone is phonemic in Cantonese, it makes the 'same' words with different tones not homonyms (sounding identical), but 'minimal pairs', that is, two words whose meaning is different due to a change of one sound between. What this description also overlooks – or downplays – is that the very same principles are true of most languages; for example, an easy equivalent might be English homonyms like 'pore, poor, pour' or 'rain, reign, rein' or 'raise, rays, raze', which, in Spanish, say, would be rendered differentially as 'poro, porbre, verter'; 'lluvia, reinado, reinda' and 'aumento, rayos, arrasar', respectively. And a similar phonemic (meaning-producing) feature of English prosody is stress, in words such as '*record*' (noun) and '*record*' (verb). (And this is not to mention the relative challenge of the idiosyncrasies of English spelling.) Of course, the real value in pointing to grammatical and phonetic characteristics such as these does not lie in their linguistic validity or significance, but rather in their *perceived* oddity and, therefore, *implied* exoticity. Once again, in the context of tourism, language is given value (and attention) because of its symbolic rather than representational or interpersonal function. In this case, language offers itself as an ideal metasemiotic resource for communicating the touristic 'safe-adventure' trope such that the 'threat' of an unknown language can be managed – simultaneously mitigating the threat by rendering the language understandable or unnecessary (that is, 'everyone speaks good English') and by playing up the 'threat' for exotic effect.

Another folk-linguistic topic commonly picked up by guidebooks is the aesthetic merits of different languages – in the style of what Howard Giles and Nancy Niedzielski (1998) characterize as the 'Italian is beautiful, German is ugly' myth. In her analysis of the 1993 *Lonely Planet* guide to India, Deborah Bhattacharyya (1997: 381–382) discusses the noticeable use throughout the guidebook of evaluative adjectives ('fascinating' vs. 'little to see'; 'spectacular' vs. 'dull') to describe tourist sites. In glossaries, we see local languages falling under the same purview; they are objectified – and thereby become commodified – like any other monument, landscape or spectacle. As such, they too are subject to aesthetic evaluation. Sometimes, as in Extracts 6.11–6.13, this is done explicitly in the context of judgments about difficulty, intelligibility and the considerable effort required to master such languages:

> The visual appearance of Polish is pretty fearsome for people outside the Slavonic circle, and it's no doubt a difficult language to master. It has a complicated grammar, with word endings changing depending on case, number and gender, and the rules abound in exceptions.
>
> (Extract 6.11, Source: *LP, Poland*, p. 47)

> The Cantonese dialect is a harsh-sounding, guttural and tonal language that is almost impossible for most visitors to attempt without considerable prior knowledge.
>
> (Extract 6.12, Source: *IG, Hong Kong*, p. 286)

> The lingo has a laconic, poetic originality and a prolific profanity.
>
> (Extract 6.13, Source: *IG, Australia*, p. 389)

The first two extracts above express overtly negative views of Polish and Cantonese, referring to them as 'fearsome', 'difficult', 'complicated' and somehow irregular ('abounds in exceptions') (Polish), and 'harsh-sounding', 'guttural' and 'impossible... to attempt' (Cantonese). In the third case (Strine 'Broad Australian English') the term 'lingo' is used for connoting a language that is not fully developed or 'substandard' in another way (for example, used by some subcultural types), especially in contrast to ideological hegemony of 'standard' English (e.g. Milroy, 2006). This is reinforced by the additional reference to 'laconic', that is, somewhat restricted, though potentially pleasing ('poetic') creativity, and by focusing on the apparent richness of another typical feature of what makes language 'bad language' (Andersson and Trudgill, 1990) – swearing ('profanity').

Most attempts of the guidebooks to characterize destinations from a linguistic point of view are riddled with other problems. Consider the following two examples:

In the families of Celtic languages, Welsh bears most similarity to largely defunct Cornish and defiant Breton, the language of the north-western corner of France.

(Extract 6.14, Source: *Rough Guide, Wales*, p. 471)

Whereas Swahili developed in East Africa as a way for all the tribes to communicate, in West Africa the languages of the former colonial powers – French in Senegal and English in Gambia – have become each country's common language (or *lingua franca*).

(Extract 6.15, Source: *IG, Gambia & Senegal*, p. 323)

Travel guides generally include some social-historical background on the linguistic situation in the destination, for example, the languages spoken in the destination, those classified as official or national and those considered to be indigenous languages. It is here that evaluation arises in more subtle ways, such as when we read that Cornish is 'defunct' or that Breton is 'defiant' (Extract 6.14). As we noted in Chapter 1, this kind of anthropomorphism is a common device for attributing pejorative blame or maleficent intention to a language rather than its speakers. Similarly, the potted linguistic history of Gambia and Senegal in Extract 6.15, arguably obscures the calculation and violence of colonial language policy through the choice of terminology like 'developed' and 'have become' which gives agency to abstracted languages independent of the actions of the colonizers. Although, over time, languages accrue tremendous symbolic and economic power, it is ultimately people who exercise power *through* language and, historically speaking, it is not languages that conquer and colonize – but their speakers. Generally speaking, the metadiscursive representation of languages in guidebooks is largely de-politicized, which is not to say, of course, de-ideologized. The only exception we came across in our survey was in fact the Rough Guide's account of Welsh, which includes the 1536 illegalization of the language by the English King Henry VIII and the Victorians' 'barbaric' Welsh Not policy. (Incidentally, the author of this guidebook was English.)

Understandably perhaps, guidebooks almost always indicate how widespread the use and proficiency of English is in any country, while at the same time encouraging readers to attempt to speak some of the local language. It is this underlying tension – you should learn some of the local language, but you don't *have* to – which confirms the underlying ludic quality of the guidebook glossary and which explains their largely inconsistent, perfunctory content and organization (see below). Nonetheless, this constant reassurance is also characteristic of so much of tourism discourse (see Chapters 1 and 2) where tourists are continually being promised either a home-from-home experience ('it's just like home') or the oxymoronic 'safe adventure'. In this case, we are also reminded of the political-pragmatic realities of being monolingual English speakers: any incentive or motivation to speak a 'foreign' language is ironically undermined by the increasing availability of English speakers, many of whom are personally and professionally committed to exploiting their own second-language skills. That is, according to guidebooks, unless tourists find themselves outside the 'civilized' spaces of the young, urban bourgeoisie.

Cantonese, Mandarin and English are the official languages of Hong Kong. English is widely understood and spoken, so English-speakers will find it easy to get around, although expect communication difficulties with taxi drivers and residents in remoter rural areas.

(Extract 6.16, Source: *DK, Hong Kong*, p. 136)

While English is quite widely spoken in tourist resorts, some knowledge of Spanish goes down well and is needed if travelling off the beaten track.

(Extract 6.17, Source: *TC, Mexico*, p. 185)

Although many Mexicans speak some English, it is good to have some basic Spanish phrases at your disposal; in remote areas, it is essential.

In general, Mexicans are delighted with foreigners who try to speak the language and they'll be patient – if sometimes amused.

(Extract 6.18, Source: *IG, Mexico*, p. 381)

Fortunately, staff at most tourist offices and hotels are fluent English speakers; bus drivers and staff at guesthouses, hostels and restaurants may not be – though they'll often fetch someone who can help. Finns who speak Finnish to a foreigner usually do so extremely clearly and 'according to the book'. Mistakes made by visitors are kindly tolerated, and even your most bumbling attempts will be warmly appreciated.

(Extract 6.19, Source: *LP, Finland*, p. 319)

Discussions about the level of English to be expected in holiday destinations – and the concomitant expectation that the host population will indeed be able to speak at least enough English to facilitate the tourist experience – also emphasize the unidirectional nature of global tourist flows (cf. Appadurai, 1990). Those who receive the tourists are expected to take on board the tourist language(s) while the tourists do not have time to learn more than a few words of the host language before jetting off to another destination. While Phipps (2007) has high expectations for the commitment of tourists to learn host languages, we remain less convinced.

In Extracts 6.18 and 6.19, what is striking is less the reassurances of English, as the stereotypic portrayal of host attitudes to tourists' attempts at using the local language. We are told, for example, that the use of Spanish in Mexico 'will go down well' and that the Mexicans will be 'delighted' and 'patient', just as the Finns are supportive, tolerant and 'warmly' appreciative of any attempts to speak Finnish. These clearly generalized statements problematically render local people a homogenous community and one that is uniformly predisposed to tourists. Once again, the expectation is that hosts will serve tourists and like them. The fact that a few words will suffice emphasizes the liminality of the tourist experience: the host language can be dipped into or rather *crossed* into using the phrases provided in the guidebook. The reported patience of hosts when tourists do try and speak reiterates the reality that the host language is intended for creating only a fleeting, playful involvement between the two parties – the hosts are just letting the tourists have a go. As we shall show in a moment, this next tourist conceit is consistent with the kind of commercial rhetoric that typically legitimates and promotes language learning.

This metadiscursive framing of local people also highlights the unequal relations of power that typically characterize host–tourist exchanges where responsibility for the success of the exchange almost always lies with the hosts – it is they who must carry what Rosina Lippi-Green (1997) calls the 'burden of communication'. And, for tourists (or business people), who typically want to be in command of their travel experience, this presents them with something of a double-bind: in choosing to cross into the other language they must also relinquish some control, which they are promised in the form of endless choice – or, at least, the appearance thereof (see Thurlow and Jaworski, 2006). Although potentially transformative and enjoyable even, intercultural exchange is typically unpredictable and uncomfortable – two sensations that tourism marketing deliberately downplays even if it must some-times invoke the 'risk factors' in order to leverage the symbolic currency of an exotic adventure.

In both the specific language sections and elsewhere in the guide-books, comments and information about other aspects of linguaculture are sometimes made, apparently in an attempt to encourage a more sophisticated sociolinguistic or communicative competence (Hymes, 1971). The *Insight Guide to Senegal*, for example, contains a section enti-tled Manners and Customs, in which West African greeting practices are explained, while the guide to Hong Kong has a box or inset containing a lay explanation of face, popularized from Goffman's (1963) original work. Consider also the advice in Extract 6.21 about how to behave when visiting a Maori religious site.

> As the Maori are a tribal Polynesian people, they have a unique pro-tocol which should be observed on a marae (religious site).... The important things to remember when visiting a marae are to take off your shoes before entering a meeting house and greeting your hosts with a 'hongi' – a traditional Maori welcome where you press noses to signify friendship. Visitors to marae are often welcomed with a powhiri (formal welcome) and a wero (challenge).
>
> (Extract 6.21, Source: *IG, New Zealand*, p. 327)

In this extract, in addition to the basic explanation of the necessity to remove one's shoes and exhortation to respect the Maori culture, the text is 'linguascaped' with several Maori words glossed into English. While this use of the language surely has the effect of further exoti-cizing the image of the *marae* and of Maori culture generally, our own fieldwork in New Zealand suggests that visitors are rarely expected to use

Figure 6.2   A unilateral exchange: New Zealand Tourism's 'hongi' website banner (April 2008)

these words. It is also highly unlikely that they will perform the *hongi* in earnest unless as a part of a commodified ritual (Jaworski, 2009). What is compelling, however, is obviously the romance and mystery of this particular cultural rich point by which, according to tradition, a person becomes one with the *tangata whenua* (that is, 'a local') rather than remaining *manuhiri* ('a visitor').[5] As an icon of the quintessential tourist hospitality discourse, the *hongi* has not surprisingly been taken up as a central resource for the selling of New Zealand as a tourist destination (see Figure 6.2). Needless to say, what the guidebook fails to mention is that the *hongi* obliges visitors also to share in the duties and responsibilities of their hosts. In other words, communicative 'crossing' is only ever fleeting, decontextualized, stylized or commodified and unilateral (cf. Bell, 1999).

Speaking tourist: Semantic and ideological fields

Having considered the publishers' perspectives on the language sections of their guidebooks and having examined the general metadiscursive framing of the local linguacultues covered, we now turn to focus more specifically on the actual content of glossaries. The guidebooks we have looked at all include some information about the languages spoken in the destination country, and all but three of them included a glossary of useful/key/essential words and phrases for the tourist. Even destinations like Australia (Strine), New Zealand (Maori) and Wales (Welsh), perceived as mainly English-speaking destinations, featured either general or specific language information in this way.

Table 6.1 Main glossary content categories, together with number of items in each category and percentage of overall dataset

Content category	Items	%
Time/days/numbers	697	27.2
Getting around/directions	578	22.6
Eating out	291	11.4
Biographical information (e.g. my name is, I am from, I like, I don't like)	204	8.0
Shopping	169	6.6
Accommodation	164	6.4
Essentials/basics (e.g. yes, no, please, thank you, when, where)	155	6.1
Health/emergencies	108	4.2
Greetings/leave-takings	103	3.7
Language difficulties	75	2.9
Pronouns	24	0.9
Total	**2568**	**100**

All the different words, phrases and terms presented in the different guidebook glossaries – nearly 2600 different items – can be clustered in to one or other of the eleven main content categories we list in Table 6.1. It is in this way that we see how the most common tourist activities are identified and prioritized by guidebooks: tourists will spend a lot of time moving from place-to-place (getting around/directions) and finding and staying in hotels, campsites and the like (accommodation). As well as doing lots of eating and drinking (eating out) they will also buy things (shopping). Tourists are expected to at least meet and greet hosts (greeting, leave-taking) and to say a little bit about themselves (biographical information). It is also possible that they will need to get medical or other official help (health/emergencies) and that they may have problems understanding their hosts (language difficulties).

What is striking about this overview of a sample of different guide-book glossaries is not only the limited prescription of communicative topics but also assumptions made about the nature of the relationship between visitors and local people. The vocabularies on offer are clearly restricted to the functional requirements of service transactions (that is, 'how much is ...?', 'where can I find ...?' and so on); alternatively, they encourage a level of relational engagement that seldom ventures beyond the superficial courtesies of greeting rituals (for example, 'hello', 'good morning', 'my name is ...', 'I am from ...'). Almost never is there a vocabulary made available which might otherwise help facilitate a more substantial, extended exchange or conversation – even at the most basic level, say, of 'I like my job because...', 'This is the first time I've...', 'I believe that...' and so on. There is certainly little in these glossaries that might move visitors towards the kind of intercultural, cross-lingual encounter with the Other which sits at the heart of tourism mythology and which the guidebooks themselves consistently imply. Instead, glossaries leave tourists stranded in a permanent state of greeting, introduction and purchase – perhaps appropriate to the liminal, fleeting nature of most host–tourist encounters.

On close inspection, the glossaries suggest to us that apart from the most phatic exchanges (greetings, leave-takings, expressions of thanks and so on) and the tourist-centred needs of getting to a specific location, getting a good night sleep (possibly in a room with a view), finding a meal and a toilet, getting a good bargain in a shop or at a market, the most likely situation in which the tourist will want to speak to a host is in an emergency. To some extent, this goes some way to contradict the mythology of travel as always safe and pleasurable. The preponderance of words and phrases related to accidents, illness and all sorts of other mishaps could provide a useful script for any travel insurance company advert.

The following is a relatively unordered list of the English language phrases to be used in case of an emergency. Many occur in our sample repeatedly (for example, 'Call a doctor!'), while some only once (for example, 'rapist' – Hong Kong):

Help!
Watch out!
Thief!
Fire!
Stop!
Call a doctor!
Call the police!
Call an ambulance!
Call the fire department!
Where is the nearest hospital?
I want to contact my embassy
Could I use the telephone?
Could you help me, please?
I'm ill
I'm sick
I'm injured
I do not feel well

I feel ill
I have a headache
I have a stomach ache
I need to rest
I have a fever
I'm allergic to penicillin
I'm allergic to antibiotics
The child is/the children are sick
We need a doctor
I need a prescription for . . .
    cold
    cough
    cut
    flu
    hayfever
    headache pills
hospital
nausea
sore throat
dentist
doctor
thermometer
drug store
medicine
pills
accident
ambulance
emergency
police
policeman
foreign affairs police
pickpocket
rapist
I've been robbed
I've/we've been mugged
They stole my . . .
I'm lost

It is doubtful whether a selection of words and phrases from the above list can indeed be effective in solving tourists' health problems and other mishaps when no other means of communicating with local people are available, but it may fulfil the publishers' aforementioned aim of providing their itinerant readers with general background information and ways of seeking practical assistance. Thus, these parts of glossaries provide tourists with some reassurance of finding help when needed, while at the same time acting as subtle reminders that indeed not all travel is always 'safe'. A particular tone of urgency and demand is established by the use of grammatical mood/modality. Most phrases, as in the list above and elsewhere, are those suggested for the use by tourists to hosts (rather than vice versa). This is evidenced in the range of requests for specific information, actions, goods and services. They appear as commands (for example, 'Help!'), demands (for example, 'We need a doctor'), questions with politeness formulae (for example, 'Could you help me, please?'), indirect requests in the form of a statement (for example, 'I'm sick'), single words ('doctor') and so on. The majority of the expressions are speech acts to be performed 'bold on record', that is, with little if any redressive action to preserve the addressee's face, which is warranted by gaining maximum efficiency (Brown and Levinson, 1987). The image of a rather blunt tourist emerges not only in situations when they may be in an emergency situation, however, but also when they simply seem to be tired or bored of too much attention from apparently overbearing hosts. It is in such circumstances that guidebooks offer help with expressions like: 'Go away!' (Finland) and 'Leave me alone!' (Senegal; Poland).

It is only very occasionally that phrases suggesting a more considerate attitude to hosts are included (again, apart from a large number of greeting formulae such as 'How are you?' and 'Glad to meet you', which can obviously be used reciprocally by hosts and tourists). Such rare examples include modalized requests like 'May I sit here?', 'Can you please help me take a photo?' or 'Is it ok to take a photo?' A few questions for biographical information included in the glossaries are probably meant to allow tourists the comprehension of what is being said to them, revealed, for example, by potential answers to the question 'Where are you from?' In other instances, material that would appear to facilitate a more convergent, conversational move does not quite live up to expectation. For example, it is not made clear when it may or may not be appropriate to ask someone 'What's your name?', 'How old are you?' or 'Are you married?' Certainly, in the linguacultures with which we ourselves are most familiar, questions about age are socially delicate just as questions about marital status are highly context sensitive. So, although questions such as these may appear relatively innocuous in the context of a guidebook glossary, their pragmatic force, especially in the context of a potentially/or relatively powerful tourist to a potentially or relatively powerless host, may take on sinister and coercive overtones leading to what Jenny Thomas (1983) refers to as socio-pragmatic failure: language use which violates the cultural expectations of the addressee in terms of their assessment of the socio-cultural context of the interaction. When the size of imposition, social distance, relative rights and obligations, cost and benefits are miscalculated in a foreign language situation, the result may be saying the wrong thing, in a wrong way to the wrong person.

What is generally quite striking about the glossaries is their randomness. This is evident in some of the more idiosyncratic words and expressions we find linked mysteriously to specific destinations such as 'Charity has already been made' (Senegal) and 'tampons' (Mexico) and 'male genitals' (New Zealand). With regards to the latter, there is also the listing of Maori place names presumably translated for comic effect rather than for conversational application (for example, 'Burnt Penis' and 'Eat People'). By the same token, we can't help but wonder at the crisis-management listings' random selection of 'penicillin' and 'antibiotics' as opposed to any number of other life-threatening allergies or conditions. Why, too, are no prescription translations offered for common ailments like diarrhoea or menstruation pains?

These idiosyncrasies aside, we finish by listing here the range of phrases related specifically to language use:

Do you speak English/French?
Does anyone speak English?
Does anyone here speak English?
I speak only English
I speak a little French
I don't speak Polish/Wolof/French/Spanish . . .
I (don't) understand
Do you understand (me)?
Please speak more slowly
Could you speak more slowly please?
What did you say?
Could you repeat that, please?
Please write that down (for me)
What does it mean?
What is this called?
How do you say . . . (in Finnish)?
How do you pronounce it?

A clear and probably not mistaken assumption behind such formulae is that the English-speaking tourists expected to use them are monolingual. Yet, they convey a paradox giving tourists tools to admit their linguistic ineptitude, or to request communication in English through the language of the host. Other than appearing courteous to their hosts, such usage has little pragmatic value. Of course, some tourists may demonstrate varying degrees of competence in the host language, and especially when it is quite rudimentary, formulae requesting reformulation or further explanation (for example, 'Could you speak more slowly please?', 'Please write that down (for me)' or 'How do you pronounce it?') may come in handy to ease their communication problems. In other words, we do not mean to be totally dismissive of guidebook glossaries.

Formulaic language that, apart from word lists, constitutes the core of the glossaries is taught and learnt early in the beginning stages of foreign language study. Formulae are useful because they can be used frequently and give the impression of fluency in a foreign language (Coulmas, 1981; Davies 1987; Jaworski, 1990; Weinert 1995). They are also seemingly easy to learn; they can be memorized as singular items before grasping the full or even partial understanding of the grammatical system. 'Students of English, for instance, might learn and use formulas such as *don't mention it* or *God bless you* long before they learn to produce imperative or subjunctive structures' (Schmidt, 1983; Davies, 1987: 76).

This is not to say that all formulae are successfully learnt and used by all learners, including tourists exposed to written lists with no or scant guidance on the pronunciation of the target expressions. Languages differ in the meaning, distribution, frequency of occurrence and social colouring of their respective formulae (Tannen and Öztek, 1981). Moreover, 'item learning' in the beginning stages of foreign language instruction, as opposed to 'system learning' in the later stages, facilitates transfer (or borrowing) from one's native language (Ringbom, 1985), and may lead to pragmatic failure in the target language (Thomas, 1983; see also Pawley and Syder, 1983).

Not all of the formulaic expressions, or formulaic sequences (Wray and Perkins, 2000) in the guidebooks are of the same order. As in other contexts, some are entirely fixed strings (for example, 'How are you?') while others are strings with open slots (for example, 'Do you like...?', 'Where is the...?', 'They stole my...'). In the latter case, additional knowledge of relevant vocabulary items is quite indispensable. Sometimes, these items are provided in the glossaries, though of necessity, they are quite limited in scope.

As a general rule, the language information contained in the guide-books is laid out for tourists to speak to hosts (that is, the base word or phrase is in English, which is then translated into the host language). In this sense too, the glossaries tend to re-inscribe the host roles of server and sounding-board. Once again, this is a one-way street. For the most part, glossaries promote a conversational exchange pattern whereby the tourist speaks rather than listens. The exceptions, interestingly, are the Maori items, which, in both the guidebooks we looked at (two different publishers), were presented as Maori being translated into English (see above). Otherwise, the language sections provide few phrases oriented to listening and understanding. Thus, tourists seem to be offered some very basic tools to utter a few fixed phrases in the host language, that is, assuming that they need to speak at all; as the publishing representative quoted in Extract 6.6. reminds us, tourists may also prefer simply to point at phrases in glossaries in much the same way as popular booklets like *The Wordless Travel Book* encourage them to do (see Figure 6.3).[6]

Take a look at our own hypothetical compilation of a typical range of 'conversational' phrases offered in the guidebooks:

Welcome! Hello Glad to meet you. **How are you?** Very well, thanks. **What's your name?** My name is…**Where are you from?** I'm from…I'm a tourist/student I'm from Europe. **How old are you?** I'm 25 **Are you married?** How do you say…No (not so) Yes I want…No. I don't want it. **Do you like**…? I like it very much I don't like…May I? It doesn't matter. Can you please help me take a photo? Is it ok to take a photo? Goodbye

Any conversation based on this vocabulary would unavoidably be some-thing of a one-way street; this is clearly not a vocabulary of *exchange* but merely of encounter whereby the local person (imagined in bold) remains, for the most part, 'unspoken' and unknown. Certainly, the DK Eyewitness promise made in Figure 6.1 of becoming somehow 'indige-nous' seems highly improbable if this is all the small talk one can muster. Guidebook glossaries are, in Thurlow's (2004: 83) terms, only ever 'cod-ified, fixed regimes of translated truth which…promote the literal and denotative, the formulaic and reductive, at the expense of the subtle, the complex, the messy, the "lived" '. In fact, it is not unreasonable to suggest that the very *raison d'être* of guidebooks is, somewhat ironi-cally in the case of glossaries, to minimize or at least mitigate contact with local people. It is in much the same way that Daniel Boorstin (1964: 91) commented some time ago on the effect travel agencies

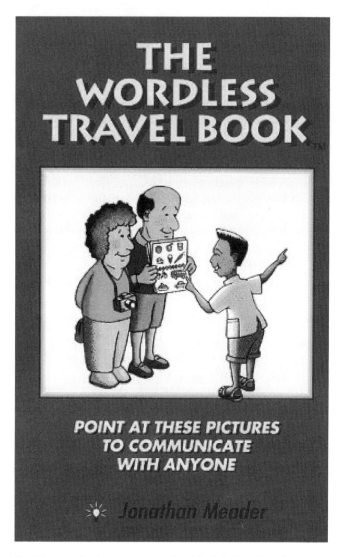

Figure 6.3   Why speak when you can point: *The Wordless Travel Book*

had in 'insulating the tourist from the travel world' (cf. Bhattacharyya, 1997). And herein lays the central contradiction of guidebooks. It is clear from the inclusion of language glossaries in the guidebooks that guidebook writers do feel that they need to cater for the eventuality of host–tourist interaction. Thus, it is possible to argue that guidebooks give out conflicting messages insofar as, on the one hand, they carry glossaries to aid host–tourist communication, but on the other, the need for tourists to interact with hosts is reduced if they use a guidebook.

Glossaries function primarily to fulfil the ludic and identificational needs of tourists, which we talked about in more detail before (for example, Chapter 5), and in this regard they are more than adequate. To be fair, tourists who want to go further can always turn to a phrase book or a language course. As a whole, however, guidebooks usually play with the backstage frisson, the mythologized desire of tourists to seek the otherwise illusive authenticity of a 'real' connection or a 'genuine' encounter with the 'true' Other. In this way, language glossaries promote themselves as resources for cracking the code of the local and for *crossing* into alterity. There is inevitably a satisfying and enjoyable sense of mastery in both these processes; it is an almost narcissistic – which is not to say necessarily inconsiderate or maleficent – delight.

Travel narrows the mind: The language of encounter

There is a kind of double-performativity to guidebooks: first, through their iconicity as quintessential tourist texts; second, through their scheduling of the tourist itinerary and their scripting of the host–tourist encounter (cf. Jack and Phipps, 2003). In other words, and to follow both Goffman (1963) and Butler (1990), the performance of the tourist identity is established in part through the reiterative act of purchasing, carrying and following the guidebook itself. Guidebooks are the epitome of the 'how to tour/how to be a tourist' text, just as having an inflight magazine helps an airline to establish its identity as an international or global player (Chapter 1). By the same token also, the language glossary is a key part of securing the generic, recognizable format of the guidebooks. More importantly, however, it is through tourists' decision to learn or attempt some of the language tokens in these glossaries, with whatever degree of success, that they are again able to perform their identity as tourists. The community of practice distinguishes and establishes itself, in part, through its pleasurable crossings into the local language that, although motivated by a desire to play at being local, inevitably mark them out as visitors.

As generic practices in themselves, the word and phrase listings included towards the end of virtually all guidebooks are fairly unique, with nothing of the attempted scope of dictionaries or language course books, little of the relative detail in phrasebooks, they typically share the superficial, incidental quality of glossaries. In the rote learning tradition of the audio-lingual language learning methods and with the pretence of the 'real-life' notional-functional method (see Pennycook, 1989, for a critical review), this is language instruction that stops well short of communicative competence and that seldom goes much further than a foreign-language translation of 'Do you speak English?' (cf. Phipps, 2007). Language is, in the process, abstracted and rendered simultaneously representative of and autonomous from its cultural context. As such, it is not only the local language that is reduced, packaged and glossed but also, of course, the local culture more generally. These are, after all, the quintessential texts of the quintessential 'culture industry of otherness' (Favero, 2007). What guidebook glossaries ultimately do is, not unlike newspaper travelogues (Chapter 4) and television holiday shows (Chapter 5), commodify the local 'languaculture' (or 'linguaculture') in Mike Agar's (1994) terms. Intended to highlight the inseparability of language and culture, Agar explains: 'Culture is in language, and language is loaded with culture' (p. 38). In the case of guidebooks, however, the tourist linguascape is presented as almost totally disembedded from the cultural context of any plausible, extended host–tourist relationship even though the expectation or promise is that these languacultural snippets might eventually be deployed in the service of intercultural exchange. Even then, however, these presumed relationships (or interactions) are predicated on certain key assumptions about the objectives of tourism and the relations of power by which tourism is organized.

As publishers themselves note, the space available for language sections is so limited that providing the language for extended interactions is not really a practical proposition. Guidebooks are therefore typically designed to offer only 'the basics' or 'the essentials' and glossaries function rather as linguascaping resources, that is, they serve to give a flavour of the languages spoken in the destination country, just as TV travel shows play 'local' music as background on items about a particular country. For Tim Edensor (2001: 73), 'guidebooks are a kind of master script for tourists which reduces disorientation and guides action'. It is possible therefore to see their glossaries in a similar light – as providing a more literal linguistic script to accompany the mediating master script of the guidebook as a whole. Where the guidebook advises tourists where to go, what to see, what to eat and so on, the glossaries tell them what to say while they are going, seeing and eating. As we have already mentioned, however, these are by no means totalizing texts, and nor are tourists complete dupes; nonetheless, they might be understandably susceptible to the authoritative, expert voice with which guidebooks are usually written. As such, we are inclined to think of glossaries in the way that de Certeau (1984:121) talks of maps losing the richness of narrative detail and 'colonizing space'. Inger Birkeland (2005: 82) summarizes de Certeau's position well:

> In the modern map...the storyteller and tour describer have disappeared. The itinerary is lost in favour of an abstract view from above. The map authorizes legitimate and dominant knowledge in modernity, and mapping relates to power over place, to dominant technologies in a society and imperialism, in which knowledge is power.

Ask any person why they go on holiday or vacation overseas and eventually, after the obvious 'getting away', 'escaping',/'relaxing'/and so on, the more lofty ideals of 'broadening the mind', 'seeing other cultures', 'getting to know other peoples' invariably follow. More often than not, it is this second rationale by which tourists are better able to leverage the cultural capital (or cachet) that comes with educational-cum-intercultural self-improvement. As such, these explanations offer themselves as potential identity resources – arguably even more so for those looking to style themselves 'committed travellers' (for example, back-packers) rather than 'mere tourists' (for example, package holiday makers). Not surprisingly, it is in these sorts of ways that tourism discourse is seen to service class ideologies.

The mythology – or ideology – of tourism is that it broadens the mind and that we seek through our travels to meet, engage with and come to understand local people and their cultural ways. And yet, as we have seen throughout, the generic/mediated representations of tourism time and again depict and enable only the most superficial contact with local people.

For the most part, the language instruction in the glossaries centres on the transactional demands of service encounters rather than the interactional demands of conversational relationship. And yet, a close examination of the language information provided in tourist guidebooks shows that there is rarely sufficient information to conduct anything but the most rudimentary of conversations. Although tourists might be encouraged to believe they are becoming global communicators and acquiring a global linguistic repertoire of tourism by using the language sections, the focus on the practicalities of travel and transactional language contrasts with the common myth of travel broadening the mind.

Much of what is said about language(s) in these guidebooks is similar to the commodifying rhetoric of the wider language-learning market. Estimated to be a global industry worth tens of billions of dollars (for example, in 2007, Britain's English language teaching revenue alone was estimated at US$10 billon – a third of the worldwide revenue and not counting teaching actually in the UK; see *Language Travel Magazine*, 2008).[7] Typically, the marketing for this industry is as liberal in its claims as any other form of marketing. Take, for example, DK Eyewitness' *15-Minute Spanish*, one of a series of more comprehensive language-learning resources to supplement their well-known travel guides and phrase books.[8] The front and back covers of this particular booklet contain the following commitment to readers:

> Order a meal. Book a room. Buy a ticket. Ask directions. Make conversation.
>
> Learn Spanish in just 15 minutes a day.
>
> In just 15 minutes a day you can speak and understand Spanish with confidence.
>
> Real-life examples cover every vacation and business situation.
>
> (Extract 6.22)

Not only do these courses make the highly questionable promise of being able to 'learn Spanish' in a total of three hours (over twelve weeks), but they also promote an image of language-use as being uncontentious and trouble-free, with the exception perhaps of lessons like 'At the Doctor', 'At the Hospital' and 'Police and Crime' (for example, 'I've been robbed' or 'He had short, black hair and a beard'). For the most part, the experience of speaking the foreign language is also presented as a transaction; this is language learning designed almost exclusively to facilitate service or business encounters. In keeping with the types of categories we see in guidebook glossaries, the twelve weekly themes covered in *15-Minute Spanish* include Eating and Drinking, Getting Around, Accommodation, Shopping, Work and Study, Health, Services and, of course, Travel. Even the lessons 'Hello' and 'Socializing' have a corporate quality to them (see Figure 6.4). It is, we think, no coincidence that a lesson is devoted to the verb *querer* ('want').

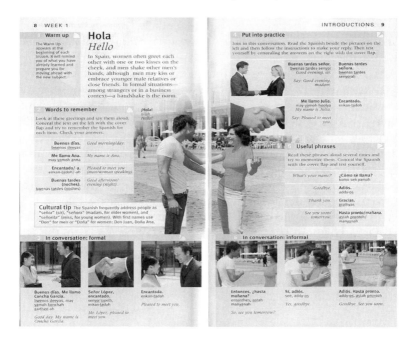

Figure 6.4   The rules of engagement: First lesson from DK Eyewitness' *15-Minute Spanish*

Thus the language displayed in travel guides – and even phrase books and some language courses – is frequently commodified and the opportunity to try out another language is sold (in both senses of the word) as part of the holiday experience. In one sense, it serves to exoticize the destination, to provide the tourist with a *frisson* of *dépaysement* (a – slightly disorienting – change of scenery which may include, among other factors, the physical setting, climate, cuisine, as well as people, language and culture), which is always part of the product to be consumed on holiday. On the other hand, the translations and explanations provided help to make the exotic seem more familiar and less daunting, thus contributing to the all important relaxation aspect of the holiday (cf. Edensor, 2001).

Regardless of the symbolic value of local people in tourist mythology, for the most part they are apparently of real value insofar as they provide a basic service (that is, they serve food, provide a room, can give directions) or perform a cultural token (that is, they demonstrate a greeting ritual, they display...). Following Edward Said (1979: 142), therefore, glossaries present themselves as quintessentially Othering or 'Oriental-izing' technologies whereby the human (that is, host) is transformed into the specimen.

The possibility of discovering the 'true Italy', as Miss Lavish expresses it in *Room With a View*, continues to be the tantalizing object of tourism's desire. This is a yearning which hinges on the tourist never-ending pursuit of authenticity (MacCannell, 1999 [1976]), something numerous scholars have themselves given up hope of determining or admitting as a viable goal in tourism (Boorstin, 1964; Frow, 1997). How-ever, as N. Coupland et al. (2005) have convincingly argued in the context of the richly contested heritage tourism, authenticity, or more appropriately, various layers of authenticit*ies*, are successfully embed-ded in the personal and institutional discourses performing heritage and other forms of tourism, for example, through the materiality of the sites, tourists' routine behaviour, tour guides' talk and banter with the tourists and so on.

In the texts examined in this chapter, the question for us is that of setting conflicting expectations in the mediation of an authentic – or sincere – encounter with hosts. As we have demonstrated, the hyper-bolic promise of 'going native' and the (linguistic) resources put at the tourists' disposal do not often match. In the end, the monolingual tourist *framed* by the guidebook glossary in hand, staggering through the unfamiliar setting of a destination, trying out a few formulaic phrases on a local person may be met with bemused sympathy or genuine offer of help in the situation of crisis (Franklin, 2003). We too have benefited from the combination of kind hosts and an odd phrase picked up from a guidebook glossary in a range of tourist contexts. What we wanted to problematize here, though, is the inevitably consistent format and con-tent of the glossaries in creating a sense of hegemonic ideology in the nature of the host–tourist interaction. In her interpretation of Antonio Gramsci's (1971: 349) notion of hegemony as 'collectively attaining a single cultural "climate" ', Monica Heller (2003b) demonstrates how the dominant categories of francophone identity in Canada are challenged and reshaped through actors' discursive and interactive acts transform-ing their 'collective will' (p. 29). We do not have any data that give us a systematic and reliable access to the way tourists enact their interactions with hosts as mediated through guidebook glossaries. Yet, we argue that whatever the tourist practices in this regard may be (which we offer as a potentially useful and intriguing empirical question), the ubiquity and uniformity of guidebook glossaries constitutes a genre-specific textual frame fostering a 'single cultural 'climate' around host–tourist contact.

As we have seen in other genres of tourism discourse (television holiday shows and newspaper travelogues), these texts construe an ideology of tourism repeatedly premised on a largely asymmetrical model of communication placing the tourist in charge and the host in a subordinate and servile if sympathetic position of the exoticized 'Other'.

> Symbolic capital, a transformed and thereby disguised form of physical 'economic' capital, produces its proper effect inasmuch, and only inasmuch, as it conceals the fact that it originates in 'material' forms of capital which are also, in the last analysis, the source of its effects.
>
> (Bourdieu, 1977: 6, 183)

What we see in guidebooks is yet another instance of the 'language of global mobility' being deployed, and metadiscursively framed, in a way which not only consistently misrepresents the nature of communication (that is, language, social interaction and intercultural exchange), but which, to follow Pierre Bourdieu (1977), repeatedly 'mis-recognizes' the politically and economically (self-)interested practices of tourism discourse. It is precisely in this way that these supposedly 'innocent', 'harmless', 'practical' or 'well-meaning' glossaries of guidebooks legitimate themselves as such, while also constructing powerful (for example, cosmopolitan, commanding, charming) identities for tourists and while reproducing the interactional order and power relations of the tourism economy. In fact, Bourdieu (1990) himself remarks on the tendency under post-industrial capitalism for concealing self-interested privilege and wealth in the symbolic cachet of apparently philanthropic or charitable acts. In this regard, we cannot help but think of 'eco-tourism' and other 'alternative' tourisms; having said which, it is the same kind of 'do-good' or 'global village' rhetoric that often justifies tourism as a whole. It is the same ideology that underpins Mark Twain's (1869) hackneyed sentiment in *The Innocents Abroad*:

> Travel is fatal to prejudice, bigotry, and narrow-mindedness, and many of our people need it sorely on these accounts. Broad, wholesome *charitable* views of men and things cannot be acquired by vegetating in one little corner of the earth all one's lifetime.
>
> (our emphasis)

Tourists and writers are not alone in perpetuating this mythologization of travel in general and of local language play in particular. Phipps (2007: 12) writes eloquently of the 'languaging' of tourism that she characterizes as 'the full, embodied and engaged interaction with the world that comes when we put the languages we are learning into action'. In this case, to be fair, her optimism is directed at those tourists who are motivated to take language classes rather than those who rely on phrasebooks and guidebook glossaries. (Surprisingly, she fails to consider these more informal language-learning practices, which are, no doubt, more common – in both senses of the word.) Nonetheless, Phipps' account of language(s) in tourism presents a kind of Habermasian 'ideal communication' predicated on the privileging and romanticizing of orality (cf. Ong, 1982) and on the assumption (or hope?) that language learning is necessarily a cosmpolitanizing process – the 'good' kind of cosmopolitan that is (cf. Beck, 2002; Featherstone, 2002 – also, Hannerz, 1996). In this regard, her aspirations for language-learning are not dissimilar to the expectations of Mark Twain and the principles of Intercultural Communication scholarship: that contact, 'dialogue' and 'communion' are somehow sufficient conditions for mutual understanding and social change (see Thurlow, 2004, for more on the problems with this perspective). Accordingly, Phipps makes much of the transformative potential in being able to order a coffee in Portugal in Portuguese without appearing to recognize the inherent privilege of this pleasure (that is, of sojourning in Portugal) or its Eurocentrism. (Phipps offers little explanation for her choice of Italian and Portuguese language courses as those she targeted for participant observation – as opposed, say, to ones with less obvious cultural capital or familiarity.) There is also a tremendous, unreflected privilege in the nostalgic yearning of rich-country citizens for orality when so many poor-country citizens seek basic literacy. Ultimately, and in the light of Bourdieu's comments about mis-recognition, it is perhaps telling that Phipps also resorts to framing – and, effectively, legitimizing – her own and tourists' self-interested use of local languages as acts of 'courtesy' and 'charity' (p. 179), however well-intended. As Bourdieu also notes (ibid.: 6), everything typically ends up taking 'place as if agents' practice...were organized exclusively with a view to concealing from themselves and from others the truth of their practice'.

Whatever the motives of individual tourists are, languages and the language learning industry are inevitably and unavoidably caught up in the political economy of global capitalism. And the same is true of the seemingly innocent guidebook glossary. This hand-in-glove relationship manifests itself overtly in the modern history of language learning as an offshoot of World War II-related military needs and the commercial-cum-diplomatic interests of Cold War US politics. And language learning is not less embedded within the industrial-military complex today, as the following two examples show. First, from a 2007 press release by one of the world's largest language-learning corporations:

> Rosetta Stone Inc., creator of the No. 1 language-learning software, has leveraged its revolutionary language-learning platform to offer a military-specific program: *Arabic – Military Edition*.[9]

Then this from a 2007 article in the business section of the *New York Times* titled 'Not lost in translation: A few phrases in another language can go a long way':

> With corporate travelers now doing business in all four points of the globe, developing some fluency in foreign languages is getting to be as important as taking along a laptop on an overseas trip. On a visit to Moscow a friendly *kak dela* (how are you doing?) can be an icebreaker when meeting a Russian contact, and an *obrigado* (thank you) when you exit a session in São Paulo may be just enough Portuguese to charm your Brazilian host.[10]

Whether it is a tourist ordering coffee in Lisbon or a business person exiting a meeting in São Paulo, a grasp of Portuguese – phrasebook or classroom learned – serves primarily as an act of traveller identification in the service of self-interested 'convergence' needs (cf. Le Page and Tabouret-Keller, 1985; Giles et al., 1991; Kristiansen and Giles, 1992), as does the US soldier's use of Arabic on the streets of Baghdad. In the not-so-particular context of tourism, local languages present themselves as something of a contradiction: on the one hand, they are a highly desirable eroticizing resource to be enjoyed and, on the other hand, they are an inconvenient obstacle – or threat – to be overcome. In either case, efforts to master [sic] these languages continue, in the best/worst traditions of colonialism (cf. Pennycook, 1989; 1994), to be a methodology for the taming or 'conquering' of other peoples.

Conclusion
Tourism Discourse and Banal Globalization

> ...banal nationalism cover[s] the ideological habits which enable the established nations of the West to be reproduced.... these habits are not removed from everyday life, as some observers have supposed. Daily, the nation is indicated, or 'flagged', in the lives of its citizenry. Nationalism, far from being an intermittent mood in established nations, is the endemic condition.
>
> – Billig, 1995: 6.

> ... 'banal' cosmopolitanism occurs beneath the surfaces, behind the persisting facades of national spaces and sovereignties where the main signifiers on display continue to proclaim national mentalities, identities and forms of consciousness.
>
> – Beck, 2004: 134.

At one point, we had thought of using the phrase 'banal globalization' for the title of this book; that we didn't had more to do with the logistics of publication, because our original reasons for liking the phrase have remained unchanged. Instead, we use it here as a way to round off the book, reflecting on some of the central themes or topics that have arisen in the previous six chapters as well as moving ourselves a little nearer to the more ethnographic, sociolinguistic dimension of our research covered in Jaworski, Thurlow and Ylänne (forthcoming). We also want to return to the 'bigger picture' for a moment.

The first, and most straightforward reason for invoking the notion of 'banal globalization' is to put our ideas into conversation with Mike Billig's well-known thesis on 'banal nationalism' (Billig, 1995) and Ulrich Beck's more recent thinking about 'banal cosmopolitanism'

(Beck, 2002, 2004, 2006; Beck and Sznaider, 2006).[1] For Billig, 'banality' refers to the everyday representations and discursive accomplishments of national identity; for example, displaying flags in house windows, international football matches, 'national' weather maps on TV and in newspapers, popular expressions and turns of phrase and so on. The power and influence of banal nationalism lies precisely in its ubiquity, repetition, ordinariness and familiarity and, thus, its tendency to go largely unnoticed. These performances of national identity are in contrast to – but complicitously implicated in – large-scale, state-organized or sanctioned structures (for example, immigrant control), as well as the more obvious, aggressive performances of nationalism by extremist or separatist groups (for example, the British National Party). For Billig, it is the more covert, unremarkable, unquestioned nature of the many contemporary nationalisms that gives them their ideological power. Like Billig, we too are convinced that – based on our own empirical evidence – the nation state is by no means in decline as a hugely influential organizing principle. We return to the issue of the nation in just a moment.

In his notion of 'banal cosmopolitanism', Ulrich Beck invokes the banal partly in the same sense as Billig talks of the everyday routinization of nationalism, but also in contradiction to it. The banality of cosmopolitanism is, for Beck, also a matter of its undermining and circumventing nationalism through the mundane, localized manifestations and experiences of 'global processes and phenomena' (Beck, 2002: 28), such as popular music and food (cf. Tomlinson, 1999; Pennycook, 2007). However, Beck also means to distinguish this kind of cosmopolitanism – what he calls 'really existing cosmopolitanism or the cosmopolitanization of reality' (Beck, 2006: 18) – from the kind of abstracted cosmopolitanism (he uses the term 'normative') which promotes an ideal of international and intercultural harmony. This second kind of 'philosophical' cosmopolitanism he dismisses as an elitist one of choice as opposed the first kind of 'social scientific' cosmopolitanism which is instead a matter of coerced choice and unconscious decisions. This is an everyday, banal cosmopolitanism that arises as a direct and unavoidable consequence of the *reality* of 'global flows', currents of information, symbols, money, education, risks and people (Beck, 2002: 29). It is the 'natural' consequence of globalization and the concommitant de-territorialization of the nation state. Beck thus sees banal cosmopolitanism *replacing* banal nationalism.

In keeping with some of these ideas of Billig and Beck, we choose to invoke the banal ourselves for framing and understanding tourism discourse as rooted in everyday, textual enactments of globalization, be they institutional, interpersonal or mediatized. By 'everyday', we do not mean to say that these enactments are either foolish or inconsequential: on the contrary. It is, we suggest, at the level of 'innocent' texts and 'harmless' (inter)actions that globalization – or, more precisely, global capitalism – is actually realized. These discursive practices may well be trite (for example, postcards, newspaper travelogues, guidebooks) but they are far from trivial. Just as 'small talk' is always pragmatically speaking 'big talk' (J. Coupland, 2000) and just as reiterative performances of gender solidify and naturalize the 'heteronormative matrix' (Butler, 1990), so too do the mundane genres and textual practices of tourism turn out to be *global* in their reach and in their impact.

It is not only Bill Gates, Ban Ki-moon or Barak Obama who 'do' globalization, who make it happen; nor is it they alone who should be held responsible for its 'human consequences' (Bauman, 1998). First of all, it is 'we' who invest these leaders with the power they have through our political or consumer choices. These individual names are after all only metonymic substitutes for institutions and the organized collectives whose interests they represent and protect (that is, industrialists, politicians, CEOs of large multinational corporations, lobbyists and NGOs). Second, we greatly misunderstand the nature and power of globalization and global capitalism if we also fail to see our own complicity and the ways in which these same political-economic realities (and inequalities) are realized in small, mundane, everyday, social (inter)actions of our 'ordinary' lives.

In taking up the term 'banal globalization', we therefore mean to align ourselves with both Billig and Beck insofar as the everyday experiences and mundane enactments of global capitalism are concerned. However, we are less certain of the strong de-territorialization position that Beck adopts. Nor is he alone: David Harvey, for example, talks of the 'annihilation of temporal and spatial barriers' (Harvey, 1990: 278; see also Bauman, 2000). Part of our unease with this stance is that, in our own data, we find signs that nationalism – banal or otherwise – is far from replaced and often only temporarily *displaced* (see Sheller and Urry, 2006, on 'reterritorialization'; also our own Chapter 3). This is not to say that we deny the kinds of global flows that Beck describes (see also Appadurai, 1996) and the kinds of heightened 'liquidity', about which Bauman (2000) writes; these are undoubtedly real and unquestionably have real consequences.

Notwithstanding our reservations about de-territorialization, we do see a number of different ways in which nationality, cosmopolitanism and globalization are connected to, and realized in, tourism discourse; the contours of this 'banal globalization' we can outline in the following interwoven statements of principle:

- The political economy and the material consequences of *global capitalism* are represented by and organized through *globalization* as a neoliberal ideology (or system of representation and legitimation) about/in the service of global capitalism (cf. Fairclough, 2002, 2003). Globalization discourse unavoidably establishes relations of power and inequality that inevitably favour capital.
- Globalization and global capitalism are *banally* enacted (or performatively produced) in everyday, routinized, individual, textual practices; as such, they have as much to do with *communication* (that is, everyday social interactions) as they do with *communications* (that is, mass media and technologies). Globalization is thereby a micro-level, textual accomplishment as well as a macro-level multinational or governmental one.
- Tourism, as the world's single largest international trade and as a truly global cultural industry (Urry, 2002), is a major site (a social, cultural and economic domain) for the banal enactments of globalization. Tourism is a deeply 'semiotic industry' committed to the production, commodification and representation of culture and cultural *difference*; language is clearly an essential resource in this cultural production.
- Nationalism, with its tropes of 'pure culture' and 'cultural ownership', is still a major semiotic resource and organizing principle in/for tourism. Constantly needing to (re)produce *difference* (something 'exotic') and *distance* ('away from home'), tourism relies on being able to accentuate or de-accentuate nationality, internationality and globality for strategic effect. Nationality is thus 'globalized' through its commodification and promotion – its being sold back to people – in tourism discourse's performance of cosmopolitan, 'global' identities.
- Tourism discourse both produces and draws on the mythologies of cosmopolitanism as a principal legitimation strategy and as a marketing ploy. Like cosmopolitanism, tourism discourse (and its agents) may be charged with perpetuating a bourgeois, racialized, gendered idealization/romanticization of mobility (cf. Kaplan, 1996; Ahmed, 2000; Skeggs, 2004); it does so largely at the expense of, or to the exclusion of, those who don't get to travel for leisure, those people on the move who don't come home at the end of the stay.

- The mythology of cosmopolitanism is central to both globalization and tourism discourse as an aspirational identity/marketing strategy; however, it is the most abstracted, aestheticized, 'global-village' kind of cosmopolitanism that usually unites the two discourses. This easy cosmopolitanism (or 'cosmopolitanism lite') seeks only the most contained, risk-free kind of difference – 'friendly locals', 'safe adventures' and so on. To borrow phrases used by others, this type of cosmopolitanism represents little more than 'global sampling' (Hutnyk, 2000: 22) or 'coffee-table globalism' (Roberts, 1998: 67).

As a staunch proponent of de-territorialization, Ulrich Beck (2002: 31) bluntly asks, 'So why do we expect that political loyalties and identities will continue to be tied exclusively to a nation?' Well, as far as tourism is concerned, one might simply answer that this is because there is still *frisson* or cultural capital to be had from the crossing of borders, from the experience of Otherness (theirs and mine) and from the exoticization of 'different' cultures. A longer answer might also comment on the economic – not to mention political and military – gain to be had. It's a little too soon to be dancing on the grave of nationalisms – banal or otherwise (witness, for example, the efforts to get the planet out of the 'global' economic crisis in 2009 orchestrated as a meeting of the twenty most powerful *national* economies). The imagination that imagines nations is still hard at work. This is not to say that location remains such a determining factor or that collectivity isn't being diversified.

The significance of national points of reference in the otherwise 'global' discourses of tourism appears to be at the forefront of much of our own analysis. In Chapter 1, for example, we considered how the unifying genre of inflight magazines (with their huge investment in international English) constructs the cosmopolitan, global jet-setter as transcending national boundaries. In fact, we could argue that there would be no cosmopolitan traveller if there were no national boundaries to cross in the first place. As such, and with reference to the frequent claims of globalization, we find ourselves in agreement with Hannerz (1996: 90) who continues to view the nation as an important point of reference for the construction of individual and group subjectivities. Given their ubiquity and the consistency of their format, it is tempting to think of inflight magazines as embodying concerns expressed by global sceptics or critics about the levelling or 'smothering' effects of so-called 'global culture' (Appadurai, 1990; Held and McGrew, 2000). According to the perspective taken by 'globalists', globalization – both cultural and economic – is driven more by companies than by countries these days (Held and McGrew, 2000: 17). Nevertheless, it seems that countries still continue to direct companies. Structures of sovereignty and national identity may be shifting (Heller, 2010b) but nation states evidently remain important in wielding political and military power (Giddens, 1999), and especially in some areas of cultural-media production such as the national press and sports (cf. Bishop and Jaworski, 2003). As we have found in the inflight magazines, the nation continues to work as an important cultural resource – the (inter)national 'flag-carrier' is itself a manifestation of this impulse. According to James Lull (2001: 153), appealing to nationality gives people a necessary 'shared sense of difference', and, as Stuart Hall (1991: 22) notes, identity is inevitably 'negotiated against difference'.

The national as a basis for tourist Self- and Other-identification is likewise manifested in our Chapters 4, 5 and 6, where we focus on the *representations* and *imaginations* of host–tourist interactions. Tourists crossing into local languages merely stylize themselves as hosts in playful moments of liminal/liminoid suspension of their true (or technical) *national* identities, and these exchanges are pre-figured by the pervasive ethnotyping of hosts (for example, 'Italians are passionate about food', p. 172; 'Italians are noisy by nature and so are children', p. 147), the mapping of languages onto national speech communities (for example, 'Although many Mexicans speak some English, it is good to have some basic Spanish phrases at your disposal ...' p. 203), or by hosts positioning themselves as members of national groups ('Harvey Nichols Gambia Branch', Figure 2.7, p. 64). Meanwhile, traders in Gambia buy into the myth of global citizenship through their knowledge of the commercial landscape in the UK (in the same way as the traders in Senegal use the references from France). Gambians too stylize themselves 'global' through their use of English, which is of course part of their post-colonial legacy, but especially through their displays of cultural references to English football, weather, geography and so on (cf. Lawson and Jaworski, 2007). However, knowing this, with few exceptions, the asymmetry of economic globalization does not allow them to shrug off their territorialized (or territorially constrained) national identity as 'Gambians'.

National identities are also reconfirmed and maintained in more localized forms of mobility where hosts and locals view themselves and their language varieties as 'same' – as in the case of Polish agritourism (Jaworski and Lawson, 2005). Hosts and tourists participate in the co-construction of a shared, albeit imagined national identity (cf. Anderson, 1983), in the newly discovered 'friendships' of like-minded peers through a shared local language. In this sense, therefore, the contemporary appeal of national identity may be regarded not only in terms of a reactionary, defensive response to fears and anxieties about the 'runaway world' of globalization (Giddens, 1999). The nation (and national identity) is instead re-imagined as a means of experiencing and expressing the 'international' and the 'global'.

In fact, in dismissing some of the exaggerated claims of, or anxieties about, globalization, Anthony Smith (2000: 180) notes that the 'greatest obstacle' to the emergence of any putative 'global culture' is the persistence of modern and even pre-modern myths and sentiments. From what we have begun to see in the different data examples we discuss here, the tenacity of national identity is apparent – and clearly desirable to many. Tourism may promote an aura of globe-trotting and tourists (or local people) may aspire to jet-setter lifestyles, but nationality still has a strong hold on subjectivities and offers, offering itself as an important point of reference. In this way, and just as Smith (2000) talks about the nationalization of pre-modern ethnicities from the 19th century onwards, there appears to be a *globalization of nationality* which puts a 'global' spin on traditional, modernist constructs such as nation state and national language.

It is precisely for this reason also that, just as Rampton (1995) argues for linguistic crossing to create new 'inter-ethnicites', we propose that tourist crossing – both linguistic and territorial – creates *new internationalisms*, which entail tourists playing with global identities but not fully embracing them (Chapters 4 and 5) and exploiting the double standard of dealing with the 'exotic' in a familiar semiotic landscape (Chapter 2). While the popular notion of the 'international jet-setter' is a largely modernist construct relying as it does on earlier discourses of the nation state and of elite, privileged technologies of travel, it is precisely this 'ideal' to which new internationals aspire through the mediated, consumerist discourses of glossy magazines, celebrity-oriented TV holiday shows and so on. In fact, we would further argue that appeals to global citizenship are fundamental to both the economy of global capitalism and the mythology of globalization; nevertheless, it is an image and identity that remain rooted in structuring processes of national identification. We therefore agree with Lull's (2001: 15–16) observation that '[n]ation is a discursive product that is perpetually marketed back to its own people and to other nations. Nation thus continues to function as a defining, unifying, reinforcing, reassuring socio-political and cultural resource of extraordinary importance'.

Certainly, in the semiotic landscape of tourism, much of what takes the appearance of being global is, more often than not, tour operators, tourists and hosts in pursuit of the *cachet* of globalization and the *cash* of global capital. All the while, it is implicit that the context and conditions for social life are shifting and being steadily transformed as a result of the economic and ideological re-orderings of global capitalism and worldwide interconnectedness of capital and (mass) communication (Thompson, 2000). At the level of human interaction, however, we are less certain of the kind of interconnectedness invoked by the popular notion of the 'global village', which appears to remain more at the level of myth than universal reality. In other words, it is *aspirational* rather than actual, with people talking globalization into existence. For us, then, tourism sustains globalization as a discourse, and ideological construction, an identity resource.

Like Michael Billig (also a discourse analyst), the appeal of 'banal globalization' is partly motivated by our methodological preference for a *linguistically-oriented*, micro-analysis of everyday discourse. It is in this way that we believe we are able to both complicate and contribute to the broad, generalizations of social theory – and, especially, globalization theory – by attending to the 'on-the-ground' *texturing* of both tourism and global capitalism. In other words, our work as critical discourse analysts directs us to examine the properties of texts (for example, lexical, grammatical and code choices), the organization of communicative practices (for example, the spread of different formats and design features in multimodal texts), the discursive representation and construction of discourses (for example, nationalism, neoliberalism, globalization, global capitalism). At each turn, we want to understand how ideologies and hegemonic inequalities are represented in texts – whether spoken or written, mediatized or mulitmodal – but also how the same texts are involved in the (re)production of these ideologies and hegemonic inequalities. What makes this work interesting is that the 'hidden agendas' we mean to reveal are, almost always, right in front of our noses and not so hidden after all. They reveal themselves partly through an academic attention to detail, and a critical eye for repetition and patterning.

An approach like this and a book such as ours clearly presents opportunities as well as limitations. As we acknowledged from the start, we do not claim to represent all tourisms or all tourists. In working across a selection of very common tourist genres, our goal has been to examine *some* of the ways tourism, as a mode of global mobility, is commonly textualized (that is, represented and discursively organized). This, we believe, provides a unique mapping of the kinds of global processes and rhetorical strategies which underpin the symbolic economy and language ideologies of both tourism and globalization. To this end, we have analysed and interpreted each genre with the help of key sociolinguistic and discourse analytic concepts, and by framing these with relevant social/critical theoretical perspectives. The underlying questions that have concerned us throughout are, in simple terms, these:

- What is the role of language in tourism?
- How is language represented in tourism discourse?
- How does language shape the discourses of tourism?
- How is globalization represented in tourism discourse?
- How does tourism discourse shape the discourses of globalization?
- What is the role of discourse in globalization?

In addressing these questions and by offering some tentative answers in our analytic chapters, we have also tried to maintain a balance between representing different points of view and subject positions. The three chapters in Part I were deliberately chosen to articulate three different 'voices' or agentive types involved in the global re-orderings of every-day life. The institutional voice in Chapter 1 was represented through the self-presentation of airlines in their inflight magazines. The voice of hosts was present in the commercial signs and business cards of Gambian entrepreneurs. Finally, the voice of tourists was heard in our analysis of postcard messages. Moving on to Part II, we considered three different media formats – TV holiday shows in Chapter 4; news-paper travelogues in Chapter 5; language glossaries in guidebooks in Chapter 6 – with a specific focus on the representation of language and linguistic interactions *between* hosts and tourists. Therefore, in Part I, cutting across different genres, we identified communicative strategies through which various 'players' of globalization stylize themselves and their intended addressees as such, and in Part II, we examined the mediatized *models* of interactions between these global players.

In seeking the economic and cultural capital to be made through the opportunities afforded by globalization, we find a number of similar themes and discourses running through the different genres and media formats. One is, as suggested above, the pervasive interplay between the discourses of nationality and cosmopolitanism. And it is through the micro-analysis of our textual data that we see how the paradoxes, ten-sions, ironies or dialectics of globalization are at work. In other words, our 'middle-ground' position aligns with Mimi Sheller and John Urry's (2006) 'new mobilities' paradigm, accepting the need to reconsider all aspects of social life through an anti-sedantrist perspective but without subscribing to an extreme de-territorializing view of globalization. This, we believe, is what is borne out in the recurring balancing act between the global and the local in our data. In fact, and as we noted above (see especially Chapter 3), we have attempted to demonstrate empirically the textual enactments of post-modern 'interspatiality', as well as to make a broader claim that there is in fact no other way to manifest and make sense of these interspatial relations other than through discourse. Getting on an international flight, visiting an exotic souvenir market or even 'having lunch with the Disney characters' (p. 115), is only prefigured in, and made meaningful through, the mytholgies or ideologies of travel surrounding acts of physical, sensory, embodied movement, transaction and consumption.

What we see in the different genres of tourism discussed in Chapters 1–3 is the commonality of different tropes and points of reference signposting globalization as an identity resource for the imagined community of practice of tourists (or self-styled cosmopolitans). At a very general level these are: homogenizing textual formats (genres) for 'doing' globalization; globalization of the nation; heavy mediation of aspirational 'global' identities; and pervasive orientation to 'home' – the 'here-and-there-ness' – implied and acted out in the moments of travel and international encounters.

Likewise, in Chapters 4–6, we find time-and-time again instances of mediated interactions recontextualizing and commodifying language as play, a symbolic resource for tourists to imagine themselves as a global community of practice moving freely, effortlessly and pleasurably across spaces of ethnic, linguistic and cultural difference. Thus, in reflecting on some of the different issues, topics or 'findings' in our six, closely related case studies, we see three major, interlocking themes emerging that point us to ways textual practices mediate and establish the symbolic/cultural capitals of tourism and its 'regimes of truth' (Foucault, 1980) about global mobility in general: language, identity and relationship. To recap:

(1) Language, alongside other semiotic modes, works in the textual mediation of global mobility by promoting the ideology of globalization and 'textualizing' all tourism, especially relying on homogenizing the textual formats (genres) of the discourses on the move. Different genres, codes, styles and registers are recontextualized, borrowed and hybridized, frequently implying language learning, primacy of form over meaning, relational (yet commodified) goals

overriding instrumental ones (masquerading as 'friendship'), 'playing' with language rather than 'owning' language as linguascape in the production of difference and distinction. Yet, the dominant ideologies of language such as the clear hierarchy of languages for communication (in our data it is predominantly English) and languages for play (all the others) is firmly rooted in the language market where specific linguistic items and repertoires have real value embedded in the broader market of economic exchange and tourism industry. Language is both a commodity and a means of other commodity exchanges.

All of these linguistic processes have a profound effect on the re-ordering of space, creating new sense of place-ness while new linguistic styles and genres come to be enacted and consumed in private, public, commercial and media contexts. Blommaert et al. (2005) develop the idea of space as organized along different hierarchically ordered scales of social structure (for example, local, national, transnational, global, ethnic, political and so on). These scalar spaces are filled with various sorts of material and symbolic attributes and constitute an active, contextualizing (Gumperz 1982; Goodwin and Duranti, 1992) semiotic source of indexical meaning; while people move between differently ordered spaces, they effect different indexical values providing meaning to individual, situated acts of linguistic behaviour. Movement through space of linguistic and communicative resources and skills affects the value of the linguistic skills and repertoires of speakers. For example, commercial texts, such as trade signs and business cards discussed in Chapter 2 or postcard messages discussed in Chapter 3, become indexes of new place-based and personal identities, signalling economic disparities, local and global allegiances of social actors and vast differences in their cultural capital.

(2) Tourist identities are refashioned as an imagined, global communities of practice. Being a tourist involves learning how to be a tourist, how to look for, read, interpret cultural signs, symbols and artefacts, and how to speak, write and interact in tourist spaces. The acts of learning are typically framed as acts of 'crossing' and identity play, frequently aiming to elevate Self at the expense of Other. Yet, old allegiances appear intact, as tourists' transient here-and-there identities are underpinned by the promise and desire to return 'home' – the most coveted of all places.

Thus, in responding to Ulrich Beck's adage that 'The national outlook ... is becoming false' (Beck, 2006: 18), we re-emphasize the sentiment expressed by Julia Harrison (2003: 9) insisting that it is only the 'vagabonds' (to use Bauman's phrase) who are the real transnationals. They, she argues, are materially uprooted, unanchored: they don't have homes to go back to, no pension schemes to draw on, their sense of identity, of citizenship, is involuntarily dislocated and often irreversibly so. Everyone else, as Bauman says, is a 'tourist'.

(3) Tourism relationships are premised on a neocolonial myth of contact. The light-hearted, ludic and fleeting encounters between tourists and hosts across all our data (see especially Part II) suggest *encounters* not relationships, *contact* not engagement, *service* not commitment. These forms of interactions are pre-figured by the mythologies of tourism premised on the idea of tourists 'going native', yet the tourist industry is one of cultural otherness (Favero, 2007), where 'new' interactions are highly scripted and take place in a succession of brief, stylized encounters. Governed by and perpetuating global inequalities, the neocolonial agenda driving tourism offers globalization as a lifestyle resource, yet in most types of mass tourism only one party in the encounter may exercise a discourse of mastery, while the other must appear (self-style) as subservient, romanticized, eroticized and pre-modern.

As ways of contemplating cultural difference in the contemporary globalized habitats of the world, the touristic ways of seeing leave us with localities and individuals emptied of their political dimensions and, thus, of the links holding them together. Only in such a way can the world appear to us as a beautiful sight, devoid of all disturbing post-colonial tensions of politics, injustice, poverty, dependency and subalterneity that characterize it. This is indeed a 'wonderful world', but unfortunately what we 'see', is not all there is to 'know' about it (Favero, 2007: 77)

And so to finish, we will step back a little from our data, our texts, to view things with a more overtly critical eye and to consider briefly where we may be headed next.

Tourism discourse, it seems, finds itself caught between, on the one hand, its deep-seated mythology, its own aspirational marketing of 'cosmopolitization' (the promise of intercultural contact and understanding) and, on the other hand, its old-fashioned, elitist cosmopolitanism that Mike Featherstone (2002: 1) caricatures as the voyeuristic, parasitic cultural tourist who 'dabbles rootlessly in a variety of cultures' and is marked by their 'incapacity to form lasting attachments and commitments to place and others [and an] inability to participate in a community for which one feels obliged to make sacrifices.'

As an aside, the new wave of 'luxury' tourism appears to do away altogether with the pretence of intercultural encounter and any superficial engagement with local culture (see Thurlow and Jaworski, 2006, 2010; Jaworski and Thurlow, 2009b). While Phaedra Pezzullo's (2007) fascinating work points to some of the more reassuringly positive opportunities for contact in contemporary travel, the rise of high-end, super-elite travel is unabashedly about 'me' – about *my* well-being, *my* needs, *my* preferences, *my* space, *my* cultural enrichment and *my* spiritual enlightenment. It is seldom about 'our' (that is, other tourists) and it barely is ever about 'their' (that is, local people). There is no 'dialogical imagination' (Beck, 2002: 18) in luxury travel, partly because there is no dialogue and partly because any of the 'contradictions within and between cultures' (which Beck describes) are so completely sanitized or so highly aestheticized.

In many ways, we might think of (much) contemporary tourism as a kind of colonial backlash, a reaction to the discomfort experienced as a result of the gradual decentring and de-privileging of the old power bases. In these terms, tourism discourse is to global inequality as colour blindness is to racism; where the one hinges on its mythology of interculturality, the other relies on its rhetoric of multiculturalism. Yet both are neoliberal, neocolonial slights of hand conveniently serving the interests of the privileged (those who choose to travel and those who pass as 'un-raced') by usually concealing their historical origins and material consequences, and by 'containing' difference under an earnest guise of celebration and respect (cf. hooks, 1992; Jordan and Weedon, 1995).[2] If, as the rumbling Euro-American rhetoric would have it, China is in the economic ascendancy; one way to contain it, to massage our fear of this unknown, is to know it, to visit it, to tour it – in other words, to turn it into a destination, a playground, a spectacle. And, if 'travel broadens the mind' and exposes us to 'different cultures', how can our travels be a bad thing?

Since the early 1990s, discourse analysts have been tracking – and exposing – the complex, contradictory ways people find to express racist attitudes while professing not to be racists in the face of a collective disapprobation of racism (van Dijk, 1992; Wetherell and Potter, 1992). In a supposedly post-colonial world that appears to promote the notions of 'global village' and 'global warming', we are similarly faced with the challenge of reconciling our culpability and responsibility. Like complex

'I'm not a racist, but…' discourses, tourism discourse offers an all too human way out, reinventing itself according to the times: 'eco-tourism', 'alternative tourism', 'sustainable tourism' and so on. Meanwhile, 'cultural tourism' (or 'ethno-tourism') recasts itself as 'township tourism', 'educational tourism', 'heritage tourism' or 'toxic tourism'. Even the seemingly carefree 'luxury tourism' is reorganizing itself nostalgically around *Out of Africa* safaris, *Golden Age* cruises and *Grand Tours*. The colonial past is thus commodified, romanticized and unapologetically marketed back to the children, grandchildren and great-grandchildren of the old Empires. Who could have imagined that the US decedents of slaves would nowadays find themselves crossing the Atlantic as 'slave tourists' to Gambia? Tourism discourse is perfectly suited for the age of flexible accumulation; it is quick to identify and leverage symbolic capital from just about anything, anywhere and anyone. Everything, everywhere and everyone is a potential destination.

Appendix
Summary of Data and Analytic Procedures

Chapter 1

Based on several online listings (for example, Swartz 1999; Mosley 2001), we approached approximately 120 international airlines for copies of their most recent inflight magazines. Of these, 72 airlines responded and sent us copies of their magazines (an alphabetical listing of these airlines and their country of origin is presented below). With only one or two exceptions, all the inflight magazines were from June/July/August 2001 and represented the following crudely delineated regions: Asia and Australasia/Oceania ($n = 14$), Africa and Middle East ($n = 15$), Americas and Caribbean ($n = 11$), and, accounting for almost half of the data-set, Europe ($n = 32$). This uneven geographical spread is itself representative of the unequal distribution of the international airline industry as a whole, and, in a broader sense, of the asymmetrical patterning of global flows.

All 72 magazines were analysed by two principal raters and two secondary raters using content analytic procedures, and coding for categories such as the names of magazines, the wording of any cover strap lines, the use of forms of address in welcome letters, the principle images used on covers and the language(s) used throughout each magazine. More specifically, the format of each magazine was also carefully coded to identify each of its main components (for example, feature articles, adverts, airline information, inflight entertainment). Feature articles were also coded for their content in order to identify the relative thematic orientation of the magazine – principally in terms of domestic and foreign coverage.

Airlines from which magazines were obtained

Adria Airways (Slovenia)
Aer Lingus (Ireland)
Aeroflot (Russia)
Air Atlanta (Iceland)
Air Baltic (Latvia)
Air Canada
Air France
Air Malta
Air New Zealand

Air Zimbabwe
Alitalia (Italy)
American Airlines
ANA (Japan)
Austrian Airlines
Avianca (Colombia)
BMI (UK)
British Airways
BWIA (West Indies)
Cathay Pacific (Hong Kong)
Continental Airlines (USA)
COPA Airlines (Panama)
Croatia Airlines
ČSA Czech Airlines
Cyprus Air (Greek)
Delta Airlines (USA)
EgyptAir
El Al (Isreael)
Emirates (UAE)
Estonian Airways
Ethiopian Airlines
EVA Air (Taiwan)
Finnair (Finland)
Garuda Indonesia
Gulf Air (Bharain)
Iberia (Spain)
Icelandair
Iran Air
JAL (Japan)
JAT (Serbia/Yugoslavia)
Kenya Airways
KLM (Netherlands)
Korean Air
Kuwait Airways
LAB (Bolivia)
Lithuanian Airlines
LOT Polish Airlines
Malaysia
Malev (Hungary)
MEA (Lebanon)
Northwest Airlines (USA)
Olympic (Greece)
Polynesian Airlines
Qantas (Australia)
Qatar Airways
Royal Air Maroc (Marocco)
Royal Brunei
Royal Jordanian
Sabena (Belgium)

SAS (Scandinavia)
Singapore Airlines
South African Airways
Sri Lankan Airlines
Swissair
TAP (Portugal)
TAROM (Romania)
Thai Airways
Tunis Air
Turkish Airlines
Ukraine International Airways
United Airlines (USA)
USAir (USA)
Virgin Atlantic (UK)

Across the whole sample, the total number of feature articles devoted to *foreign* travel destinations was 126; these were divided into two categories: (a) cities ($n = 68$; 54 per cent) and (b) continents, countries, regions, states, archipelagos and islands ($n = 58$; 46 per cent). Destinations covered in feature articles across all the magazines were as follows: Cities: London (8), Madrid (6), New York and Paris (5), Rome (4), Hong Kong and Budapest (3), Beijing, Berlin, Buenos Aires, Cairo, Chicago, Milan and Taipei (2), Amsterdam, Bangkok, Barcelona, Beirut, Cancún, Cape Town, Dubai, Düsseldorf, El Salvador, Kraków, Lagos, Las Vegas, Lisbon, Manchester, Munich, Moscow, New Delhi, Santiago, Seoul, Shanghai, Singapore, Strasbourg, Tokyo, Venice and Vienna (1). Countries and so on: France (6), USA (5), UK (4), Australia, California, New Zealand and Spain (3), China, Indonesia, Italy and Japan (2), Africa, The Azores, Canada, Egypt, Germany, Greece, Hungary, India, Jordan, Korea, Madeira, Malawi, Laos, Russia, Scandinavia, Serbia, Surinam, Tahiti, Taiwan, Thailand, Togo, Vietnam and Zambia (1).

Nine categories of cover image were identified, as summarized in Table 1.1. In each case, 'celebrity' was taken to mean either an internationally or nationally recognized or otherwise public figure – usually someone featured inside the magazine. The remaining covers featuring people involve visually identifiable but otherwise unnamed models, usually women, and in several other cases children

Table 1.1   Categories and distribution of cover images

Non-specific/non-photographic design	$n = 18$	25%
Landscape	$n = 17$	24%
Female celebrity	$n = 10$	14%
Female other	$n = 6$	8%
Male celebrity	$n = 7$	7%
Male other	$n = 2$	3%
People as scenery	$n = 8$	11%
Child	$n = 3$	4%
Male & female celebrity	$n = 1$	1%

Table 1.2   Principal content categories of inflight magazines

1. Travel and destination information (for example, general tourist features, travelogues, specific articles about cities or places covered by the airline's network)
2. Lifestyle/ 'culture' (for example, features on fashion, food and drink, films, interviews)
3. Games (for example, some sort of puzzle or crossword)
4. Passenger/inflight information (for example, practical information about airports, visas, local climate and currency)
5. Airline news (for example, new routes, mergers, code-sharing agreements)
6. Business information (for example, information about international finance and investments, and interview articles with business people)

and men. In a separate category, we have included covers representing people as 'scenery', that is, images where people are not the main content and are usually depicted in groups, in a long shot and generally more anonymously than the individual models. The remaining two categories, accounting for nearly a half of all the covers in the sample, are landscapes and other inanimate images such as food and drink, aeroplanes and so on.

Chapter 2

The data discussed in this chapter was collected as part of Adam's field trip to Gambia 23 October–7 November 2003. The images from Senegal were taken by our research associate Sarah Lawson in October 2003.

Chapter 3

Our original corpus consisted of 609 postcards sent by friends, relatives and work colleagues to recipients in the UK (or now residing in the UK) while on holiday, although 61 of the cards were from work-related trips, such as conferences and extended fieldwork abroad, and six of the cards in the corpus were sent from senders' visits to see family. The cards were collected by Virpi and with the help of Sarah Lawson (our research associate at the time) using a snowball technique, starting with personal contacts and then through inviting departmental administrators at Cardiff University to hand over any cards being displayed on their office notice boards. The corpus was first coded electronically; both sides of the cards were scanned and stored. The written texts were then coded using semantic categories to enable subsequent more detailed content- and other corpus-based analyses. The topics covered in the postcard texts were initially mapped out in a content analysis; we then examined the writers' discursive identifications of themselves, the recipients and aspects of the trip/holiday. The analytic categories we refer to in Chapter 3 emerged from this process and the extracts reproduced preserve the senders' original spelling and layout. In Table 3.2, we show a summary of the main topics covered across the corpus.

Table 3.1   Primary themes of postcards' front-side images

urban/town/village	190 (32%)
Sea view	128 (21%)
rural/wildlife	125 (21%)
famous site	63 (11%)
local people	26 (4%)
hotel	10 (2%)
map	10 (2%)
cartoon	9 (1.5%)
fictitious characters	9 (1.5%)
souvenirs, local artefacts	4 (0.7%)
painting	4 (0.7%)
food	3 (0.5%)
other	15 (2.5%)

Table 3.2   Postcard message categories and frequency of occurrence

Category	Number of occurrences
Activities	348
Weather	305
'Revoir' (see you soon)	221
Place	200
General comments about holiday	199
Phatic comment	180
In-group joke/joke	160
Reference to picture	147
Food and drink	125
Nature, landscape	104
Accommodation	92
Journey	86
Greeting	61
Reference to locals	30
Health	19
Reference to other tourists	16
Reference to tourist experience	12
Learning a foreign language	6

We also broadly categorized the range of images shown on the front sides of the postcards (Table 3.1).

Chapter 4

Newspaper sources

Anderson, A. 2002. Park and ride. *The Guardian*. 23 February 2002. pp. 16–17. (Location: Swiss Alps).

Anderson, Alf. 2004. The right kind of snow. *The Guardian.* 13 March 2004. pp. 12–13. (Location: Swiss Alps Grindelwald).

Anonymous. 2005. Gluhwein snifters. *The Sunday Times.* 6 November 2005. p. 27. (Location: Swiss Alps).

Ashdown, Paddy. 2002. If this is faking it, then I'm all for it. *The Independent.* 3 February 2002. p. 19. (Location: Swiss Alps).

Barrell, Sarah. 2001. La dolce vita. *The Guardian.* 3 February 2001. pp. 4–5. (Location: Italy).

Bleach, Stephen. 2002. On the cheap. *The Sunday Times Travel.* 28 January 2001. p. 9. (Location: Bangkok).

Boase, Tessa. 2001. Feelgood factory. *The Guardian.* 3 February 2001. p. 12. (Location: Italy).

Boase, Tessa. Upstairs downstairs in Mafia country. *The Daily Telegraph Travel.* 23 February 2002. p. 5. (Location: Sicily).

Bray, Roger. 2000. Round the Horn. *The Guardian.* 23 December 2000. pp. 8–9. (Location: Swiss Alps/Zermatt).

Brown, Helen. 2006. Water music. *The Independent.* 4 March 2006. pp. 10–11. (Location: Engadine/St Moritz).

Cox, Jonathan. 2003. It's party time. *The Sunday Times.* 22 June 2003. p. 2. (Location: Lucerne, Lucerne International Music Festival, August 14th–September 20th).

Fenn, Patricia. 2001. Raiding the larder. *Guardian Travel.* 3 February 2001. pp. 10–11. (Location: Italy).

Garbett, Will. 2001. Europe's country trails. *The Guardian.* 4 March 2001. p. 9. (Location: Bernese Alps – Feature on 'Walks on the wild side – from the Alps to Madeira's banana canals').

Green, Richard. 2002. On the cheap. *The Sunday Times Travel.* 10 February 2002. p. 8. (Location: Malta).

Henry, Georgina. 2001. Peace in our time. *The Guardian.* 3 February 2001. p. 6. (Location: Tuscany).

Holford, Nicky. 2000. White weekends. *The Guardian.* 25 November 2000. pp. 10–11. (Location: Swiss Alps – A 'winter break' feature on Italy, France, and Switzerland).

Holford Nicky. 2002 Emotional peaks. *The Guardian.* 9 February 2002. p. 13. (Location: Swiss Alps/Verbier).

Kennedy, Douglas. 2002. Get into the grove. *The Sunday Times.* 6 January 2002. p. 5. (Location: Engadine/St Moritz).

Langley, Lee. 2002. A novel form of escapism. *The Daily Telegraph Travel.* 23 February 2002. p. 7. (Location: Madeira).

Lazell, Jeremy. 2000. Tinsel towns. *The Sunday Times,* 3 December 2000. pp. 2–3. (Location: Germany).

Mills, Simon. 2005. Skiing as it used to be. *The Guardian.* 12 November 2005. pp. 6–7. (Location: Swiss Alps/Champéry).

Mallalieu, Ben. 2002. Beyond the oompah. *The Guardian.* 16 February 2002. p. 13. (Location: Bavaria).

Mallalieu, Ben. 2005. Outside favourite. *Guardian Travel.* 10 September 2005. pp. 12–13. (Location: Ljubljana).

Milnes, Anthea. 2001. There's nothing like a bit of Romansch. *The Independent.* 23 June 2001. p. 5. (Location: Graubünden).

Newsom, Sean. 2003. Moritz for mere mortals. *The Sunday Times*. 26 January 2003. p. 8. (Location: St Moritz).

Newsom, Sean. 2004. Bargain time on the piste. *The Sunday Times*. 15 February 2004. p. 10. (Location: Swiss Alps).

Newsom, Sean. 2005. White frontiers *The Sunday Times*. 2 October 2005. p. 21. (Location: Swiss Alps).

Newsom, Sean. 2006. A place to chill. *The Sunday Times*. 19 February 2006. pp. 24–25. (Location: Swiss Alps).

Rufford Nick. 2002. A ski pass to the stars. *The Sunday Times*. 8 December 2002. p. 8. (Location: Swiss Alps).

Scott, Alistair. 1999. Klosters – fit for a prince? *The Sunday Times*. 12 December 1999. p. 7. (Location: Swiss Alps/Klosters).

Scott, Alistair. 2000a. Apartment life for the smart skier. *The Sunday Times*. 5 November 2000. p. 6. (Location: Swiss Alps).

Scott, Alistair. 2000b. High life: the best bars in the Alps. *The Sunday Times*. 31 December 2000. p. 6. (Location: Swiss Alps).

Scott, Alistair. 2001. The high art of lunch. *The Sunday Times*. 18 February 2001. p. 9. ('10 top alfresco eateries' in the Alps).

Stewart, Stanley. 2001. On the cheap. *The Sunday Times Travel*. 11 February 2001. p. 8. (Location: St Petersburg).

Sykes, Lisa. 2003. Fair share. *The Sunday Times Travel*. 28 January 2001. pp. 1–2. (Location: Lesotho).

Thomas, Andrew. 2003. Roll on, king Mekong. *The Sunday Times Travel*. 14 December 2003. p. 3. (Location: Laos).

Wangford, Hank. Dancing in the streets. *Guardian Travel*. 30 September 2000. pp. 2–3. (Location: Buenos Ares).

Warwick, Samantha. 2002. The ultimate blind date. *The Guardian*. 27 April 2002. p. 9. (Location: Zürich).

Chapter 5

The data we used in the current study come from 18 episodes of the BBC's *Holiday* and 10 episodes of ITV's *Wish You Were Here?* broadcast between November 2000 and April 2001. (See Endnote 5.1 for more background on these programmes.) The programmes comprised 106 episodes featuring 33 destinations (countries or regions), broadly reflecting the most popular destinations of UK holiday-makers (National Statistics, 2002). Perhaps not surprisingly, the most popular destination on the programmes was the UK, where the question of a language barrier in communicating with hosts was also far less likely to arise. Notably, in episodes featuring the UK, most interviews were with other tourists, rather than hosts, although British tourists, tour operators and expatriates were also occasionally interviewed in 'foreign' episodes. We chose not to include any of these interactions in our data analysis. Many other popular destinations, such as Ireland, the USA, parts of the Caribbean or of Canada, are, of course, largely 'English-speaking' and whatever interactions were undertaken with hosts in these locations were invariably conducted in English. In other locations, however, English was spoken by the majority of the local population as a second or foreign language. It was predominantly these settings that our examples come from.

Across all the 106 episodes of the programmes analysed, we identified 246 instances of interaction between tourist-presenters and hosts. For our purposes, we defined 'interaction' as any form of mutual engagement between a tourist and a host. This may have been verbal (often non-reciprocal, with only one participant assuming a speaking role) or nonverbal, for example, when the tourist and host make eye-contact, or when a tourist-presenter gets a massage from a host. We excluded from the category 'interaction' the ubiquitous, one-sided act of tourist gazing – in a more literal sense than the way it has come to be used in tourism studies, following Urry (2002). Our sample included 63 instances of the use and/or representation of languages other than English, which constituted approximately 26 per cent of all interactions with locals in the total sample.

Chapter 6

Our discussion in this chapter is based on data from three related sources. The main focus of our analysis is on a corpus of all lexical items and phrases from the glossaries of nineteen travel guides published between 1999 and 2003. This largely random sample of guidebooks was not intended to be strictly representative but rather based on some of the destinations we ourselves were working in for this book and for our sister publication (see Jaworski *et al.*, forthcoming). Having said which, the sample did cover six different destinations in Europe, Asia, Africa, Australasia and the Americas, fourteen different languages and five different guidebook publishing companies, sometimes with two or three different companies on the same destination: the *DK Eyewitness* (DK), *Insight Guides* (IG), *Lonely Planet* (LP), *Rough Guides* (RG) and *Thomas Cook Traveller* (TC) series.

Our analysis of this main linguistic corpus was also informed by asking each of the five guidebook publishers to tell us briefly about their rationale for including glossaries, how they decide what to include, and any information they had about the actual use of the glossaries by tourists. In addition, we were interested in isolating all metalinguistic or metacultural commentary included in the guidebooks we had chosen for our corpus. To this end, we also looked at a few additional

Table 6.2 Summary of sample guidebook countries, publishers and languages

Target country	Publisher	Non-English Language
Finland	IG	Finnish/Swedish
Hong Kong (and Macau)	DK, LP	Cantonese/Mandarin
Mexico	DK, LP, TC	Spanish
New Zealand	DK, IG, LP	Maori
Poland	DK, IG, LP	Polish
Gambia and Senegal	IG, LP	Diola/French/Fula/Malinke/Mandinka/Wolof
Australia	DK, IG	–
Wales	RG	Wesh

guidebooks: two on Australia (DK Eyewitness, Insight Guide) and one on Wales (Rough Guide).

To analyse the content of the language sections of the travel guides, all the different lexical items from the glossaries were input into an SPSS database, including the semantic (for example, transport) or syntactic (for example, pronouns) heading they were classified under by the guidebook authors themselves. The number of lexical items in any one guide varied considerably, depending on the space allocated by the publisher. Unsurprisingly, guides also differed in the way they classified words or how they titled their categories, for example, 'getting around' vs. 'transport'; 'greetings and civilities' vs. 'essentials'.

We eventually arrived at the listing of 46 initial categories in Figure 6.1 (p. 207), which was then clustered into eleven superordinate categories. These superordinate categories were standardized so that words and phrases were linked semantically and functionally rather than by their original guidebook category listing.

Complete list of guidebooks surveyed

Auger, T. (2002). *DK eyewitness travel guides: New Zealand*. London: Dorling Kindersley Limited.

Czerniewicsz-Umer, T., Omilanowowska, M. and Majewski, J. S. (2001). *DK eyewitness travel guides*: *Poland*. London: Dorling Kindersley Limited.

Dowling, C. and Bell, B. (2002). *Insight guide: New Zealand*. Singapore: APA Publications.

Dydynski, K. (2002). *Lonely planet: Poland*. Melbourne: Lonely Planet Publications Pty Ltd.

Else, D. (1999). *Lonely planet: Gambia & Senegal*. Melbourne: Lonely Planet Publications, Pty Ltd.

Fallon, S. (2002). *Lonely planet: Hong Kong & Macau*. Melbourne: Lonely Planet Publications Pty Ltd.

Fitzpatrick, L., Gagliardi, J., and Stone, A. (2002). *DK eyewitness top 10 travel guides: Hong Kong*. London: Dorling Kindersley Limited.

Griffiths, C. and Bell, B. (2000). *Insight guide: Poland*. Singapore: APA Publications.

Harding, P., Bain, C., and Bedford, N. (2002). *Lonely planet: New Zealand*. Melbourne: Lonely Planet Publications, Pty Ltd.

Inman, N. (2002). *DK eyewitness travel guides*: *Mexico*. London: Dorling Kindersley.

King, M. (2002). *Mexico*. Peterborough: Thomas Cook Publishing.

Laughton, F., Hennessy, H., and Bell, B. (2002). *Insight guide: Australia*. Singapore: APA Publications.

Noble, J., Forsyth, S., Greensfelder, B., Konn, M., Lepe, M., Lyon, J., Matter, M., Murphy, A., Nystrom, A. D., Wagle, V., and Wright, A. (2002). *Lonely planet: Mexico*. Melbourne: Lonely Planet Publications, Pty Ltd.

Pike, J. and Bell, B. (2003). *Insight guide: Mexico*. Singapore: APA Publications.

Ross, Z. (2002). *DK eyewitness travel guides*: *Australia*. London: Dorling Kindersley Limited.

Ross, Z. and Hennessy, H. (2003). *Insight guide: Finland*. Singapore: APA Publications.

Rutherford, S. (2000). *Insight guide: Finland*. Singapore: APA Publications.

Sweeny, P. (1999). *Insight guide: Gambia & Senegal*. Singapore: APA Publications.

Notes

Introduction: Mediating Global Mobility: Language, Tourism, Globalization

1. With its specific focus on the representation and mediatization of tourism, this book distinguishes itself in a number of important ways from our sister publication *Language, Tourism and Globalization* (Adam Jaworski, Crispin Thurlow, and Virpi Ylänne, forthcoming), which is ethnographically oriented and focuses more on the face-to-face, interactional accomplishment of tourist encounters. Theoretically and empirically speaking, however, the books are complementary steps towards establishing a properly sociolinguistic analytic perspective on tourism rooted in linguistically oriented discourse analysis (see Jaworski and Coupland, 2006, for an overview of this perspective).

2. These figures were based on the following sources: WTO's *World Tourism Barometer*, Volume 7(1), January 2009, available online (3 April 2009) at: <http://www.world-tourism.org/facts/eng/pdf/barometer/UNWTO_Barom09_1_en_excerpt.pdf> and the International Trade Forum's *Redefining Tourism*, available online (3 April 2008) at <http://www.tradeforum.org/news/fullstory.php/aid/866/Redefining_Tourism.html>. See also the *World Tourism Baromter*, Interim Update, September 2009, available online (4 October 2009) at: http://www.unwto.org/facts/eng/pdf/barometer/UNWTO_Barom09_update_sept_en.pdf.

3. In a report for the UK's Voluntary Service Overseas and the campaign group Tourism Concern on the representation and promotion of tourism to developing countries on television, Rice (2001) reiterates the concern that popular tourism representations (specifically, television holiday programmes) are worryingly insensitive to the environmental, social and cultural concerns of the people living in the travel destinations covered – especially in non-industrialized countries – and that they do not sufficiently raise the awareness of (potential) tourists. Perhaps critiques such as the ones we present here in, say, Chapters 4, 5 and 6 help expose some of the reasons for concern.

4. We recognize that a term like 'host' is inherently problematic and makes assumptions about (a) the relative power status of local people and their motivation to entertain, and (b) the homogeneity of inhabitants who may or may not be native or local and whose role-identities will inevitably vary. We are also not completely happy with the disparaging connotation of 'locals' – itself susceptible to the same homogenizing assumption. However, with its apt dual-meaning of a parasitic or symbiotic life-source, we have chosen to retain the label 'host' and to use 'local' only as a pre-modifier and not in its nominalized form.

5. Arguably the most important human communication code, language, is central to social life, the way we make sense of it and organize it. We are

dependent on language not just to describe the world, but also to represent the world and to justify our place in it. Even more importantly, however, language is used to *do* things: specifically, to construct identities, establish and maintain relationships and, unavoidably, to exert power and control over others. This is language as social action. To differentiate this type of language study from the sort of 'formal' language linguists study, the technical term *discourse* is usually preferred. In this sense, discourse analysts are less concerned with the way language is structured (for example, its sound system, lexicon, morphology and syntax), but rather with the way verbal communication is used in everyday contexts. Again, for an introductory account of 'language as discourse' see the opening chapter of Jaworski and Coupland's (2006) *Discourse Reader* and Coupland and Jaworski's (2009) *The New Sociolinguistics Reader*.

1   Elite Mobility and Global Lifestyles: Inflight Magazines

1. In their essay about guidebooks, Jack and Phipps (2003) borrow the notion of *apodemic literature* (that is, writing 'away from home'), which appears to have some of the same qualities as our own 'discourses on the move'. See also Chapter 6 for more on their ideas in this regard.
2. Our IATA figures were found in the organization's 2008 *Annual Report* available (3 April 2009) online at <http://www.iata.org/NR/rdonlyres/84158349-7772-4892-86AB-836DE73E0A52/0/IATAAnnualReport2008.pdf>. As we noted in the Introduction, it is important to recognize that figures such as these cannot possibly represent different individuals; it is inevitable that many of the same people are buying air tickets and that air travel is by no means accessible to all.
3. The Inflight Marketing Bureau <www.inflight-marketing.com> is a professional organization that represents the European inflight media industry.
4. For this kind of industry insight we rely on a article from 29 July 2008 in the *Kuwait Times* 'What's the future for in-flight magazines?' available (22 October 2009) online at <http://www.kuwaittimes.net/read_news.php?newsid=MzIwMjIyNzQy>.
5. For colour reproductions of these maps, please visit the following website: <http://faculty.washington.edu/thurlow/inflightmagazines/>. These were made available for the publication of Thurlow and Jaworski (2003).
6. A copy of McArthur's *Universal Corrective Map of the World* is available (28 August 2006) online at <http://www.flourish.org/upsidedownmap/> and a copy of a 14th-century *Mappa Mundi* at <http://www.cwru.edu/affil/GAIR/canada/pg41.jpg>.

2   Borrowed Genres and the Language Market: Trade Signs and Business Cards

1. In writing this chapter and in thinking about our data, we wanted to avoid the ethnocentric tendency to talk of 'our shops' and 'their stalls', 'our high streets' or 'our malls' and 'their markets'. The exoticizing, Orientalizing idea of the 'third world' marketplace is such a common trope in tourism that, we

think, works to sustain the privileged gaze of the (Western) tourist – their consumption of cultural Other and their production of difference.

2. In a chapter such as this one we are especially conscious of the inadequate terminology for accurately, fairly and respectfully distinguishing between the geographic and social domains of global capitalism. 'Grassroots', for example, carries some awkward, problematic connotations but we use it as a familiar shorthand for the experiences and perspectives of people organizing their lives outside, and in spite of, the traditional centres of global power – often those relatively disenfranchised or marginalized people within rich countries, and those people living in poor countries. By the same token, we know to avoid the problematic Third World/First World and Developing/Developed binaries. Our preference would be to talk about Rich Countries and Poor Countries. Although Western is largely unspecific and inaccurate, we opt for this as a convenient stand-in for the rich countries of North America, Europe and Australasia. In this mix, it should not be forgotten that, after Germany and the UK, the other great touring nation of the world is Japan (World Tourism Organization figures).

3. In thinking about these misspelled tradesigns, we are reminded of the deliberate misspelling of knock-off logos (e.g. Gillehe for Gillette, SQNY for SONY and adadas for adidas) while otherwise meticulously recreating the typographic style. See TheChive.com for good examples of this; available (20 October 2009) online at <http://thechive.com/2008/12/name-brand-knock-off-fail-30-photos/>.

4. Any doubt about the comparative scale of inequality between the economies of business cards in Gambia and in the global core is quickly dispelled by <http://creativebits.org/cool_business_card_designs> (accessed 17 December, 2008).

5. Zulu beadwork is itself a product of 19th-century colonialism and, indeed, more ancient globalizations; see <http://www.marques.co.za/clients/zulu/history.htm>.

3   Transient Identities, New Mobilities: Holiday Postcards

1. A potted history of the picture postcard is offered by Annette Pritchard and Nigel Morgan (2005) and a much more extensive history of the so-called 'Golden Age of postcards' from Bjarne Rogan (2005). For a wonderful visual history and impressive collection see Phillips' (2000) *The Postcard Century*. The Golden Age of postcards (approximately 1870/1895 to 1920/1930) reached its peak around 1914, when, according to Pritchard and Morgan (2005), over 880 million cards were posted that year. According to Rogan, many of these cards would have been 'local cards' (for example, depicting the sender's town, familiar buildings and activities of local interest) while many others would have been 'tourist cards', usually depicting typical motifs such as landscapes, cathedrals, hotels/liners, folkloric activities/artefacts and 'ethnic locals'. Rogan makes the interesting connection between modern postcards and modern-day text-messaging – both in terms of their communicative form (that is, short, economical messages) and function (that is, relationally oriented), but also given the moral panic which errupted around them – see this

newspaper comment quoted by Rogan (p. 3) from *The Standard* (London, UK) in 1899:

> The illustrated postcard craze, like the influenza, has spread to these islands [Great Britain] from the Continent, where it has been raging with considerable severity.

The post-WWI decline of postcards is associated with the rising cost of postage stamps and the increasing popularity of hand-held cameras.

2. We are drawn to the notion of the exorbitant with its obvious meaning of excess but also for its etymological trace of *ex orbita* – out of a groove or rut.

3. There is an irony in reading Jack and Phipps's (2005: 31) metaphoric description of having to 'dust off' the supposedly neglected material culture and restoring it to its rightful place; it wasn't that long ago that sociolinguists and discourse analysts were claiming to do the same with language (see Eggins and Slade, 1997).

4   Linguascaping the Exotic: Newspaper Travelogues

1. Just as we struggle with the slightly pejorative connotations of 'locals', our particular interpretation of 'lot' as a collective noun for local people is akin to 2008 public discussion in the US media about a presidential debate when the White Republican candidate John McCain referred to the Black Democratic candidate Barak Obama as 'that one'. For many, especially Black, USAmericans this passing remark was racially coded in the way that ethnic majority people might refer to a ethnic minority person as 'you people'. Without ever being sure of speaker intent, most of us remain unaware of the *social voices* we inherit and which unavoidably speak through us (cf. Bakhtin, 1986). For more on the original story, see <http://www.newsday.com/news/printedition/nation/ny-usthat095875399oct09,0,6989531.story> (accessed 17 December 2008).

5   Language Crossing and Identity Play: Television Holiday Shows

1. Both these programmes have now been cancelled. In 2006, BBC producers announced that they were, according to a newspaper article at the time, 'to axe its flagship travel show *Holiday* as part of a major shake-up of its schedules'. See 'Daily Mail' (25 November 2006). ' "Holiday" programme axed after 37 years'. Available (5 April 2008) online at: http://www.dailymail.co.uk/pages/live/articles/news/news.html?in_article_id=418633& in_page_id=1770. In the meantime, *Wish You Were Here* was axed in 2003, again following a major reshuffle of the ITV's primetime schedule. In 2008, the ITV relaunched the programme (as *Wish You Were Here – Now and Then*), now presented by the son of Judith Chalmers – the previous show's presenter for nearly 20 years. This latest incarnation is a twenty-five-part series where the show's presenters revisit destinations originally visited by Judith and the other original *Wish You Were Here* Presenters to see how much they have changed. As such,

and judging from the destinations being covered at the time we were com-pleting this book, the basic 'geopolitical format' remains largely unchanged: Benidorm, New York, Mallorca, Pisa and Brittany; Torremolinos, Marrakech, Blackpool, Madeira and San Francisco; Ibiza, Croatia, Banff, Lisbon and Torbay; Costa Brava, Boston, Cyprus, Malta and Dublin. See the ITV's own website for more: <http://www.itv.com/Lifestyle/WishYouWereHere/>.

2. Holiday destinations featured in the programmes used: UK (16), Spain (14), Caribbean (11), Italy (9), France (8), USA (6), Greece (5), Eire (3), Portugal (3), Austria (2), Canada (2), Egypt (2), Germany (2), Hong Kong (2), Maldives (2), South Africa (2), Australia (1), Cyprus (1), Dubai (1), Ecuador (1), Fiji (1), Finland (1), India (1), Kenya (1), Malta (1), Mauritius (1), Mexico (1), Netherlands (1), South Korea (1), Sweden (1), Switzerland (1), Thailand (1), Turkey (1).

3. The extracts were transcribed using a simplified version of Jefferson's tran-scription conventions for spoken data (Atkinson and Heritage, 1999). The following conventions were used:

[	overlapping speech;
=	contiguous speech;
underline	emphatic speech;
CAPS	louder than normal voice/shouting;
?	utterance interpreted as a question/rising intonation;
:	lengthening;
(.)	short pause;
(1)	pause measured in seconds;
(smiles)	nonverbal and other contextual information;
((unclear))	unclear speech, uncertain transcription;
yes (italics)	translation

6 The Commodification of Local Linguacultures: Guidebook Glossaries

1. E. M. Forster's *A Room with a View* is regarded by some as one of the first literary examples of critical tourism writing.

2. In his book *Tristes Tropiques* Claude Lévi-Strauss (1961: 44) wrote, 'I should have liked to live in the age of real travel, when the spectacle on offer had not yet been blemished, contaminated, and confounded.' A wistful com-plaint which speaks volumes about the problematic epistemologies of that generation of anthropologists.

3. A selection of British newspaper comment on the changing nature of guide-books in the face of market trends, technological developments and media convergence:

The Times (9 April 2005). 'The new breed of travel guidebooks' (Annabelle Thorpe). Available (1 April 2008) online at <http://travel.timesonline.co. uk/article/0,,10299-1558911.html>.

The Sunday Times (7 August 2005). 'Podcasting: The beginning of the end for guidebooks?' (Stephen Bleach). Available (1 April 2008) online at <http:// travel.timesonline.co.uk/article/0,,10299-1558911.html>.

The Guardian (2 October 2007). 'BBC worldwide snaps up lonely planet guidebooks'. Available (1 April 2008) online at: <http://www.guardian.co.uk/media/2007/oct/02/bbc.books>.

4. Lonely Planet Publications. (2007). *Lonely planet Australian language & culture*. Other Language Guide series include, the 'real talk', 'fast talk', and 'phrase-book' series.

5. Interpretations of the *hongi* abound; we have borrowed ours from the official New Zealand's tourism website and a page titled *Powhiri: New Zealand's welcoming spirit*, available (1 April 2008) online at: <http://www.newzealand.com/travel/about-nz/culture/powhiri/the-ceremony/hongi-embrace.cfm>.

6. In addition to Jonathan Meader's *The Worldless Travel Book*, there are two other well-known publications:

   Franklin, Mark. (2005). *The Universal Phrase Book: A picture dictionary for international travelers*. New York: Sterling.
   Graf, Dieter. (1999). *Point It: Traveller's language kit: picture dictionary*. Munich: Graf Editions.

7. *Language Travel Magazine* (August 2008). 'Special report: The bigger picture'. Available (5 April 2009) online at: <http://www.hothousemedia.com/ltm/ltmbackissues/nov08web/nov08specreport.html>. See also UK Government Press release (17 January 2008). 'English: The world's language'. Available (5 April 2009) online at: <http://www.number10.gov.uk/Page14289>.

8. Bremón, Ana. (2005). *15-minute Spanish*. London, New York, Munich, Melbourne and Delhi: Dorling Kindersley. For more about this series see the Dorling Kindersley website at: <http://us.dk.com/nf/Search/AdvSearchProc/1,,S195,00.html>.

9. Rosetta Stone. (3 December 2007). '*New Rosetta Stone Arabic* – Military edition program dramatically reduces time to train for deploying soldiers'. Press release available (1 April 2008) online at <http://www.rosettastone.com/global/press/news-20071203-rs>.

10. *New York Times*. (20 February 2007). 'Not lost in translation: A few phrases in another language can go a long way'. Available online at <http://www.nytimes.com/2007/02/20/business/worldbusiness/20language.html?pagewanted=print>.

Conclusion: Tourism Discourse and Banal Globalization

1. We cannot fail to acknowledge John Tomlinson's (1999: 119–120) passing use of the term 'banal globalization' which he uses to characterize the connection of the local and the global in practices such as the consumption of 'foreign' food and the supposed emergence of a 'globalized youth culture'. The problem for us, however, is that Tomlinson resorts to framing these mundane moments of globalization as an ontological expression of a kind of 'cosmopolitan disposition' – in his words: an 'awareness of the wider world as significant for us in our locality, the sense of connection with other cultures and even, perhaps, an increasing openness to cultural difference' (ibid.: 200) It is for this reason that we are drawn to Beck's idea of 'banal cosmopolitanism' which he distinguishes

from the kind of *cosmopolitanization* (Beck's term) which Tomlinson describes (hopes for?).
2. In thinking of 'colour-blind racism' (Bonilla-Silva, 2002) and the 'celebration of difference' (hooks, 1992; Jordan and Weedon, 1995), Celia Lury (1997: 83) offers the following nice example of a commodified cosmopolitanism extracted from a 1994 brochure for Habitat, the British household furnishing retailer:

> Experiencing different cultures and ways of life is now an everyday occurrence. In this catalogue we celebrate the skills and visual inspiration of many countries, with simple designs that can reflect how you live.

Needless to say, examples of this kind of 'containment for control' abound, most notably in so-called 'Diversity Management' programmes (see Lorbiecki and Jack, 2000) and in the institutionalization of Diversity in higher education (cf. Ferguson, 2008).

References

Abbink, J. (2000). Tourism and its discontents: Suri-tourist encounters in southern Ethiopia. *Social Anthropology*, 8, 1–17.

Abram, S. (1997). Performing for tourists in rural France. In S. Abram, J. Waldren and D.V. L. MacCleod (eds), *Tourists and tourism: Identifying with people and places* (pp. 29–49). Oxford: Berg.

Agar, M. (1994). *Language shock: Understanding the culture of conversation*. New York: William Morrow and Company.

Ahmed, S. (2000). *Strange encounters: Embodied others in postcoloniality*. London: Routledge.

Aiello, G. and Thurlow, C. (2006). Symbolic capitals: Visual discourse and intercultural exchange in the European capital of culture scheme. *Language and Intercultural Communication*, 6, 148–162.

Alber, J. L. (1985). Bonjour de Neuchâtel où il fait beau et chaud. Essai d'interprétation d'un corpus de cartes postales de vacances. (Greetings from Neuchâtel where it is fair and warm: attempted interpretation of vacation postcards). *Travaux Neuchatelois de Linguistique (TRANEL)*, 8, May, 69–94.

Anderson, B. (1983). *Imagined communities: Reflections on the origin and spread of nationalism*. London: Verso.

Anderson, C. (2003). Phillipson's children. *Language and Intercultural Communication*, 3(1), 81–95.

Anderson, L. and Trudgill, P. (1990). *Bad language*. Oxford: Basil Blackwell.

Androutsopoulos, J. (2007). Style online: Doing hip-hop on the German-speaking Web. In P. Auer (ed.), *Style and social identities: Alternative approaches to linguistic heterogeneity* (pp. 279–317). Berlin: Mouton de Gruyter.

Appadurai, A. (1986). Introduction: Commodities and the politics of value. In A. Appadurai (ed.), *The social life of things: Commodities in cultural perspective* (pp. 3–63). Cambridge: Cambridge University Press.

Appadurai, A. (1990). Disjuncture and difference in the global cultural economy. *Theory, Culture and Society*, 7, 295–310.

Appadurai, A. (1996). *Modernity at large: Cultural dimensions of globalization*. Minneapolis, MN: University of Minnesota Press.

Arnheim, R. (1982). *The power of the centre*. Berkeley: University of California Press.

Aston, G. (ed.). (1988). *Negotiating service: Studies in the discourse of bookshop encounters: The PIXI Project*. Bologna: Cooperativa Libraria Universitaria Editrice Bologna.

Atkinson, M. and Heritage, J. (1999). Jefferson's transcript notation. In A. Jaworski and N. Coupland (eds), *The discourse reader* (pp. 158–166). London: Routledge.

Austin, J. L. (1961). *How to do things with words*. Oxford: Clarendon.

Bærenholdt, J. O., Haldrup, M., Larsen, J. and Urry, J. (2004). *Performing tourist places*. Aldershot: Ashgate.

Bakhtin, M. (1981). *The dialogic imagination: Four essays.* (Edited by M. Holquist; Translated by C. Emerson and M. Holquist). Austin, TX: University of Texas Press.

Bakhtin, M. M. (1984). *Problems in Dostoevsky's poetics.* (Translated by C. Emerson). Minneapolis, MN: University of Minnesota Press.

Bakhtin, M. M. (1986). *Speech genres and other late essays.* (Edited by C. Emerson and M. Holquist; Translated by V. W. McGee). Austin, TX: University of Texas Press.

Baudrillard, J. (1994). *Simulacra and simulation.* Ann Arbor, Mich: University of Michigan Press.

Bauer, L. and Trudgill, P. (eds) (1998). *Language myths.* New York: Penguin Books.

Bauman, R. (1977). *Verbal art as performance.* Rowley, MA: Newbury House.

Bauman, R. (2004). *A world of others' words: Cross-cultural perspectives on intertextuality.* Oxford: Blackwell Publishing.

Bauman, R. and Briggs, C. (1990). Poetics and performance as critical perspectives on language and social life. *Annual Review of Anthropology,* 19, 59–88.

Bauman, R. and Briggs, C (2009). Poetics and performance as critical perspectives on language and social life. In N. Coupland and A. Jaworski (eds), *The new sociolinguistics reader* (pp. 607–614). Basingstoke: Palgrave Macmillan.

Bauman, Z. (1998). *Globalization: The human consequences.* Cambridge: Polity.

Bauman, Z. (2000). *Liquid modernity.* Cambridge: Polity.

Beck, U. (1992). *Risk society: Towards a new modernity.* London: Sage.

Beck, U. (2002). The cosmopolitan society and its enemies. *Theory, Culture and Society,* 19, 17–44.

Beck, U. (2004). Cosmopolitical realism: On the distinction between cosmopolitanism in philosophy and the social sciences. *Global Networks,* 4, 131–156.

Beck, U. (2006). *The cosmopolitan vision.* Cambridge: Polity.

Beck, U. and Sznaider, N. (2006). Unpacking cosmopolitanism for the social sciences: A research agenda. *The British Journal of Sociology,* 57, 1–23.

Belk, R. W. (1997). Been there, done that, bought the souvenirs: Of journeys and boundary crossing. In S. Brown and D. Turley (eds), *Consumer research: Postcards from the edge* (pp. 22–45). London: Routledge.

Bell, A. (1999). Styling the other to define the self: A study in New Zealand identity making. *Journal of Sociolinguistics,* 3, 523–541.

Bell, A. (2009 [1997]). Language style as audience design. In N. Coupland and A. Jaworski (eds), *The new sociolinguistics reader* (pp. 265–275). Basingstoke: Palgrave Macmillan.

Bhattacharyya, D. P. (1997). Mediating India: An analysis of a guidebook. *Annals of Tourism Research,* 24, 371–389.

Billig, M. (1991). *Ideology and opinions.* London: Sage.

Billig, M. (1995). *Banal nationalism.* London: Sage.

Birkeland, I. (2005). *Making place, making self: Travel, subjectivity and sexual difference.* Aldershot: Ashgate.

Black, J. (1997). *Maps and politics.* Chicago: Chicago University Press.

Blackledge, A. J. (2005). *Discourse and power in a multilingual world.* Amsterdam/Philadelphia: John Benjamin.

Blommaert, J. (ed.) (1999). *Language ideological debates.* Berlin: Mouton de Gruyter.

Blommaert, J. (2003). Commentary: A sociolinguistics of globalisation. *Journal of Sociolinguistics*, 7, 607–623.

Blommaert, J. (2005). *Discourse: A critical introduction*. Cambridge: Cambridge University Press.

Blommaert, J. (2007). Sociolinguistics and discourse analysis: Orders of indexicality and polycentricity. *Journal of Multicultural Discourse*, 2, 115–130.

Blommaert, J. (2009). A sociolinguistics of globalization. In N. Coupland and A. Jaworski (eds), *The new sociolinguistics reader* (pp. 560–573). Basingstoke: Palgrave Macmillan.

Blommaert, J., Collins, J. and Slembrouck, S. (2005). Spaces of multilingualism. *Language & Communication*, 25, 195–216.

Blommaert, J. and Verschueren, J. (1998). *Debating diversity: Analysing the discourse of tolerance*. London: Routledge.

Boissevain, J. (1989). Tourism as anti-structure. In C. Giordano et al. (eds), *Kulturanthropologisch 30. Ein Festschrift für Ina-Maria Greverus* (pp. 145–159). Frankfurt: University of Frankfurt.

Boissevain, J. (ed.) (1996a). *Coping with tourists: European reactions to mass tourism*. Oxford: Berghahn Books.

Boissevain, J. (1996b). Introduction. In J. Boissevain (ed.), *Coping with tourists: European reactions to mass tourism* (pp. 1–26). Oxford: Berghahn Books.

Bonilla-Silva, E. (2003). *Racism without racists: Color-blind racism and the persistence of racial inequality in the United States*. Lanham, MD: Rowman & Littlefield.

Boorstin, D. (1964). *The image: A guide to psuedo-events in America*. New York: Harper.

Bourdieu, P. (1977). *Outline of a theory of practice*. (Translated by R. Nice). Cambridge: Cambridge University Press.

Bourdieu, P. (1984). *Distinction: A social critique of the judgement of taste*. (Translated by R. Nice). London: Routledge.

Bourdieu, P. (1990). *The logic of practice*. Stanford: Stanford University Press.

Bourdieu, P. (1991). *Language and symbolic power*. (Edited by J. B. Thompson; Translated by G. Raymond and M. Adamson). Cambridge: Polity.

Bourdieu, P. (1993). *The field of cultural production: Essays on art and literature*. (Edited by R. Johnson). Cambridge: Polity.

Bourdieu, P. and Wacquant, L. (2001). Commentary: NewLiberal speak: Notes on the new planetary vulgate. *Radical Philosophy*, 105, 2–5.

Brown, D. (1996). Genuine fakes. In T. Selwyn (ed.) *The tourist image: Myths and myth making in tourism* (pp. 33–47). Chichester: John Wiley & Sons.

Brown, G. (1990). Cultural values: The interpretation of discourse. *English Language Teaching Journal*, 44, 11–17.

Brown, M. (2000). *Closet space: Geographies of metaphor from the body to the globe*. London: Routledge.

Brown, P. and Levinson, S. (1987). *Politeness: Some universals in language usage*. Cambridge: Cambridge University Press.

Bruner, E. M. (2005). *Culture on tour: Ethnographies of travel*. Chicago: University of Chicago Press.

Bruner, E. M. (2005 [1996]). Tourism in the Balinese borderzone. In *Culture on tour: Ethnographies of travel* (pp. 191–210). Chicago: University of Chicago Press.

Budach, G., S. Roy and M. Heller. (2003). Community and commodity in French Ontario. *Language in Society*, 32(5), 603–627.

Butler, J. (1990) *Gender trouble: Feminism and the subversion of identity.* New York: Routledge.

Butler, J. (1993). *Bodies that matter: On the discursive limits of 'sex'.* London: Routledge.

Callinicos, A., Rees, J., Harman, C. and Haynes, M. (eds) (1994). *Marxism and the new imperialism.* London: Bookmarks.

Cameron, D. (1995). *Verbal hygiene.* London: Routledge.

Cameron, D. (2000a). Styling the worker: Gender and the commodification of language in the globalized service economy. *Journal of Sociolinguistics,* 4, 323–347.

Cameron, D. (2000b). *Good to talk? Living in a communication culture.* London: Sage.

Cameron, D. (2001). *Working with spoken discourse.* London: Sage.

Cameron, D. (2009 [1990]). Demythologising sociolinguistics. In N. Coupland and A. Jaworski (eds), *The new sociolinguistics reader* (pp. 106–118). Basingstoke: Palgrave Macmillan.

Casey, B. (1993). Genre. In Kenneth McLeish (eds), *Key ideas in human thought.* London: Bloomsbury.

Castells, M. (2000[1996]). *The rise of the network society* (2nd ed.). Oxford: Blackwell.

Chandler, D. (1997). *An introduction to genre theory.* April 04, 2002, from <http://www.aber.ac.uk/media/Documents/intgenre/intgenre.html>.

Cheshire, J. and Moser, L. (1994). English as cultural symbol: The case of advertisements in French-speaking Switzerland. *Journal of Multilingual and Multicultural Development,* 15, 51–69.

Chmielewska, E. (2010). Semiosis takes place or radical uses of quaint theories. In A. Jaworski and C. Thurlow (Eds), *Semiotic landscapes: Image, text, space.* London: Continuum.

Cilauro, S., Sitch, R. and Gleisner, T. (2004) *Molvania: A land untouched by modern dentistry – A jetlag travel guide.* London: Atlantic Books.

Clifford, J. (1997). *Routes: Travel and translation in the late twentieth century.* Cambridge: Harvard University Press.

Cohen, E. (1972). Towards a sociology of international tourism. *Social Research,* 39, 179–201.

Cohen E. (1973). Nomads from affluence: Notes on the phenomenon of drifter–tourism. *International Journal of Comparative Sociology,* 14(1/2), 89–103.

Cohen, E. (1979). A phenomenology of tourist types. *Sociology,* 13, 179–201.

Cohen, E. (1985). The tourist guide: The origins, structure and dynamics of a role. *Annals of Tourism Research,* 12, 5–29.

Cook, I. and Crang, P. (1996). The world on a plate: Culinary culture, displacement and geographical knowledges. *Journal of Material Culture,* 1, 131–153.

Coulmas, F. (1981). Introduction: Conversational routine. In F. Coulmas (ed.), *Conversational routine: Explorations in standardized communication situations and prepatterened speech* (pp. 1–17). The Hague: Mouton.

Coupland, J. (ed.) (2000). *Small talk.* London: Pearson Education.

Coupland, N. (1985). 'Hark, hark the lark': Social motivations for phonological style-shifting. *Language and Communication,* 5, 153–172.

Coupland, N. (1999). 'Other' representation. In J. Verschueren, J.-O. Östman and C. Bulcean (eds) *Handbook of Pragmatics* (pp. 1–24). Amsterdam/Philadelphia: John Benjamins.

Coupland, N. (2001). Dialect stylisation in radio talk. *Language in Society*, 30, 345–375.

Coupland, N. (2003a). Introduction: Sociolinguistics and globalisation. *Journal of Sociolinguistics*, 7, 465–472.

Coupland, N. (ed.) (2003b). Language and globalisation. Special issue of the *Journal of Sociolinguistics 7/4*.

Coupland, N. (2007). *Style: Language variation and identity*. Cambridge: Cambridge University Press.

Coupland, N. (2009). Dialect style, soial class and metacultural performance: The pantomime Dame. In N. Coupland and A. Jaworski (eds), *The new sociolinguistics reader* (pp. 311–325). Basingstoke: Palgrave Macmillan.

Coupland, N. (ed.) (2010). *Handbook of language and globalization*. Oxford: Wiley-Blackwell.

Coupland, N. and Jaworski, A. (2004). Sociolinguistic perspectives on metalanguage: Reflexivity, evaluation and ideology. In A. Jaworski, N. Coupland and D. Galasiński (eds), *Metalanguage: Social and ideological perspectives* (pp. 15–51). Berlin: Mouton de Gruyter.

Coupland, N. and Jaworski, A. (eds) (2009). *The new sociolinguistics reader*. Basingstoke: Palgrave Macmillan.

Coupland, N. and Ylänne-McEwen, V. (2000). Talk about the weather: Small talk, leisure talk and the travel industry. In J. Coupland (ed.), *Small talk* (pp. 163–182). London: Pearson Education.

Coupland, N., Garrett, P. and Hywel B. (2005). Wales underground: Discursive frames and authenticities in Welsh mining heritage tourism events. In A. Jaworski and A. Pritchard (eds), *Discourse, communication and tourism* (pp. 199–222). Clevedon: Channel View.

Crang, P. (1997). Performing the tourist product. In C. Rojek and J. Urry (eds), *Touring cultures: Transformations of travel and theory* (pp. 137–154). London: Routledge.

Cresswell, T. (2006). *On the move*. New York: Routledge.

Cronin, M. (2000). *Across the lines: Travel, language, translation*. Cork: Cork University Press.

Cutler, C. (1999). Yorkville crossing: White teens, hip hop, and African American English. *Journal of Sociolinguistics*, 3, 428–442.

Cutler, C. (2009). Yorkville crossing: White teens, hip hop, and African American English. In N. Coupland and A. Jaworski (eds), *The new sociolinguistics reader* (pp. 299–310). Basingstoke: Palgrave Macmillan.

Davies, E. (1987). A contrastive approach to the analysis of politeness formulas. *Applied Linguistics*, 8, 75–88.

Davis, J. (1992). *Exchange*. Minneapolis, MN: University of Minnesota Press.

De Botton, A. (2002). *The art of travel*. London: Hamish Hamilton.

De Certeau, M. 1984. *The practice of everyday life*. Berkeley: California University Press.

De Cordova, R. (1990). *Picture personalities: The emergence of the star system in America*. Chicago: University of Illinois Press.

De Garzia, S. (1964). *Of time, work and leisure*. Garden City, NY: Anchor Books.

De Mooij, M. (1998). *Global marketing and advertising: Understanding cultural paradoxes*. Thousand Oaks, CA: Sage.

De Swaan, A. (2002). *Words of the world: The global language system*. Cambridge: Polity.

Deleuze, G. (1990). *Negotiations*. New York: Columbia Univeristy Press.

Demont-Heinrich, C. (2005). Language and national identity in the era of globalization: The case of English in Switzerland. *Journal of Communication Inquiry*, 29, 66–84.

Dillon, G. L. (2006). Clipart images as commonsense categories. *Visual Communication*, 5, 287–306.

Dilworth, L. (2003). 'Handmade by an American Indian': Souvenirs and the cultural economy of southwestern tourism. In H. K. Rotham (ed.), *The culture of tourism, the tourism of culture* (pp. 101–117). Albuquerque, NM: University of New Mexico Press.

Doorne, S. and Ateljevic, I. (2005). Tourism performance as metaphor: Enacting backpacker travel in the Fiji Islands. In A. Jaworski and A. Pritchard (eds), *Discourse, communication and tourism* (pp. 173–198). Clevedon: Channel View.

Douglas, M. (1996). *Purity and danger: An analysis of concepts of pollution and taboo*. London: Ark.

Du Gay, P. and Pryke, M. (eds) (2002). *Cultural economy*. London: Sage.

Dürmüller, U. (2001). The presence of English in Swiss universities. In U. Ammon (ed.), *The dominance of English as a language of science: Effects on other languages and language communities* (pp. 389–403). New York: Mouton de Gruyter.

Dunn, D. (2005). 'We are not here to make a film about Italy, we are here to make a film about me ...' British television holiday programmes' representations of the tourist destination. In D. Crouch, F. Thompson and R. Jackson (eds), *The media and the tourist imagination: Converging cultures* (pp. 154–169). London: Routledge.

Dunn, D. (2006). Singular encounters: Mediating the tourist destination in British television holiday programmes. *Tourist Studies*, 6, 37–58.

Eastman, C and Stein, R. F. (1993). Language display. *Journal of Multilingual and Multicultural Development*, 14, 187–202.

Eckert, P. and McConnell-Ginet, S. (1992). Think practically and look locally: Language and gender as community-based practice. *Annual Review of Anthropology*, 21, 461–490.

Eckert, P. and McConnell-Ginet, S. (2003). *Language and gender*. Cambridge: Cambridge University Press.

Edensor, T. (1998). *Tourists at the Taj: Performance and meaning at a symbolic site*. London: Routledge.

Edensor, T. (2001). Performing tourism, staging tourism: (Re)producing tourist space and practice. *Tourist Studies*, 1, 59–81.

Edwards, E. (1996). Postcards: Greetings from another world. In T. Selwyn (ed.), *The tourist image: Myths and myth making in tourism* (pp. 197–221). Chichester: John Wiley & Sons.

Eggins, S. and Slade, D. (1997). *Analysing casual conversation*. London: Cassell.

Fairclough, N. (1992). *Discourse and social change*. Cambridge: Polity.

Fairclough, N. (1993). Critical discourse analysis and the marketization of public discourse: The universities. *Discourse & Society*, 4, 133–168.

Fairclough, N. (1995). *Media discourse*. London: Edward Arnold.

Fairclough, N. (1999). Global capitalism and critical awareness of language. *Language Awareness*, 8, 71–83.

Fairclough, N. (2001). *Language and Power*, 2nd edition. London: Pearson.

Fairclough, N. (2002). Language in new capitalism. *Discourse & Society*, 3, 163–166.

Fairclough, N. (2003). *Analysing discourse: Textual analysis for social research*. London: Routledge.

Fairclough N. (2006). *Language and globalization*. London: Routledge.

Favero, P. (2007). 'What a wonderful world!': On the 'touristic ways of seeing', the knowledge and the politics of the 'culture industries of otherness'. *Tourist Studies*, 7, 51–81.

Featherstone, M. (1991). *Consumer culture and postmodernism*. London: Sage.

Featherstone, M. (2002). Cosmopolis: An introduction. *Theory, Culture and Society*, 19, 1–16.

Feifer, M. (1985). *Going places*. London: Macmillan.

Ferguson, R. A. (2008). Administering sexuality; or, the will to institutionality. *Radical History Review*, 100, 158–169.

Flink, J. J. (1988). *The Automobile Age*. Cambridge, MA: MIT Press.

Foucault, M. (1980). *Power/knowledge*. New York: Pantheon.

Foucault, M. (1998[1976]). *The History of Sexuality Vol. 1: The Will to Knowledge*. London: Penguin.

Franklin, A. (2003). *Tourism: An introduction*. London: Sage.

Franklin, A. and Crang, M. (2001). The trouble with tourism and travel theory. *Tourist Studies*, 1, 5–22.

Friedrich, P. (1989). Language, ideology, and political economy. *American Anthropologist*, 91, 295–312.

Frow, J. (1997). *Time & commodity culture: Essays in cultural theory and postmodernity*. Oxford: Clarendon.

Gal, S. and Irvine, J. T. (1995). The boundaries of language and disciplines: How ideologies construct difference. *Social Research*, 62, 967–1001.

Galasiński, D. and Jaworski, A. (2003). Representations of hosts in travel writing: *The Guardian* travel section. *Journal of Tourism and Cultural Change*, 1, 131–149.

Garrett, P., Evans, B. and Williams, A. (2006). What does the word 'globalisation' mean to you? Comparative perceptions and evaluations in Australia, New Zealand, the USA and the UK. *Journal of Multilingual and Multicultural Development*, 27, 392–342.

Gendelman, I. and Aiello, G. (2010). Faces of places: Façades as global communication in Post-Eastern Bloc urban renewal. In A. Jaworski and C. Thurlow (eds), *Semiotic landscapes: Image, text, space*. London: Continuum.

Giddens, A. (1990). *The consequences of modernity*. Cambridge: Polity.

Giddens, A. (1991). *Modernity and self-identity: Self and society in the late modern age*. Cambridge: Polity.

Giddens, A. (1999). *The runaway world: The Reith Lectures revisited*. September 06, 2001, from <http://www.lse.ac.uk/Giddens/pdf/10-Nov-99.pdf>.

Gilbert, D. (1999). 'London in all its glory – or how to enjoy London': Guidebook representations of imperial London. *Journal of Historical Geography*, 25, 279–297.

Giles, H. and Niedzielski, N. (1998). Italian is beautiful, German is ugly. In L. Bauer and P. Trudgill (eds), *Language myths* (pp. 85–93). Middlesex: Penguin.

Giles, H., Coupland, N. and Coupland, J. (1991). Accommodation theory: Communication, contexts, consequences. In H. Giles, N. Coupland and

J. Coupland (eds), *Contexts of accommodation: Developments in applied sociolinguistics* (pp. 1–68). Cambridge: Cambridge University Press.

Goffman, E. (1963). *Interaction ritual: Essays on face-to-face behavior*. Garden City, NY: Anchor Books.

Goffman, E. (1974). *Frame analysis: An essay on the organization of experience*. New York: Harper and Row.

Goffman, E. (1981). Footing. In E. Goffman, *Forms of talk* (pp. 124–159). Oxford: Blackwell.

Goodwin, C. and Duranti, A. (1992). Rethinking context: An introduction. In A. Duranti and C. Goodwin (eds), *Rethinking context: Language as an interactive Phenomenon* (pp. 1–42). Cambridge: Cambridge University Press.

Graburn, N. (1989). Tourism: The sacred journey. In V. Smith (ed.), *Hosts and guests: The anthropology of tourism* (2nd ed.) (pp. 171–185). Philadelphia: University of Pennsylvania Press.

Graddol, D. (2002). *The English language and globalization*. Paper presented at the Language and Global Communication Seminar, Centre for Language and Communication, Cardiff University, July 2002.

Gramsci, A. (1971). *Selections from the prison notebooks of Antonio Gramsci*. (Edited and translated by Q. Hoare and G. N. Smith). New York: International Publishers.

Granovetter, M. (1985). Economic action and social structure: The problem of embeddedness. *American Journal of Sociology*, 91, 481–510.

Grice, H. P. (1975). Logic and conversation. In P. Cole and J. Morgan (eds), *Syntax and semantics: Vol. 3, speech acts* (pp. 41–58). New York: Academic Press.

Gumperz, J. J. (1982). *Discourse strategies*. Cambridge: Cambridge University Press.

Gupta, A. and Ferguson, J. (1992). Beyond 'culture': Space, identity and the politics of difference. *Cultural Anthropology*, 7, 6–23.

Hall, S. (1996a). The problem of ideology: Marxism without guarantees. In D. Morley and K.-H. Chen (eds), *Stuart Hall: Critical dialogues in cultural studies* (pp. 25–46). London: Routledge.

Hall, S. (1996b). Introduction: Who needs 'identity'? In S. Hall and P. du Gay (eds), *Questions of cultural identity* (pp. 1–17). London: Sage.

Halliday, M. A. K. (1978). *Language as social semiotic: The Social interpretation of language and meaning*. London: Edward Arnold.

Hanefors, M. and Mossberg, L. (2000). Travel shows and image making. In M. R. Robinson, N. Evans, P. Long, S. Sharpley and J. Swarbrooke (eds), *Management, marketing and the political economy of travel and tourism* (pp. 179–189). Sunderland: Centre for Travel and Tourism in association with Business Education Publishers.

Hannerz, U. (1996). *Transnational connections: Culture, people, places*. London: Routledge.

Harding, M. (2004, May 19). Revamping a staid image to stay afloat. *The Guardian*, p. 5.

Hardt, M. and Negri, A. (2000). *Empire*. Cambridge, MA: Harvard University Press.

Harold, C. (2004). Pranking rhetoric: 'Culture jamming' as media activism. *Critical Studies in Media Communication*, 21, 189–211.

Harrison, J. (2003). *Being a tourist: Finding meaning in pleasure travel*. Vancouver: University of British Columbia Press.

Harvey, D. (1989) *The condition of postmodernity: An enquiry into the origins of cultural change.* Oxford: Blackwell.

Harvey, D. (1990). Between space and time: Reflections on the geographical imagination. *Annals of the Association of American Geographers*, 80, 418–434.

Harvey, D. (2006). *Spaces of global capitalism: Towards a theory of uneven development.* London: Verso.

Harvey, P. (1992). Bilingualism in the Peruvian Andes. In D. Cameron, E. Frazer, P. Harvey, M. B. H. Rampton and K. Richardson (eds), *Researching language: Issues of power and method* (pp. 65–89). London: Routledge.

Held, D. and McGrew, A. (2000). The great globalization debate: An introduction. In D. Held and A. McGrew (eds), *The global transformations reader: An introduction to the globalization debate* (pp. 1–45). Cambridge: Polity.

Held, D., McGrew, A., Goldblatt, D. and Perraton, J. (2000). Rethinking globalization. In D. Held and A. McGrew (eds), *The global transformations reader: An introduction to the globalization debate* (pp. 54–60). Cambridge: Polity.

Heller, M. (1999). Heated language in a cold climate. In J. Blommaert (ed.), *Language ideological debates* (pp. 143–170). Berlin: Mouton de Gruyter.

Heller, M. (2003a). Globalization, the new economy and the commodification of language and identity. *Journal of Sociolinguistics*, 7, 473–498.

Heller, M. (2003b). Actors and discourses in the construction of hegemony. *Pragmatics*, 13, 11–31.

Heller, M. (2009). A study on transnational spaces. In P. Auer and J. Schmidt (eds), *Language and space: An international handbook on linguistic variation.* Berlin: Mouton de Gruyter.

Heller, M. (2010a). Language as resource in the globalised new economy. In N. Coupland (ed.), *Handbook of language and globalization.* Oxford: Wiley-Blackwell.

Heller, M. (2010b). *Paths to post-nationalism: A critical ethnography of language and identity.* New York: Oxford University Press.

Herbert, R. (1990). Sex-based differences in compliment behavior. *Language in Society*, 19, 201–224.

Hill, J. (1985). The grammar of consciousness and the consciousness of grammar. *American ethnologist*, 12, 752–737.

Hill, J. (2001[1998]). Language, race, and white public space. In A. Duranti (ed.), *Linguistic anthropology: A reader* (pp. 450–464). Malden, MA: Blackwell.

Hill, J. (2008). *The everyday language of white racism.* Oxford: Blackwell.

Hill, J. and Hill, K. C. (1996). *Speaking Mexicano: Dynamics of a syncretic language in Central Mexico.* Tuscon, AZ: University of Arizona Press.

Hodge, R. and Kress, G. (1993). *Language as ideology* (2nd ed.). London: Routledge.

Holmes, J. (1988a). Compliments and compliment responses in New Zealand. *Anthropological Linguistics*, 28, 485–508.

Holmes, J. (1988b). Paying compliments: A sex-preferential politeness strategy. *Journal of Pragmatics*, 12, 445–465.

Holmes, J. and Meyerhoff, M. (eds) (1999). Communities of practice in language and gender research. Special Issue of *Language in Society*, 28(2).

Hoogvelt, A. (1997). *Globalization and the postcolonial world: The new political economy of development.* London: Macmillan.

hooks, b. (1992). Eating the other: Desire and resistance. In *Black Looks: Race and Representation* (pp. 21-39). Boston: South End Press.

House, J. (2003). English as a lingua franca: A threat to multilingualism? *Journal of Sociolinguistics*, 3, 556–578.

Hutnyk, J. (1996). Magical mystical tourism. In R. Kaur and J. Hutnyk (eds), *Travels worlds: Journeys in contemporary cultural politics* (pp. 94–119). London: Zed Books.

Hutnyk, J. (2000). *Critique of exotica: Music, politics and the culture industry*. London: Pluto.

Hymes, D. (1971). *On communicative competence*. Philadelphia: University of Pennsylvania Press.

Irvine, J. T. (1989). When talk isn't cheap: Language and political economy. American Ethnologist, 16, 248–267.

Irvine, J. and Gal, S. (2000). Language ideology and linguistic differentiation. In P. V. Kroskrity (ed.), *Regimes of language* (pp. 35–83). Santa Fe, NM: School of American Research Press.

Irvine, J. and Gal, S. (2009). Language-ideological processes. In N. Coupland and A. Jaworski (eds), *The new sociolinguistics reader* (pp. 374–377). Basingstoke: Palgrave Macmillan.

Jack, G. and Phipps, A (2003) On the uses of travel guides in the context of German tourism to Scotland. *Tourist Studies*, 3, 281–300.

Jack, G. and Phipps, A. (2005). *Tourism and intercultural exchange: Why tourism matters*. Clevedon: Channel View.

Jacquemet, M. (2005). Transidiomatic practices: Language and power in the age of globalization. *Language & Communication*, 25, 257–277.

Jaffe, A. (1999a). Packaged sentiments: The social meanings of greeting cards. *Journal of Material Culture*, 4, 115–141.

Jaffe, A. (1999b). *Ideologies in action: Language politics on Corsica*. Berlin: Mouton de Gruyter.

Jaffe, A. (2000). Introduction: Non-standard orthography and non-standard speech. *Journal of Sociolinguistics*, 4, 497–513.

Jaffe, A. (2007). Corsican on the airwaves: Media discourse, practice and audience in a context of minority language shift and revitalization. In Sally Johnson and Astrid Ensslin (eds) *Language in the media* (pp. 149–172). London: Continuum.

Jaffe, A. and Walton, S. (2000). The voices people read: Orthography and the representation of non-standard speech. *Journal of Sociolinguistics*, 4, 561–587.

Jakobson, R. (1960). Closing statement: Linguistics and poetics. In T. A. Sebeok (ed.), *Style in language* (pp. 350–377). Cambridge, MA: MIT Press.

Jaworski, A. (1990). The acquisition and perception of formulaic language and foreign language teaching. *Multilingua*, 9, 397–411.

Jaworski, A. (2007). Language in the media: Authenticity and othering. In S. Johnson and A. Ensslin (eds) *Language in the Media: Identity, Representation, Ideology* (pp. 271–280). London: Continuum.

Jaworski, A. (2009). Greetings in tourist–host encounters. In N. Coupland and A. Jaworski (eds), *The new sociolinguistics reader* (pp. 662–679). Basingstoke: Palgrave Macmillan.

Jaworski, A. and Coupland, J. (2005). Othering in gossip: 'you go out you have a laugh and you can pull yeah okay but like…'. *Language in Society*, 34, 667–694.

Jaworski, A. and Coupland, N. (eds) (2006). *The discourse reader* (2nd ed.). London: Routledge.

Jaworski, A., Coupland, N. and Galasiński, D. (eds) (2004). *Metalanguage: Social and ideological perspectives.* Berlin: Mouton de Gruyter.

Jaworski, A. and Lawson, S. (2005). Discourses of Polish agritourism: Global, local and pragmatic. In A. Jaworski and A. Pritchard (eds), *Tourism, language and communication* (pp. 123–149). Clevedon: Channel View.

Jaworski, A. and Piller, I. (2008). Linguascaping Switzerland: Language ideologies in tourism. In M. Locher and J. Strassler (eds), *Standards and norms in the English Language* (pp. 301–321). Berlin: Mouton de Gruyter.

Jaworski, A. and Sachdev, I. (2004). Teachers' beliefs about students' talk and silence: Constructing academic success and failure through metapragmatic comments. In A. Jaworski, N. Coupland and D. Galasiński (eds), *Metalanguage: Social and ideological perspectives* (pp. 227–244). Berlin: Mouton de Gruyter.

Jaworski, A. and Thurlow, C. (2009a). Gesture and movement in tourist spaces. In C. Jewitt (ed.), *Handbook of multimodal discourse analysis* (pp. 253–262). London: Routledge.

Jaworski, A. and Thurlow, C. (2009b). Talking an elitist stance : Ideology and the discursive production of social distinction. In A. Jaffee (ed.), *Stance: Sociolinguistic perspectives* (pp. 195–226). New York: Oxford University Press.

Jaworski, A. and Thurlow, C. (2010a). Language and the globalizing habitus of tourism: A sociolinguistics of fleeting relationships. In N. Coupland (ed.), *The handbook of language and globalisation.* Oxford: Blackwell.

Jaworski, A. and Thurlow, C. (eds) (2010b). *Semiotic Landscapes: Language, Image, Space.* London: Continuum.

Jaworski, A., Thurlow, C. and Ylänne, V. (forthcoming). *Language, tourism and globalization: The sociolinguistics of fleeting relationships.* London: Routledge.

Jaworski, A., Thurlow, C., Ylänne-McEwen, V. and Lawson, S. (2003). The uses and representations of local languages in tourist destinations: A view from British television holiday programmes. *Language Awareness,* 12, 5–29.

Jaworski, A., Ylänne-McEwen, V., Thurlow, C. and Lawson, S. (2003). Social roles and negotiation of status in host–tourist interaction: A view from British television holiday programmes. *Journal of Sociolinguistics,* 7, 135–163.

Johnson, S. and Ensslin, E. (eds) (2007). *Language in the media.* London: Continuum.

Joos, M. (1961). *The five clocks.* New York: Harcourt, Brace and World.

Jordan, G. and Weedon, C. (1995). The celebration of difference and the cultural politics of racism. In B. Adam and S. Allan (eds), *Theorizing culture: An interdisciplinary critique after postmodernism* (pp. 149–164). London: UCL Press.

Judd, D. (1999). Constructing the tourist bubble. In D. Judd and S. Fainstein (eds), *The tourist city* (pp. 35–53). New Haven: Yale University Press.

Kandiah, T. (1998). Epiphanies of the deathless native users' manifold atavars: A post-colonial perspective on the native-speaker. In R. Singh (ed.), *The native speaker: Multilingual perspectives* (pp. 79–110). New Delhi: Sage.

Kahn, M. (2003). Tahiti: The ripples of a myth on the shores of the imagination. *History and Anthropology,* 14, 307–326.

Kaplan, C. (1996). *Questions of travel: Postmodern discourses of displacement.* Durham, NC: Duke University Press.

Kelly-Holmes, H. (2005). *Advertising as multilingual communication.* Basingstoke: Palgrave Macmillan.

Kennedy, C. (2005) 'Just perfect!' The pragmatics of evaluation in holiday post-cards. In A. Jaworski and A. Pritchard (eds), *Discourse, communication and tourism* (pp. 223–246). Clevedon: Channel View.

Kirshenblatt-Gimblett, B. (1998). *Destination culture: Tourism, museums, and heritage.* Berkeley: University of California Press.

Klien, N. (2002). *Fences and windows: Dispatches from the front lines of the globalization debate.* New York: Picador.

Kopytoff, I. (1986) The cultural biography of things: Commoditization as process. In A. Appadurai (ed.), *The social life of things: Commodities in cultural perspective* (pp. 64–91). Cambridge: Cambridge University Press.

Koshar, R. (1998). 'What ought to be seen': Tourists' guidebooks and national identities in modern Germany and Europe. *Journal of Contemporary History*, 33, 323–340.

Kotler, P. and Gertner, D. (2002). Country as brand, product and beyond: A place marketing and brand management perspective. In N. Morgan, A. Pritchard and R. Pride (eds), *Destination branding: Creating the unique destination proposition* (pp. 40–56). Amsterdam: Elsevier.

Kress, G. (1988). *Communication and culture: An introduction.* Kensington, NSW: New South Wales University Press.

Kress, G. and van Leeuwen, T. (1996). *Reading images: The grammar of visual design.* London: Routledge.

Kristiansen, T. and Giles, H. (1992). Compliance-gaining as a function of accent: Public requests in varieties of Danish. *International Journal of Applied Linguistics*, 2, 17–35.

Kroskrity, P. V. (2000). Language ideologies in the expression and representation of Arizona Tewa ethnic identity. In P. V. Kroskrity (ed.), *Regimes of language: Ideologies, polities, and identities* (pp. 329–359). Santa Fe, NM: School of American Research Press.

Kroskrity, P. V. (2004). Language ideologies. In A. Duranti (ed.), *A companion to linguistic anthropology* (pp. 496–517). Oxford: Blackwell Publishing.

Laakso, V. and Östman, J. (eds). (1999). *Postikortti Diskurssina* ['The Postcard as Discourse']. Hämeenlinna, Finland: Korttien Talo.

Laakso, V. and Östman, J. (2001). *Postikortti Sosiaalisessa Kontekstissa* ['The Postcard in its Social Context']. Hämeenlinna, Finland: Korttien Talo.

Labov, W. (1972). *Sociolinguistic patterns.* Philadelphia: University of Pennsylvania Press.

Labov, W. (2009 [1972]). Rules for ritual insults. In N. Coupland and A. Jaworski (eds), *The new sociolinguistics reader* (pp. 615–630). Basingstoke: Palgrave Macmillan.

Lanza, E. and Woldemariam, H. (2008). Language ideology and linguistic landscape: Language policy and globalization in a regional capital in Ethiopia. In E. Shohamy and D. Gorter (eds), *Linguistic landscapes: Expanding the scenery* (pp. 189–205). New York: Routledge.

Lash, S. and Lury, C. (2007). *Global culture industry: The mediation of things.* Cambridge: Polity.

Lash, S. and Urry, J. (1994). *Economies of signs and spaces.* London: Sage.

Lasn, K. (1999). *Culture jam: The uncooling of America*^{TM}. New York: Eagle Brook.

Lassen, C. (2006). Aeromobilities and work. *Environment and planning A*, 38, 301–312.

266   *References*

Lave, J. and Wenger, E. (1991). *Situated learning: Legitimate peripheral participation.* Cambridge: Cambridge University Press.

Laver, J. (1981). Linguistic routines and politeness in greeting and parting. In F. Coulmas (ed.), *Conversational routine: Explorations in standardized communication situations and prepatterned speech* (pp. 289–304). The Hague: Mouton.

Lawson, S. and Jaworski, A. (2007). Shopping and chatting: Reports of tourist–host interactions in Gambia. *Multilingua*, 26, 67–93.

Le Page, R. B. and Tabouret-Keller, A. (1985). *Acts of identity: Creole based-approaches to language and ethnicity.* Cambridge: Cambridge University Press.

Leach, E. (1964). *Rethinking anthropology.* London: Athlone Press.

Lefebvre, H. (1991 [1974]). *The production of space* (Translated by D. Nicholson-Smith). Oxford: Blackwell.

Levinson, S. C. (1988). Putting linguistics on a proper footing: Explorations in Goffman's concepts of participation. In P. Drew and A. Wootton (eds), *Erving Goffman: Exploring the intaraction order* (pp. 161–227). Cambridge: Polity.

Leví-Strauss, C. (1970). *The raw and the cooked* (Translated by J. Weightman and D. Weightman). New York: Harper & Row.

Lew, A. (1991). Place representation in tourist guidebooks: An example from Singapore. *Singapore Journal of Tropical Geography*, 12, 124–137.

Lewin, B. A., Fine, J. and Young, L. (2001). *Expository discourse: A genre-based approach to social science research texts.* London: Continuum.

Lippi-Green, R. (1997). *English with an accent: Language, ideology, and discrimination in the United States.* New York: Routledge.

Lorbiecki, A. and Jack, G. A. (2000). Critical turns in the evolution of diversity management. *British Journal of Management*, 11, 17–32.

Loti, P. and Lett, J. W. (1983). Ludic and liminoid aspects of charter yacht tourism in the Caribbean. *Annals of Tourism Research*, 10, 35–56.

Low, S. M. (2001) The edge and the center: Gated communities and the discourse of urban fear. *American Anthropologist*, 103, 45–59.

Lull, J. (2001). Superculture for the communication age. In J. Lull (ed.), *Culture in the Communication Age* (pp. 132–163). New York: Routledge.

Lucy, J. A. (ed.) (1993). *Reflexive language: Reported speech and metapragmatics.* Cambridge: Cambridge University Press.

Lury, C. (1997). The objects of travel. In C. Rojek and J. Urry (eds), *Touring cultures: Transformations of travel and theory* (pp. 75–95). London: Routledge.

MacCannell, D. (1984). Reconstructed ethnicity: Tourism and cultural identity in third world communities. *Annals of Tourism Research*, 11, 375–391.

MacCannell, D. (1999 [1976]). *The tourist: A new theory of the leisure class.* Berkeley: University of California Press.

Machin, D. (2004). Building the world's visual language: The increasing global importance of image banks in corporate media. *Visual Communication*, 3, 316–336.

Machin, D. and van Leeuwen, T. (2003). Global schemas and local discourses in *Cosmopolitan. Journal of Sociolinguistics*, 7, 493–512.

Machin, D. and van Leeuwen, T. (2007). *Global media discourse.* London: Routledge.

Malinowski, B. (1923). The problem of meaning in primitive languages. In C. K. Ogden and I. R. Richards (eds), *The meaning of meaning* (pp. 146–152). London: Routledge and Kegan Paul.

Manes, J. and Wolfson, N. (1981). The compliment formula. In F. Coulmas (ed.), *Conversational routine* (pp. 115–132). The Hague: Mouton.

Markwick, M. (2001) Postcards from Malta: Image, consumption, context. *Annals of Tourism Research*, 28, 417–438.

Massey, D. B. (1994). *Space, place, gender*. Minneapolis: University of Minnesota Press.

Massey, D. B. (2005). *For space*. London: Sage.

McCabe, S. (2002). The tourist experience and everyday life. In G. M. S. Dann (ed.), *The tourist as a metaphor of the social world* (pp. 61–76), Wallington: CAB International.

McCabe, S. (2005). Who is a tourist? A critical review. *Tourist Studies*, 5, 85–106.

McGregor, A. (2000). Dynamic texts and tourist gaze: Death, bones and Buffalo. *Annals of Tourism Research*, 27, 27–50.

Meethan, K. (2001). *Tourism in global society: Place, culture, consumption*. Basingstoke: Palgrave Macmillan.

Meinhof, U. H. (2004). Metadiscourses of culture in British TV commercials. In In A. Jaworski, N. Coupland and D. Galasiński (eds), *Metalanguage: Social and ideological perspectives* (pp. 275–288). Berlin: Mouton de Gruyter.

Mellinger, W. M. (1994). Toward a critical analysis of tourism representations. *Annals of Tourism Research*, 21, 756–779.

Meethan, K. (2001). *Tourism in Global Society: Place, Culture, Consumption*. Basingstoke: Palgrave.

Milroy, J. (2006) The ideology of the standard language. In C. Llamas, L. Mullany and P. Stockwell (eds) *The Routledge Companion to Sociolinguistics* (pp. 133–139). Abingdon: Routledge.

Morgan, N. and Pritchard, A. (1998). *Tourism, promotion and power: Creating images, creating identities*. Chichester: John Wiley.

Morgan, N. and Pritchard, A. (2005a). Security and social 'sorting': Traversing the surveillance–tourism dialectic. *Tourist Studies*, 5, 115–132.

Morgan, N. and Pritchard, A. (2005b). On souvenirs and metonymy: Narratives of memory, metaphor and materiality. *Tourist Studies*, 5, 29–53.

Morgan, N., Pritchard, A. and Pride, R. (2002). *Destination branding: Creating the unique destination proposition*. London: Elsevier.

Morrell, J. (1863). *Miss Jemima's Swiss journal: The first conducted tour of Switzerland*. London: Putnam.

Mosely, J. (2001). Major airlines @ Smilin' Jack's. Retrieved August 06, 2001, from <http://www.smilinjack.com/airlines.htm>.

Munt, I. (1994). The 'other' postmodern tourism: Culture, travel and the new middle classes. *Theory, Culture & Society*, 11, 101–123.

National Statistics. (2002) *Travel trends 2001 edition: A report on the international passenger survey*. Retrieved April 04, 2002, from <http://www.statistics.gov.uk/statbase/Product.asp?vlnk=1391>.

Negus, K. (2002). Identities and industries: The cultural formation of aesthetic economies. In P. du Gay and M. Pryke (eds), *Cultural economy* (pp. 115–131). London: Sage.

Nishimura, S., Waryszak, R. and King, B. (2006). Guidebook used by Japanese tourists: A qualitative study of Australia inbound travellers. *International Journal of Tourism Research*, 8, 13–26.

Ochs, E. (1990). Indexicality and socialization. In J. Stigler, R.A. Schweder and G. Herbert (eds), *Cultural psychology* (pp. 287–308). Cambridge: Cambridge University Press.

Ong, W. J. (1982). *Orality and literacy*. New York: Routledge.

Oren, T. and Shahaf, S. (2009). *Global television formats: Circulating culture, producing identity*. London: Routledge.

Osborne, P. D. (2000). *Travelling light: Photography, travel and visual culture*. Manchester: Manchester University Press.

Östman, J.-O. (2004) The postcard as media. *Text*, 24, 423–442.

Pawley, A. and Syder, F. H. (1983). Two puzzles for linguistic theory: Nativelike selection and nativelike fluency. In J. C. Richards and R. W. Schmidt (eds), *Language and Communication* (pp. 191–226). New York: Longman.

Peckham, S. (1998). Consuming nations. In S. Griffith and J. Wallace (eds), *Consuming passions: Food in the age of anxiety* (pp. 171–181). Manchester: Manchester University Press.

Pennycook, A. (1989). The concept of method, interested knowledge, and the politics of language learning. *TESOL Quarterly*, 23, 589–618.

Pennycook, A. (1994). *The cultural politics of English as an international language*. Harlow: Longman.

Pennycook, A. (1998). *English and the discourses of colonialism*. London: Routledge.

Pennycook, A. (2003). Global Englishes, Rip Slyme, and performativity. *Journal of Sociolinguistics*, 7, 513–533.

Pennycook, A. (2006). The myth of English as an international language. In S. B. Makoni and A. Pennycook (eds) *Disinventing and reconstituting languages* (pp. 90–115). Clevedon: Multilingual Matters.

Pennycook, A. (2007). *Global Englishes and transcultural flows*. London: Routledge.

Pezzullo, P. C. (2007). *Toxic tourism: Rhetorics of pollution, travel and environmental justice*. Tuscaloosa, AL: University of Alabama Press.

Phillips, T. (2000). *The postcard century: 2000 cards and their messages*. London: Thames & Hudson.

Phillipson, R. and Skutnabb-Kangas, T. (1999). Englishisation: One dimension of globalization. In D. Graddol and U. H. Meinhof (eds), *English in a changing world* (pp. 19–36). Milton Keynes: Association Internationale de Linguistique Appliquée.

Phipps, A. (2007). *Learning the arts of linguistic survival: Languaging, tourism, life*. Clevedon: Channel View.

Piller, I. (2001a). Identity constructions in multilingual advertising. *Language in Society*, 30, 153–186.

Piller, I. (2001b). Naturalization language testing and its basis in ideologies of national identity and citizenship. *International Journal of Bilingualism*, 5, 259–277.

Piller, I. (2007). English in Swiss tourism marketing. In C. Flores and O. Grossegesse (eds), *Wildern in luso-austro-deutschen Sprach- und Textgefilden: Festschrift zum 60. Geburtstag von Erwin Koller* [*Roughing it in the linguistic and textual wilds of Portuguese, Austrian and German: Festschrift for Erwin Koller on the occasion of his 60th birthday*] (pp. 57–53). Braga, PT: Cehum – Centro de Estudos Humanísticos.

Pomerantz, A. (1984). Agreeing and disagreeing with assessments: Some features of preferred/dispreferred turn shapes. In J. M. Atkinson and J. Heritage (eds), *Structures of social action* (pp. 57–101). Cambridge: Cambridge University Press.

Pomerantz, A. (1998). Compliment responses: Notes on the co-operation of multiple constraints. In J. Schenkein (ed.), *Studies in the organization of conversational interaction* (pp. 79–112). New York: Academic Press.

Preston, D. (1985). The L'il Abner syndrome: Written representations of speech. *American Speech*, 60, 328–336.

Preston, D. (2000) Mowr and mowr bayud spellin': Confessions of a sociolinguist. *Journal of Sociolinguistics*, 4, 614–621.

Preston, D. R. (2004). Folk metalanguage. In A. Jaworski, N. Coupland and D. Galasiński (eds), *Metalanguage: Social and ideological perspectives* (pp. 75–101). Berlin: Mouton de Gruyter.

Pritchard, A. and Morgan, N. (2005). Representations of 'ethnographic knowledge': Early comic postcards of Wales. In A. Jaworski and A. Pritchard (eds), *Discourse, communication and tourism* (pp. 53–75). Clevedon: Channel View.

Quinlan, S. (2005). 'Never short of a smile': A content analysis of travel guidebooks. Unpublished MA thesis, University of Waterloo, Canada. Retrieved August 22, 2006, from <http://etd.uwaterloo.ca/etd/sequinla2005.pdf>.

Rampton, B. (1995). *Crossing: Language and ethnicity among adolescents*. London: Longman.

Rampton, B. (1998). Language crossing and the redefinition of reality. In P. Auer (ed.), *Codeswitching in conversation* (pp. 290–317). London: Routledge.

Rampton, B. (1999). Styling the other. Introduction. *Journal of Sociolinguistics*, 3, 421–427.

Rampton, B. (2009a). Crossing, ethnicity and code-switching. In N. Coupland and A. Jaworski (eds), *The new sociolinguistics reader* (pp. 287–298). Basingstoke: Palgrave Macmillan.

Rampton, B. (2009b). Speech community and beyond. In N. Coupland and A. Jaworski (eds), *The new sociolinguistics reader* (pp. 694–713). Basingstoke: Palgrave Macmillan.

Rassool, N. (2007). *Global issues in language, education and development: Perspectives from postcolonial countries*. Clevedon: Multilingual Matters.

Rhodes, L. (1999). Inflight magazines: Changing the way travellers read. *Journal of Magazine and New Media Research*, 1. Available (6 April 2009) online at <http://aejmcmagazine.bsu.edu/journal/archive/Fall_1999/Rhodes.html>.

Rice, A. (2001). *Tourism on television: A programme for change*. London: Tourism Concern and Voluntary Service Overseas.

Richards, G. and Wilson, J. (eds) (2004). *The Global Nomad: Backpacker Travel in Theory and Practice*. Clevedon: Channel View Publications.

Ringbom, H. (1985). Transfer in relation to some other variables in L2-learning. In H. Ringbom (ed.), *Foreign language learning and bilingualism* (pp. 9–21). Åbo: Åbo Akademi.

Roberts, M. (1998). Baraka: World cinema and the global culture industry. *Cinema Journal*, 37, 62–82.

Robins, K. (2000 [1997]). Encountering globalization. In D. Held and A. McGrew (eds), *The global transformations reader: An introduction to the globalization debate* (pp. 195–201). Cambridge: Polity.

Rogan, B. (2005). An entangled object. The picture postcard as souvenir and collectible, exchange and ritual communication. *Cultural Analysis*, 4, 1–27.

Rojek, C. (1997). Indexing, dragging and the social construction of tourist sights. In C. Rojek and J. Urry (eds), *Touring cultures: Transformations of travel and theory* (pp. 52–74). London: Routledge.

Romaine, S. (1988). *Language in society: An introduction to sociolinguistics*. Oxford: OUP.

Rubin, A. M., Perse, E. M. and Powell, R.A. (1985). Loneliness, parasocial interaction, and local television news viewing. *Human Communication Research*, 12, 155–180.

Said, E. (1979). *Orientalism*. New York: Vintage Books.

Sassen, S. (1991). *The global city: New York, London, Tokyo*. Princeton, New Jersey: Princeton University Press.

Sassen, S. and Roost, F. (1999). The city: Strategic site for the global entertainment industry. In D. R. Judd and S. S. Fainstein (eds), *The tourist city* (pp.143–154). New Haven and London: Yale University Press.

Schechner, R. (1985) *Between theater and anthropology*. Philadelphia: University of Pennsylvania Press.

Schieffelin, B. B., Woolard, K. A. and Kroskrity, P. V. (eds) (1998). *Language ideologies: Practice and theory*. New York: Oxford University Press.

Schivelbusch, W. (1986). *The railway journey: The industrialization of time and space in the 19th century*. Berkeley: University of California Press.

Schmidt, R. W. (1983). Interaction, acculturation and the acquisition of communicative competence: A case study of an adult. In N. Wolfson and E. Judd (eds), *Sociolinguistics and language acquisition* (pp. 137–174). Rowley, MA: Newbury House.

Schmitt, B. H. and Simonson, A. (1997). *Marketing aesthetics: The strategic management of branding, identity and image*. London: Simon and Schuster.

Schultz, M., Hatch, M. J. and Mogens H. L. (eds) (2000). *The expressive organization: Linking identity, reputation and the corporate brand*. Oxford: Oxford University Press.

Scollon, R. and Wong Scollon, S. (2003). *Discourses in place: Language in the material world*. London: Routledge.

Sebba, M. (1998). Phonology meets ideology: The meaning of orthographic practices in British Creole. *Language Problems and Language Planning*, 22, 19–47.

Selwyn, T. (ed.) (1996). *The tourist image: Myths and myth making in tourism*. Chichester: John Wiley & Sons.

Sheller, M. and Urry, J. (2006). The new mobilities paradigm. *Environment and Planning A*, 38, 207–226.

Shohamy, E. (2006). *Language policy: Hidden agendas and new approaches*. London: Routledge.

Silverstein, M. (1998). Monoglot 'standard' in America: Standardization and metaphors of linguistic hegemony. In D. Brenneis and R. K. S. Macaulay (eds), *The matrix of language: Contemporary linguistic anthropology* (pp. 284–306). Boulder, CO: Westview.

Silverstein, M. (2001 [1981]). The limits of awareness. In A. Duranti (ed.), *Linguistic anthropology: A reader* (pp. 382–402). Oxford: Blackwell Publishers.

Silverstein, M. and G. Urban (1996). *Natural histories of discourse*. Cambridge: Cambridge University Press.

Skeggs, B. (2004). *Class, self, culture*. London: Routledge.

Small, J, Harris, C. and Wilson, E. (2008). A critical discourse analysis of in-flight magazine advertisements: The 'social sorting' of airline travellers? *Journal of Tourism and Cultural Change*, 6, 17–38.

Smith, A. D. (2000). Towards a global culture? In D. Held and A. McGrew (eds), *The global transformations reader: An introduction to the globalization debate* (pp. 239–247). Cambridge: Polity.

Smith, V. (ed.) (1989). *Hosts and guests: The anthropology of tourism* (2nd ed.). Philadelphia: Pennsylvania University Press.

Spafax. (2000). Inflight entertainment research solutions and audience information. Retrieved June 25, 2001, from <http://www.passengerresearch.com/ttov00.htm>.

Swales, J. M. (1990). *Genre analysis: English in academic and research settings.* Cambridge: Cambridge University Press.

Swartz, D. (1997). *Culture and power: The sociology of Pierre Bourdieu.* Chicago: University of Chicago Press.

Swartz, K. L. (1999). Airlines of the world. Retrieved June 18, 2001, from <http://www.chicago.com/air/carriers/>.

Tannen, D. (1986). Introducing constructed dialogue in Greek and American conversational and literary narrative. In F. Coulmas (ed.), *Direct and indirect speech* (pp. 311–332). Berlin: Mouton de Gruyter.

Tannen, D. (1989). *Talking voices: Repetition, dialogue, and imagery in conversational discourse.* Cambridge: Cambridge University Press.

Tannen, D. and Öztek, P. C. (1981). Health to our mouths: Formulaic expressions in Turkish and Greek. In F. Coulmas (ed.), *Conversational routine: Explorations in standardized communication situations and prepatterned speech* (pp. 37–54). The Hague: Mouton.

Thomas, J. (1983). Cross-cultural pragmatic failure. *Applied Linguistics*, 4, 91–112.

Thompson, J. B. (2000). The globalization of communication. In D. Held and A. McGrew (eds), *The global transformations reader: An introduction to the globalization debate* (pp. 202–215). Cambridge: Polity.

Thurlow, C. (2004). Relating to our work, accounting for our selves: The autobiographical imperative in teaching about difference. *Language and Intercultural Communication*, 4, 209–228.

Thurlow, C. (2006). From statistical panic to moral panic: The metadiscursive construction and popular exaggeration of new media language in the print media. *Journal of Computer-Mediated Communication*, 11. <http://jcmc.indiana.edu/vol11/issue3/thurlow.html>.

Thurlow, C. (2007). Fabricating youth: New-media discourse and the technologization of young people. In S. Johnson and A. Ensslin (eds), *Language in the media: Representations, identities, ideologies* (pp. 213–233). London: Continuum.

Thurlow, C. (2010). Speaking of difference: Language, inequality and interculturality. In R. Halualani and T. Nakayama (eds), *Handbook of critical intercultural communication.* Oxford: Blackwell.

Thurlow, C. and Aiello, G. (2007). National pride, global capital: A social semiotic analysis of transnational visual branding in the airline industry. *Visual Communication*, 5, 305–344.

Thurlow, C. and Jaworski, A. (2003). Communicating a global reach: Inflight magazines as a globalizing genre in tourism. *Journal of Sociolinguistics*, 7, 581–608.

Thurlow, C. and Jaworski, A. (2006). The alchemy of the upwardly mobile: Symbolic capital and the stylization of elites in frequent-flyer programmes. *Discourse & Society*, 17, 131–167.

Thurlow, C. and Jaworski, A. (2010). Silence is golden: Elitism, linguascaping and 'anti-communication' in luxury tourism. In A. Jaworski and C. Thurlow (eds), *Semiotic landscapes: Language, image, space*. London: Continuum.

Thurlow, C., Jaworski, A. and Ylänne-McEwen, V. (2005). 'Half-hearted tokens of transparent love': 'Ethnic' postcards and the visual mediation of host-tourist communication. *Tourism, Culture and Communication*, 5, 93–104.

Thurlow, C. and Marwick, A. (2005). Apprehension versus awareness: Toward more critical understandings of young people's communication experiences. In A. Williams and C. Thurlow (eds), *Talking adolescence: Perspectives on communication in the teenage years* (pp. 53–72). New York: Peter Lang.

Thurlow, C. and Poff, M. (2010). The language of text-messaging. In S. C. Herring, D. Stein and T. Virtanen (eds), *Handbook of the Pragmatics of CMC*. Berlin and New York: Mouton de Gruyter.

Tomlinson, J. (1999). *Globalization and culture*. Chicago: University of Chicago Press.

Turner, G. (2004). *Understanding celebrity*. London: Sage.

Turner, V. (1969). *The ritual process: Structure and anti-structure*. Chicago: Aldine.

Turner, V. (1974). *Dramas, fields, and metaphors: Symbolic action in human society*. Ithaca: Cornell University Press.

Turner, V. (1977). Variations on a theme of liminality. In S. Moore and B. Myerhoff (eds), *Secular ritual* (pp. 36–52). Amsterdam: Van Gorcum.

Urry, J. (2002). *The tourist gaze: Leisure and travel in contemporary societies* (2nd ed.). London: Sage.

Urry, J. (2007). *Mobilities*. Cambridge: Polity.

Van den Berghe, P. L. (1994). *The quest for the other: Ethnic tourism in San Cristobal, Mexico*. Seattle: University of Washington Press.

van Dijk, T A. (1992). Discourse and the denial of racism. *Discourse & Society*, 3(1), 87–118.

van Dijk, T. A. (1998). *Ideology: A multidisciplinary approach*. London: Sage.

Van Gennep, A. (1960 [1909]). *The rites of passage*. Chicago: University of Chicago Press.

Van Leeuwen, T. (2002 [1993]). Genre and field in critical discourse analysis. In M. Toolan (ed.), *Critical discourse analysis: Critical concepts in linguistics* (pp. 169–199). London: Routledge.

Van Leeuwen, T. (2005). *Introducing social semiotics*. London: Routledge.

Veblen, T. (1979 [1899]). *The theory of the leisure class*. New York: Penguin.

Ventola, E. (1987). *The structure of social interaction: A systemic approach to the semiotics of service encounters*. London: Frances Pinter.

Wallernstein, I. (1983). *Historical capitalism*. London: Verso.

Wallernstein, I. (2001). *Unthinking social science* (2nd ed.). Philadelphia, PA: Temple University Press.

Waters, M. (1995). *Globalization*. London: Routledge.

Watts, R. (1988). Language, dialect and national identity in Switzerland. *Multilingua*, 7, 313–334.

Watts, R. J. (1999). The ideology of dialect in Switzerland. In J. Blommaert (ed.), *Language ideological debates* (pp. 67–103). Berlin: Mouton de Gruyter.

Watts, R. J. (2001). Discourse theory and language planning: A critical reading of language planning reports in Switzerland. In N. Coupland, S. Sarangi and

C. N. Candlin (eds), *Sociolinguistics and social theory* (pp. 297–320). London: Longman.

Watts, R. J. and Murray, H. (eds) (2001). *Die fünfte Landessprache? Englisch in der Schweiz* ['The fifth national language? English in Switzerland']. Berne: Vdf.

Weinert, R. (1995). The role of formulaic language in second language acquisition: A review. *Applied Linguistics*, 16, 180–205.

Wenger, E. (1998). *Communities of practice*. New York: Cambridge University Press.

Wetherell, M. and Potter, J. (1992). *Mapping the language of racism: Discourse and the legitimation of exploitation*. New York: Columbia University Press.

Wolfson, N. (1983). An empirically based analysis of compliments in American English. In N. Wolfson and E. Judd (eds), *Sociolinguistics and language acquisition* (pp. 82–95). Rowley, Massachusetts: Newbury House.

Wood, D. (1992). *The power of maps*. New York: The Guildford Press.

Woolard, K. and Schieffelin, B. B. (1994). Language ideology. *Annual Review of Anthropology*, 23, 55–82

Wragg, D. (1998). *The world's major airlines*. Sparkford: Patrick Stephens.

Wray, A. (2002). *Formulaic language and the lexicon*. Cambridge: Cambridge University Press.

Wray, A. and Perkins, M. (2000). The functions of formulaic language: An integrated model. *Language and Communication*, 20, 1–28.

Wray, A., Evans, B., Coupland, N. and Bishop, H. (2003). Singing in Welsh, becoming Welsh: 'Turfing' a 'grass roots' identity. *Language Awareness*, 12, 49–71.

Yarymowich, M. (2005). 'Language tourism' in Canada: A mixed discourse. In F. Baider, M. Burger and D. Goutsos (eds), *La communication touristique: Approches discursives de l'identité et de l'alterité* (pp. 257–273) Paris: L'Harmattan.

Index

Note: The locators in **bold** refers to 'figures' and in *italics* refers to 'tables' respectively.

globalization
  anxieties, 230
  banal, 21, 224, 226–7
    enactment of, 100, 227
  cachet of, 231
  consequences of, 225
  dialectics, 232
  ethnoscape of, 5
  and global capitalism, 3–5, 227
  ideology of, 235
  ideoscape of, 46
  inequalities of, 131
  intercultural exchange, 166
  language of, 71
  mythology of, 4, 230
  peripheral space of, 79
  quintessential signs, 51–2
  signposting, 233
  sociolinguist writing, 60
  textual enactment of, 226
  theory, 59, 231
globe-trotters, 95
globe-trotting cosmopolitan, 24
glühwein, 161–2
Goffman, E., 86, 96, 125, 143, 164–5,
    169, 189, 205, 215
Golden Age Cruises, 237
Goodwin, C., 234
Graburn, N., 97–100, 116, 124–5
Graddol, D., 7, 55
Gramsci, A., 220
Granovetter, M., 89
grassroots literacy, 83
greeting
  cards, 111, 120
  exchange, 182
  formula, 36, 175, 210
Grice, H. P., 170
guidebook glossaries, 13, 110, 130,
    171, 184, 191–223
  double-performativity to, 215
  incidental quality of, 216
Gumperz, J. J., 234
Gupta, A., 92

Halliday, M. A. K., 27
Hall, S., 11, 46, 229
Hanefors, M., 163
Hannerz, U., 45, 190, 222, 228

Harding, M., 97
Hardt, M., 7, 54
Harold, C., 88
Harrison, J., 6, 96, 196, 198, 235
Harvey, D., 45, 54–7, 59, 79, 82, 87,
    91–2, 122, 140, 177, 226, 229
Harvey, P., 177
health clubs, 55
health problems, 209
hegemonically-scripted discourses, 93
Held, D., 3, 19, 49–50, 92, 228–9
Heller, M., 57–8, 60, 86, 113, 220, 229
Herbert, R., 123–4
Heritage, J., 251
heritage site, 152
heritage tourism, 220, 237
heteroglossia, 28
heteronormative matrix, 226
Hill, J., 86, 142, 172, 185
Hill, K. C., 86
HIV infection, 146
holiday travel shows, 44, 181, 189, *see
    also* television holiday shows
Holmes, J., 113, 122
homogenizing textual formats, 233
Hoogvelt, A., 3
hooks, b., 113, 236, 253
host–tourist
  communication, 215
  contact, 196, 220
  exchanges, 200, 205
  interaction, 9, 89, 189, 215,
    220, 229
  relationship, 196, 216
House, J., 38
Hutnyk, J., 7, 113, 228
Hymes, D., 205

iconization, 134, 146
ideal communication
  Habermasian, 222
identity management, 74
Idleness, 114–17
igloo supervisor, 156
illocutionary effects, 142
immigrants, 6
indirect reporting, 142
inflight entertainment, 26, 35, 238